GREAT BIBLICAL CHARACTERS ILLUSTRATED
PROFILES OF PEOPLE IN THE BIBLE

CORINNE BONNET PAOLO XELLA

GREAT BIBLICAL CHARACTERS ILLUSTRATED PROFILES OF PEOPLE IN THE BIBLE

To **Resi** and **Oswald Loretz**

Originally published in French as *Le Guide Illustré des Grands Personnages de la Bible* by Corinne Bonnet and Paolo Xella, Gremese International, Rome, 1995.

Translated from the French by:
Sandra E. Tokunaga

Jacket Design:
Carlo Soldatini

Cover:
The Fall of Adam and Eve, tenth century miniature on parchment,
San Lorenzo Royal Monastery, El Escorial

Photocomposition by:
Severini — Spoleto (PG)

Printed by:
CSR Rome

P.O. Box 14335
00149 Rome, Italy

ISBN 88-7301-050-4

CONTENTS

INTRODUCTION

The Bible, though an exceptional best-seller and the most widely published and distributed book in the world (several million copies sold annually), may still nevertheless be considered in many ways a largely misunderstood and inaccessible work. For, outside the realm of specialized circles, few are those who devote themselves to a thorough or systematic reading of the Bible, or who have access to the tools which might help them to appreciate not only the special message the Bible holds, but also its historical context. This is due to many factors. Without over simplifying, we might first mention a series of internal ones, intrinsic to the biblical text itself. A disparate, heterogeneous work by no means chronologically consistent, the Bible is more like a puzzle or overlay where the many characters juxtapose, overlap, yield to more fundamental theological considerations, or disappear entirely within the dense narrative fabric, itself constantly interrupted by digressions of a legislative, normative, scholarly or cultural nature. By external factors we mean the formidable labors applied to re-working, compiling and editing the mass of traditional belief which makes up the Bible as we know it today. Even basic familiarity with the text suffices to be immediately struck by the great differences in tone, style, and content which, to say the least, make this a most composite and eclectic work.

If biblical scholars have a wealth of research aids and tools at their disposal to assist them in the reading and study of the Great Book, the average reader is much less fortunate, and is often left to rely upon personal faith for guidance, or is abandoned to a purely instinctive interpretation. This holds particularly true for the Old Testament; the New Testament being much more familiar to the western world and more accessible to modern readers given its unity in time and space. This has brought us to focus our attention on the Old Testament and the great figures who characterize it.

Our aim here, with total respect to the Bible's theological message and historical background, is to provide keys to its reading, clues and paths to follow for lay readers in their approach to understanding and interpreting it. We have chosen a presentation by character, selecting the most significant figures from its immense narrative heritage.

Side by side with these great heroes, the biblical universe is also peopled by a multitude of other personalities who play important supportive roles in the unfolding of its stories. We have attempted to highlight the main features of these figures by leaving them in their context and studying them as they are expressed through the account of their adventures and misfortunes.

The Bible, as we are aware, is above all the story of Israel's long history and turbulent relationship with Yahweh, its national God, and for this reason it may appear that the characters are mere pawns of a divine plan and will that "crush" any expression of individuality or initiative. But God also knows how to use human strengths and weaknesses to force the course of history. In short, Man does have a primordial importance in the Old Testament which places the salvation of humanity in a deeply historical context.

It should be added here that whenever possible, when not running the risk of over-burdening the narrative, we have tried to provide the reader with a maximum of historical and interpretative data, including possible comparisons with neighboring civilizations or information about the later development of biblical heroes in successive traditions.

In addition, this guide is illustrated with a series of masterpieces depicting the great characters of the Bible and photographs of locations where events of the narrative are thought to have taken place.* The treasure represented by biblical characters in art and literature, to which we have devoted only symbolic space in each chapter, is of course so immense that the scope of our work lays no claim to even coming near an exhaustive treatment. We only hope to have set the atmosphere of the narrative and given an idea of the role these characters have played throughout our cultural history.

If this volume serves to bring readers closer to a text as fundamental to our civilization as the Bible and encourages them to pursue its reading and understanding whatever their motivations may be, we will feel our work has served its purpose and that our objective has been achieved.

* We would like to thank Professor Sever Voicu, specialist in codicology, for his precious assistance in selecting the miniatures from the Vatican Library that are reproduced in this book. We are also grateful to the Director and staff of the National Institute of Archaeology and History of Art of the Palazzo Venezia in Rome, Italy, where most of the iconographic research was carried out.

ADAM AND EVE

The Creation and the Fall of Man

So saying, her rash hand in evil hour
Forth reaching to the fruit,
she plucked, she ate;
Earth felt the wound and nature...
Gave signs of woe that all was lost.

JOHN MILTON, *Paradise Lost*, Book IX

The beginning of the Old Testament immediately confronts the reader with the fundamental themes of human questing whether it be philosophic, scientific or religious. For, the first chapters of the Book of Genesis present the origins of the universe and its organization, the birth of animal and plant life and, finally, the creation of the first human couple. This couple is destined to forever lose the gift of immortality and be driven from Eden where God intends Man and Woman to live before they commit the original sin and disobey divine will. Expelled from this paradise, the two ancestors of the human race then begin their life on earth and put the history of humanity into motion. All of Creation is presented as an exclusively divine work, of the God of Israel, who proceeds according to a very precise plan, the fulfillment of which will unfold throughout the entire Bible right up to the most recent historical events confirmed to us by the sacred text.

The Book of Genesis, particularly in its initial chapters, was the result of very complex and stratified development. Indeed, we note the influence of numerous sources of different theological leanings, these texts themselves having drawn upon more ancient material of mythological or sapiential origin. In this respect, though the events described in the Bible are indisputably original in terms of their monotheistic perspective, their elements may also be traced back quite easily to ancient Near Eastern traditions which dealt with these same fundamental questions on human existence. The various sources of the biblical text were, therefore, in a later epoch compiled and re-organized to form a relatively coherent whole. This attempt is not always completely successful from the point of view of literary form or narrative logic, but the text does reflect, nevertheless, true homogeneity particularly in terms of a common theological outlook. The events of the Book of Genesis should thus be read from a dual perspective. On the one hand, the reader should always keep in mind that the men who compiled this precious material lived in a historically

Michelangelo, *The Creation of Man*

On the sixth day of Creation God creates Man "in his own image, after his likeness" and breathes into Man's nostrils the breath of life.

μην· εἰς τὴν παροικίαν κατεδικάσθην:-

Ὑπομνήσας ἐκείνης καὶ ἀμοσιου σμιμουλῆς
ἥτις τὴν ἀπόφασιν σωματώλεξεν· ἐπεὶ τὸν θαν
τηφόρον ἰὸν ἐν τοῖς ἐμοῖς ἐπαφῆκεν ὦσιν·
ὁ φθονερὸς καὶ μιαρὸς καλοὺς σκαιωρίας· τῆς
τὴν ὀλεθρίαν μοι σπάσας ἀγγελίαν· ὁ ἐχθρὸς

well-defined religious and social context, and that they were strongly influenced by several centuries of their people's specific history culminating in the tragic Babylonian Exile. On the other hand, the biblical story should also be considered in terms of the numerous mythological traditions, Near Eastern and others, which also dealt with such fundamental themes as the origin of the universe and Man, the introduction of death in the world, in short, the "supernatural" elements that forge all of life's most important natural and cultural aspects. Who created the universe? Where does Man come from? Why must Man die? Who decided existence should have the characteristics it does today, when and why? Such are the questions all traditions seek to answer. Even minimal familiarity with ancient mythologies and those of so-called primitive peoples clearly shows that beyond the historical and cultural differences, formal or interpretative which make the biblical narrative unique, the men who related and transcribed these ancient tales were also driven by the same impassioned and tormented desire to comprehend the deepest roots of human nature.

The heroes of the first episodes of the Bible, apart from the supreme protagonist who is God, are Adam and Eve, the primeval couple, and also the knowing and crafty serpent, the embodiment of temptation. It is the serpent who causes the ancestors of mankind to fall into sin, provoking their expulsion from Eden and God's decision to give Man a mortal destiny.

The first version of these primordial events is given in chapters 1 through 2:4a of Genesis and shows God's activity performed according to a systematic plan carried out over seven days. The second version, in chapter 2:4b-3:24a represents, as we will see, a simpler and more popular version characterized by the strong anthropomorphism of the Creator, who speaks and acts just like a human being.

The first story of the Origins (significantly referred to as *toledot*, a term that literally means "generations"), begins with the creation of heaven and earth, a binominal which traditionally designates the universe as a whole. This universe, however, is completely void (the famous *tohu wabohu*), formless, and desolate. Darkness reigns everywhere, on the earth as well as on the windswept primeval ocean. The Spirit of God moves across the face of the waters, and the Lord then creates light, by separating it from the darkness. This is an undefinable energy that will be independent from the heavenly bodies, which do not yet exist. Thus night and day are born, whose names God gives them, and whose daily alternation will recall the original mixture of darkness and light from which they came. With the first succession of evening and morning, the first day of Creation is complete.

On the second day, God creates the firmament and gives it the name "sky." This is in fact the celestial dome, an immense cupola that separates the upper ocean, that is, the rainwaters, from the lower ocean, in accordance with more archaic Eastern conceptions of the cosmos which the Hebrew culture shared.

On the third day, God gathers the waters beneath the celestial dome into one place, thus separating the dry land from the vast expanse of

(*opposite page*)

Medieval miniature, *Adam and Eve*

Through the story of the primeval couple, first placed in Eden by God and then expelled from this earthly paradise, humanity has sought the reasons for its daily lot.

Marc Chagall, *The Earthly Paradise*

Representations of Eden are cultural expressions that reflect a certain epoch and geographical context. The Old Testament, for example, places the source of the Tigris and Euphrates at the heart of this paradise.

Painted from the Dutch School, *The Creation of Woman*

God, feeling he should not leave Man alone, decides to put a helpmate by his side. He therefore creates all the animals and has them pass before Adam, but none of these creatures are adequate partners for him. The Lord then has Adam fall into a deep sleep and takes a rib from his body from which he fashions Woman.

the seas. The dry land will now be the womb, the humus, where seeds may sprout, giving birth to plants and trees of all kinds.

On the fourth day God creates the stars and two great luminaries (the sun and the moon), purposely in parenthesis here so that their names will not suggest that these are gods, but rather ordinary heavenly bodies just as the stars. For, in religions of the ancient East the sun and moon were objects of very widespread worship. The sun and moon will be responsible for regulating day and night respectively and for marking a clear distinction between light and darkness.

God devotes the fifth day to the creation of the living beings that will inhabit the waters and the air, the space between the earth and the celestial dome. These aquatic and celestial creatures soon reproduce and multiply, giving birth to innumerable other species.

On the sixth day the creatures of the earth appear, those that inhabit the dry land created by the receding waters, and include all beasts that walk, creep, or crawl, from cattle to reptiles, and all other species of land animals without exception. But the finishing touch to all Creation is Man, whom God creates "in his own image, after his likeness" and therefore who is radically different from all the other creatures. For Man is similar, though of course not identical, to his Creator in terms of his spiritual potentialities. According to this first biblical tradition God creates Man "male" and "female" but it is not specified how the differentiation occurs. Man and Woman are blessed by the Lord and told to be fruitful, to multiply, and to populate the earth. They will have dominion over the fish, birds, and all the animals that inhabit the earth. As in the case of all the other living creatures, the Lord provides Man with adequate nourishment consisting of herbs and fruit from the trees. It is interesting to note that the biblical description suggests that all living creatures are vegetarian, a state which immediately suggests a typical "golden age" environment where no conflicts exist between the various creatures.

God pauses to contemplate his work and is satisfied with what he has accomplished. He

therefore decides to bring the sixth day of Creation to an end. On the seventh day (a number that symbolizes absolute fulfillment), once the creation of the universe is complete in every way, God finally ceases all activity and blesses his Creation, consecrating this a day of rest. Saturday (*sabbat*) therefore appears as a divine institution even as early as Genesis, though it will only be much later, on Mount Sinai, that God will "officially" and explicitly establish this to sanction the Covenant with Moses and his descendants (Exod. 31:12 and thereafter).

The second story of the Creation immediately follows the first version and combines two different narratives which in turn refer to various minor traditions. Without going into exaggerated detail, we will simply note here that in this version the Creation is effected according to a different sequence. In the first version the succession goes from plants, to animals, to Man, whereas in the second story there is the creation, first of all, of a particular man, Adam, followed by the creation of plants (the Garden of Eden), then animals, and finally, Woman, who is also clearly identified.

When the Lord creates heaven and earth, vegetation does not exist, no bushes, nor steppes, nor cultivated plants in the fields, and this because rain does not exist yet either, no more than man to till the earth or irrigate it. So God creates Man, "moulding" him (the verb in Hebrew used here specifically indicates the action of a potter working clay) with the dust from the ground and then breathes into his nostrils the breath of life. To more clearly understand the meaning of this passage we might note here that the Hebrew terms for "man" (*adam*) and "ground" (*adamah*) are very close, but that rather than representing a simple play on words (most probably an etymological connection between the two terms does not exist), this refers to a deeper theological concept. The term "man" is used here with the definite article to stress the fact that this is the original Man, the first man, without the indefinite, collective value. Later, however, in the list of antediluvian patriarchs, the term *adam* will be used for all humanity.

God then gives Man-Adam a habitable environment, the wonderful Garden of Eden. Though this term perhaps originally referred to a precise geographical location, it was also used as the general term meaning "steppe." The Greek translation of the Bible, the Septuagint, in any case expresses this by *paradeisos* ("garden, paradise") whereas in Hebrew it is associated with another noun that signifies "delights." Probably "place of delights," comes closest in meaning, a joyous garden overgrown with lush vegetation, plants, flowers, and fruit as beautiful to look at as they are appetizing. This wonderful oasis seems to be the exact replica on a divine scale of the magnificent gardens which were kept by Near Eastern kings, particularly in Mesopotamia, celebrated throughout history. In this garden, among all of these wonders, there are notably two very special trees: the "Tree of Life," a clear symbol of immortality, and the "Tree of Knowledge of Good and Evil," which we will return to shortly. A digression in the text then informs us that at the heart of this paradise flows a river that, after irrigating Eden, divides into four different rivers of which only the Tigris and the Euphrates are known to us. The aim of the biblical authors was quite naturally to show that the most vital arteries of earthly geography (according to conceptions of the time) originated in this garden.

With regard to pinpointing the exact location of Eden, this question has intrigued many readers over the centuries who have proposed various hypothesis. However, given the mythological nature of the story, we will not go into these here. Such details, even if they were to have any real basis, would not offer any particular interest to us in the scope of this text.

Adam is assigned the task of guarding and tending the garden. He may help himself to as much fruit as he can eat from any of the trees, with just one exception: the fruit from the "Tree of

P. P. Rubens, ***The Original Sin or Adam and Eve***
Christian tradition often gives Woman a negative role, source of the "corruption" of Man. Only the appearance of Mary helped to partially redeem womankind, often associated in the story of Genesis with the diabolical element symbolized by the serpent.

Knowledge of Good and Evil' is absolutely forbidden. If he eats the fruit from this tree, he will "surely die." These words provide the first key (among many others) to the interpretation of the episode. The fruit from this tree has the power to denature Man who, from a simple creature in the service of his Creator, will become capable of deciding for himself what is good and what is evil. He will therefore be able to act accordingly, though at the same time, without having the necessary tools to attain Absolute Truth, which God alone possesses. To eat this fruit would therefore be to commit the sin of pride, the supreme sin which would cause Man, as God had created him, "to die," transforming him into a hybrid creature, apparently gifted with divine powers yet without possessing God's divine wisdom. The term "to die" might also be interpreted here as an allusion to a corporal sentence that would not be executed immediately, but would be fatally realized at the end of a determined life cycle.

Upon closer consideration, we see that this episode is truly a story of the creation and introduction of death in the world in its sanctioning of humanity's mortal destiny. Man will pay with his life, through his mortality, for his choice of independence and his sin of insubordination, the first in an interminable series of sins committed by a creature who, by nature, rebels against any state of submission and who aspires, as if he were a god, to being supreme judge of good and evil.

At this point in the text, another version, from a different tradition, relates the creation of Woman. God feels that Man should not live alone and decides to put a helpmate by his side, a creature similar to him and adapted to his needs. Therefore, after creating all the animals, God has them pass before Man who names each one, in this way not only giving them their identity, but also asserting his authority over them. But none of these creatures are naturally adequate partners for Adam. The Lord then has Adam fall into a deep sleep and takes a rib from his body from which he fashions (the verb in the text is "to fabricate" "to create") Woman, and brings her before Man. Adam realizes that this is his true companion and greets her with great joy, naming her "Woman," in Hebrew *ishsha*, the exact parallel of the masculine term, *ish*. Man will be prepared to leave his own family for Woman, to unite with her to become one flesh. With this reference to carnal union, we note that at this point in the story, though Man and Woman are completely naked, their original innocence keeps them from feeling the slightest shame. The biblical text stresses here that any form of seduction or concupiscence is unknown to them.

Among all the beasts God creates to inhabit the garden, there is also a serpent, the shrewdest and most formidable of the animals. This serpent slyly approaches Woman and sneeringly asks her if God has *really* forbidden the couple to eat the fruit from the trees. Woman responds that no, in fact, only the fruit from the "Tree of Knowledge of Good and Evil" at the heart of the garden is forbidden, for it will cause the couple's certain death. But the serpent immediately denies this: they will not die! God knows very well that this prodigious fruit will make Man and Woman "gods" just like him if they are able to distinguish good from evil. It is simply out of jealousy that the Creator wants to keep them from this extraordinary nourishment. In fact, the serpent insinuates, human existence could well extend beyond the limits imposed by God. His tempting argument quite truly suggests that "to know good and evil" means to become independent, to know how to decide, as God does, what is right and what is wrong. However, the serpent naturally omits mentioning that though Man, because of his nature, is certainly capable of deciding for himself, there is no guarantee that he will make the right choices and, because of his limitations, he will therefore be doomed to certain failure. Though it is undeniable that the serpent wants to deceive Man and Woman, it is just as true that Man's aspiration to moral autonomy, a tragic aspiration but one inherent in his nature, is not of the serpent's invention. This desire pushes Man to make his decisions freely and is an indispensable condition if he is to fully realize himself and live out his historical and spiritual adventure to its completion.

Woman looks with new eyes at the Tree's fruit which now appears even more enticing than ever, not only because of its taste, which she imagines must be delicious, but also because of its amazing powers. She hesitates not a moment longer, tastes it, then gives the fruit to Man to eat. Immediately, their state of innocence falls away, they discover a feeling of sexual consciousness and, realizing for the first time that they are naked (physically just as well as morally), they hasten to cover themselves with fig leaves and run to hide from God's view. Their souls are worried and agitated by the fear of the consequences of their act and by the magnitude of the profound transformation it has brought about.

The Lord then intervenes and asks Man to tell him what has happened. Man responds that he was hiding because he was afraid and ashamed of his nakedness. God then asks if he had realized that he was naked after having eaten the forbidden fruit and Man admits to this, but says that Woman urged him to eat it. Woman, in turn, accuses the serpent of having beguiled her.

God then pronounces a solemn curse on the serpent, which he condemns forever more to crawl in the dust, and declares eternal enmity between the serpent and Woman. It will be Woman, in fact, who will crush the serpent's head in a famous image that, according to many scholars, prefigures the Virgin's role in the struggle against the devil, traditionally associated with the serpent. This passage in Genesis is defined as the Proto-Gospel, that is, the very first prophecy of messianic and universal dimension. Beyond the purely "physical" interpretation of the prophecy (Woman passes on eternal hostility against the serpent to her children), a moral interpretation sees in this particular episode the roots of the struggle between the human race and the diabolical entity the serpent is believed to represent.

Shop sign, ***Au Paradis***, Liege, 17th century

Popular art naturally assimilated many biblical themes such as the Fall of Man and Woman and their expulsion from paradise, a universal heritage.

After cursing the serpent, God turns to Woman. He announces that she will be condemned to live in suffering and sorrow, giving birth in pain and, as Man's seductress, living in permanent and complete subjection to him. Finally, the Lord turns on Man. For having violated the divine interdict, he will forever struggle against the arid unyielding earth whose meagre fruits will only be obtained through hard relentless toil. Man will labor for his sustenance by the sweat of his brow until, given his mortal destiny, he returns to the dust from which he was created.

Man and Woman are therefore punished by a fate which, as we can see, perfectly reflects the reality of human existence with its hardships, suffering, and pain. With the first sin, the heavenly order God had wanted to establish on earth is broken and left behind. From this moment on, instead of a life of delights in an earthly paradise, humanity must engage in a fight for survival day after day along a road leading irremediably only to death. The supreme punishment for humanity is, of course, the unconditional loss of its closeness and familiarity with God and the fact that the consequences of the wrongs committed by the first parents in human history will fall, in an inexhorable and endless chain, upon their children and upon all of their descendants.

At that moment Man-Adam choses a name for Woman, and calls her Eve, which is "living" or "life" according to biblical etymology, though the original meaning is perhaps "mother," since she will be the mother of all men. The couple are clothed in animal skins and God pronounces a statement that, after some consideration, seems to confirm to what degree the serpent has been "sincere" in his tempting invitation. "Here is Man, now become one of us, with the knowledge of good and evil!" And, since God's initial plans may in no way be altered, he expels the couple from Eden, not only as punishment, but also, he adds, to ensure that they do not eat the fruit from the "Tree of Life" as well and thus attain a condition identical to the Divine. Instead, men must remain subject to death. God therefore sends them away, out into the world, after placing cherubs with flaming swords in the garden to bar their return.

After their departure, Adam and Eve face a daily life of hardship. They come together in carnal union and have children, Cain and then Abel, whose tragic destinies will be related in the next chapter. The two ancestors of the human race have

Rembrandt, ***Adam and Eve***

Man and Woman live together in complete nakedness without the slightest embarrassment. After eating the forbidden fruit they discover a feeling of concupiscence and, realizing they are naked, hasten to cover themselves with fig leaves. Their souls are worried and agitated by fear before the magnitude of their profound transformation.

thus fulfilled their purpose in the biblical narrative and are but pale shadows of secondary importance in subsequent events. They have another child, Seth, and numerous other descendants whom we will encounter in later chapters. Though Adam and Eve will rarely appear again in the Book of Genesis, we do learn that after the birth of Seth, and the begetting of other sons and daughters, Adam dies at the age of 930 years of age, having enjoyed the extraordinary longevity which will characterize, as we will see, all humanity before the Flood.

So much has been said, written, and reflected about these passages that a succinct commentary would be inappropriate. We will simply note here that the description of this story as "a myth of suffering and punishment," as some interpreters have suggested, probably best summarizes the characteristics and final conclusions of a text whose exceptional poignance causes even its own characters to eventually give way, to virtually lose all substance and depth, under the weight of the story's greatness.

The figure of Adam will enjoy immense popularity but also inconsistent treatment in the Judeo-Christian tradition. Apocryphal literature, for example, places him in the forefront, adding a series of details to his adventure and those of his descendants which are, for the most part, foreign to the biblical narrative. Gnostic tradition, on the other hand, transforms Adam into a divine personage who, from primeval Man and king of Paradise, quite naturally goes on to becoming, after Redemption, governor of the world in the name of God. Indeed, we are confronted most everywhere, from apocryphal writings to rabbinical literature, with an ambivalent evaluation. For Adam is the venerable ancestor of humanity, the father of all men, but at the same time he is also the tragic protagonist of the original sin, the figure responsible for the irremediable Fall. This partially explains the elaborate eschatological dimension exegesis felt forced to create for him in its effort to redeem him, and through this redemption, return Adam to the original paradisical state. From this point of view, the figure of Adam tends to be identified with Man the idealist, constantly dissatisfied with his condition, forever aspiring to return to paradise lost. This at times produces a truly mystical Adam who, according to Christian tradition, must await the coming of Christ to finally be fulfilled through Him, the ultimate Adam. Only in this way will Man finally see his aspirations satisfied and rid himself of the terrible weight of his capital sin, the sin of pride.

As for Eve, though her name is never mentioned again in the Old Testament, in the New Testament she appears principally as Man's seductress. This traditionally negative role no doubt influenced the theological evaluation of women in general, particularly in the work of St. Paul, which only the appearance of Mary helped to alter somewhat.

The serpent, finally, is a creature which all cultures have drawn upon for a number of symbols. Traditionally associated with magic and death, the serpent, particularly because of its capacity to shed its skin has been universally interpreted as a symbol of self-regeneration in a vital cycle of immortality. In Near Eastern traditions, for example in the Accadian-Sumerian saga of Gilgamesh, King of Uruk, it is precisely the serpent that steals the herb of immortality just won by the king, thus tragically confirming mankind's mortal destiny. In the story of Genesis, the serpent may very well have been an allusion to a common Canaanite belief. The reptile, considered a sacred animal by Canaanite cults, was often worshipped as a household spirit in contact with the otherworld and was believed to possess the power to heal or kill anyone suffering from

Tintoretto, *The Original Sin*

The original sin is but the first in an interminable series of sins. Man shows he is a creature who, by nature, will rebel against any state of submission and aspires, as if he were a god, to being the ultimate judge of good and evil.

Gustav Klimt, ***Adam and Eve***

After their expulsion from earthly paradise, Adam and Eve, the ancestors of the human race, must face a "human" existence with its lot of daily suffering and, above all, death. Their story is thus also a myth of the origin of Man's mortal condition, which exists in all the mythologies of the world. Klimt's painting is an unfinished work.

illness. More than one Near Eastern divinity had a serpentine form, and the symbolic qualities of the serpent were perfectly illustrated in the Egyptian symbol, the uraeus (a snake and the solar disk), the Pharoah's emblem, which was supposed to have the power to burn and destroy its enemies. The biblical text, however, limits itself to presenting the serpent as simply one creature among many of God's animals. It is true, however, that the role ascribed to the serpent in the biblical story confirms the exceptional quality of the character, recognized implictly and rather naively by the editors of Genesis.

Later traditions, as we know, will identify the serpent with the devil, as the New Testament often confirms, and as the Wisdom of Solomon (2:24) already announces very significantly:

> Because of the devil's wish
> death entered the world:
> Subjected to it are those
> who belong to him.

In conclusion, let us consider the originality of Genesis, its Creation of the universe and Man, as compared to other ancient mythological traditions. Genesis is unique in that it ignores any theogonic process (explanation of the birth of gods) and makes no mention of any struggles between divinities or primeval monsters, events which normally form the basis of cosmogonies, or creations of the world. In the Bible, only a formless impersonal chaos exists upon which God exercises his Creation. Unlike the stories of creation related in Mesopotamian or Egyptian mythologies which are based upon a principle of progressive generations, Genesis stresses the individual and exclusive quality of God's activity, an action that is solitary and free. The biblical Creation is presented in a strictly monotheistic context which excludes by definition the existence of any other supernatural or divine entities.

Concerning the origin of mankind, Mesopotamian mythology affirms Man's partially divine nature when it relates that he is created from clay mixed with the blood of a dead god and that, in this way, the god's supernatural qualities are transferred to him. However, in Genesis it is God himself, a living God, who breathes life into Man and shares his divine essence with him. This was undoubtedly to emphasize the special personal and moral bond that united Yahweh and Man and which differed so radically from mythologies which often considered human beings as solely having been created to serve the gods and alleviate their fatigue. The Creation in the Bible is presented as desired by God alone, motivated by his own free will, absolute and ineffable. Though the narrative's underlying story was most certainly composed of numerous elements and traditions prevalent in Near Eastern religions, in Genesis these gave rise to an original and revolutionary version of the Creation. The text was indissolubly bound to strictly theological aims and to the destiny of the Hebrew people who saw, and still see in the story of the Creation today, the beginning of their own historical adventure. This insight helps explain why the individual heroes in Genesis inevitably lose some of the stature and importance that characterize most "first men" in other mythologies. We understand that for the sake of these theological aims the characters of the story of the Creation often appear as mere instruments, for the most part passive and unaware, of an extraordinary plan in which they play but secondary roles.

CAIN AND ABEL

Earth and Blood

They dug a ditch and Cain said,
"It is good!" and then went down alone under the dark vault.
When he had sat on his chair in the shadow
and the crypt was closed above him,
the eye was in the tomb and it looked upon him.

VICTOR HUGO, *The Conscience*

Farmer and Fratricide

Adam and Eve are expelled from Eden and must now face the "human" existence they have brought upon themselves by disobeying their Creator. They are forced to earn their daily bread through hard labor instead of having it easily at hand as before, and must now fight for their survival. With their departure from Paradise, definitive and irremediable, Man's great spiritual and cultural adventure begins, and he is called upon to create *ex nihilo* the reasons for his presence in a hostile universe where nothing is granted anyone who does not fight for it with all his strength.

The story of Genesis in this way sets out to relate not only the origins of human civilization, but also the birth of Man as a being of faith, as a thinking creature, a center of sentiments and passions. The relationship between Adam and Eve is inevitably transformed: reciprocal companionship, innocent and fraternal in a timeless existence in Eden, gives way to a highly concrete, physical, and complementary one between man, who must work very hard, and woman, whose principal function is to bear descendants.

Among the many consequences of the expulsion from Paradise, there is therefore the birth of physical love. The biblical text says simply that Adam "knew" Eve, that is, that he possessed her in the most profound and complete way, by entrusting his seed to her as one would plant seeds in the soil of the earth. We can imagine how precious this moment of intimate physical union must have been in the lives of the most solitary couple in all human history, called upon to found humanity. The mother to all creatures thus conceives, and gives birth to her first son, the ill-fated Cain. After which, we learn very expediently of a second pregnancy and the birth of a second son, Abel.

The profiles of these two brothers are quickly sketched in a few broad strokes and the great differences between them in their habits, tastes, and characters appear. Cain eventually becomes a farmer and works the land, whereas Abel chooses to be a shepherd. The farmer and the shepherd, in fact, represented two fundamental activities that characterized ancient economies for millenniums and a profoundly different ideological outlook as well as way of life was associated with each one. At season's end, each brother dutifully offers the Lord the fruits of his labor: Cain, the produce from the earth, and Abel, the first born from his flock and their fat. Without any apparent reason (though we will see, in fact, that from a historical and cultural point of view there was one), God accepts Abel's offering, and rejects Cain's. Not a word in the biblical text explains the reasons for this preference nor the possible causes for such an attitude. Many interpreters, both ancient and modern, have felt and affirmed that Abel's offering was superior to Cain's, justifying this with various arguments. In the vast extra-biblical literature of the apocryphal and pseudepigraphical texts, in other words, those not included in the official canon recognized by the Church (often because of the excess of imagination they contain), we find another rather curious explanation: Cain murdered Abel because when it came time to choose wives the more beautiful of two sisters, and the one Cain preferred, was given to Abel. The murder was therefore a crime of passion, committed out of jealousy. Whatever the case may be, surely any reader other than a theologian will find it virtually impossible to understand the profound motives of what happened; he must therefore limit himself to a few hypotheses and go on with the narrative.

Faced with God's refusal of his offering, Cain is both astounded and angry. As a forerunner of Job, he should have accepted the fact without understanding it, despite the deep lashing feelings of injustice that filled him with rage and dismay. But who could have instilled him with such faith if not this same God who punished him without any apparent reason? For, Cain thinks, "Have I not also worked and sweated day after day, laboring the arid land, planting seeds in furrows, irrigating, trembling that the weather be good, that it reward my efforts and favor my harvest? After all, have I not also respected the prophecy so dramatically revealed by the Lord to my father, Adam, according to which the earth would only yield its fruits after a thousand efforts?" And again: "Is not my labor but a continuation of Adam's, when he tilled the land in Paradise?"

Faced with Cain's desperation and rage, God decides to intervene in person. In those mythical times, in fact, contacts between heaven and earth were still possible directly, and without mediation. The Lord then reproaches Cain for his reaction and asks him to take a good look at himself and think over whether he has behaved well or not, exhorting him not to be overcome by the forces of sin. For many interpreters, this will represent the first divine enunciation of the principle of free will, though once again the biblical story, in its laconic way, says nothing to clarify nor shed any light on the background of this episode. The passage in question remains in many ways obscure, and interpretative problems are certainly not lacking. One cannot help wondering what the original farmer's sin really was: negligence, lack of faith, envy, or something else entirely?

The narrative continues at a dramatic pace. Cain speaks to his brother Abel and invites him to go out into the fields with him; as soon as they arrive, Cain kills him. Behind this short hard statement our imagination conjures up an infinite number of scenarios, though one of them prevails over all others: the jealousy and blind rage of a man who, rightly or wrongly, feels excluded and deeply rejected. Certainly nothing indicates that Abel did anything in particular to win the Lord's favor, even less to harm his elder brother. Nor does anything suggest that Cain was a bad farmer in comparison to his brother Abel, whom we imagine to be an admirable shepherd. Cain's rage against his brother appears to be the desperate though, of course, unjustifiable reaction of a person who feels he has been abandoned forever and must kill for his own survival.

After the murder, God again manifests himself to Cain and asks what has happened to his brother. Crime gives way to falsehood, as brusque as it is naive: he is not his brother's keeper, he knows nothing of him. But Abel's blood, seeping into the furrows of the ground, cries out for vengeance and God hears this urgent plea. The Lord then pronounces a terrible curse against Cain the farmer: the ground, poisoned by fratricide, will turn its back on him, he will be doomed to failure as a tiller of this soil forever! Cain must therefore abandon it, leave his home, and wander the world over as a fugitive. Cain attempts one last defense: if he is banished from his land to wander homeless, forsaken by God, any man he meets (Abel's descendants?) might easily see the divine curse upon him and kill him, without risking punishment. Upon this, without retracting his sentence, God nevertheless pronounces a word of justice as consolation, however small, for the unfortunate man: all murders will be punished, and Cain's eventual murder will be avenged seven times over. And to protect him, God puts a special mark on Cain to guard him against any man who crosses his path motivated by evil intentions.

Cain's Descendants

Cain then leaves the Lord's presence and goes to live in a land to the east of Eden, whose name, Nod, is closely related to the verb "to wander."

The story of the first crime ever committed in human history comes to an end with this episode, though another tradition giving further information about Cain's adventures and about his descendants is included in the Bible, not without a few contradictions in respect to events previously narrated. We learn from this later text that Cain marries and has a son named Enoch. Cain, the former farmer, although destined to wander forever as a vagabond, becomes a founder of cities, and even builds one which he names after his own son. We are then given more information about Cain's descendants: from Enoch is born Irad, from Irad is born Mehujael, from the latter comes Methushael and from Methushael, Lamech. The latter takes two wives, Adah and Zillah; from the first wife he has two sons, Jabal and Jubal. Jabal becomes the forefather of tent-dwelling nomadic shepherds, while Jubal becomes the predecessor of harpists and flautists. His second wife, Zillah, will give him a son, Tubal Cain, patron of metalsmiths, as well as a daughter named Naamah.

Nomadic livestock breeders are therefore traced back to Cain, as well as musicians and metalsmiths. As for Cain himself, though condemned to the life of a fugitive, he is seen founding the first urban center populated by sedentary peoples, the origins of sedentary and associative life, therefore, being attributed to him as well. Beyond their theological message, how should these events grafted onto the story's original core be considered? From a historical point of view, is there any way to reconcile them with Cain, the farmer and fratricide, as he is described in the first story?

If we were dealing with ancient mythology and not with the Old Testament, we would define Cain as a veritable "culture hero," that is, a figure responsible for significant achievements and conquests in the interest of civilization.

That this fratricide, in many ways, is an exceptional character is already suggested by his name. Initially signifying "acquired progeny" in the text (in Gen. 4:1 upon giving birth to him, Eve says, "I acquired a man from Yahweh"), Cain's name should, in fact, be interpreted as a proper noun and derivative of "metalsmith" or "metal craftsman." In Cain, therefore, two apparently opposing and contradictory aspects have merged: the farmer, linked to sedentary life and confirmed by traditions concerning his founding of cities; and the metalsmith, itinerant craftsman, no doubt an implicit allusion to his condemnation to nomadism.

To fully grasp the significance and background of this character and his adventures, we should remember that though the story of Cain and Abel takes place at the dawn of human history, the narrative was in fact written down in a much more recent epoch, much closer to our own, when urban culture was already fully developed, agricultural techniques familiar, and the skills of metallurgy largely mastered. From the story of the two brothers, the conflict clearly emerges between two opposing conceptions of life, respectively bound to agriculture (a sedentary life), and sheep farming (a semi-nomadic existence in the wake of a flock). At the time of the story's writing, the Hebrew people had already been living in Palestine for quite some time and were well-accustomed to urban life. Yet the Bible here, and at other times, tends to show a preference for the ideal of pastoral life (typical of the legendary Patriarchs of Israel), and to warn against the dangers of moral depravation and corruption inherent in urban communities (typical of the Canaanites with whom the Hebrew people had come into contact). It is also in this respect that God's preference for Abel's offering should be interpreted, in that it represented the type of life

(*opposite page*)

Medieval miniature, *Scenes from the Life of Cain and Abel*

Art certainly has not privileged the theme of the adventures of Cain and Abel, perhaps because it illustrates the most negative aspects of human nature.

G. Evrard, ***Cain and Abel***

At season's end, each brother dutifully offers the Lord the fruits of his labor: Cain, the products from the earth, and Abel, the first born from his flock and their fat. But God rejects Cain's offering who jealously murders his brother.

also led by the first nomadic patriarchs in search of pastures. Moreover, it suffices to recall that the Lord himself, in leading the chosen people, is often compared to a shepherd.

Also of extreme interest is the fact that the fundamental opposition between agriculture and sheep farming illustrated in Genesis was the object of remarkably rich literary expression in other civilizations in the ancient Orient, which undoubtedly influenced the Bible and its editors. In Sumerian documentation from Mesopotamia dating back to very ancient periods (third to second millennium B. C.), we learn of literary compositions called *tensions* or *disputes* in which two characters or two personified elements (for example Summer and Winter, two types of plants, two species of animals, etc.) took turns expounding on their particular merits in order to diminish those of the adversary. The most celebrated *dispute* was precisely the one that confronted Wheat and Cattle, in other words, the two activities which interest us here, with the resulting lifestyles they imply. Wheat was represented by its goddess, Ashnan, while Cattle was defended by its patron god, Lahar. The epilogue to the confrontation deserves particular attention: though both activities and their respective production were considered extremely precious to humanity, it was Ashnan, that is Agriculture, who was declared victorious by the acting judges, the gods. Another Sumerian text placed the farmer (Enkimdu) against the shepherd (Dumuzi) with an outcome to the confrontation which aimed at peacefully reconciling both activities and their two respective ways of life.

Frans Francken II, ***Cain and Abel***

The Bible does not explain why God prefers Abel's offering, but underlying this episode we see the conflict between two opposing conceptions of life, one bound to agriculture and the other to sheep farming. The pastoral ideal (typical of the legendary Patriarchs of Israel) was preferred to the dangers of moral depravation and corruption inherent in urban life.

It has been said that in the popular mind Cain is the archetype of the evil man, the original murderer who introduces crime into human society. Consistent with this, his descendants are also marked by morally negative aspects: Mehujael means "destroyed by God" or "destroyer of God," Methushael signifies "covetous man," Lamech is the first bigamist, and so on. Yet, beyond its moral message, the story as a whole also prompts us to ask ourselves a number of questions. Why does Cain's name, as the first murderer in human history, mean "metalsmith?" Why, in light of his terrible crime, does God mark Cain with a sign that protects him from the aggression of other men?

Our most promising lead lies precisely in focusing on the figure of the metalsmith himself. Ethnology and the history of religions tell us that in ancient cultures and in those of the so-called "primitive" peoples, the metalsmith was always a figure surrounded by very mixed feelings. He seemed to possess a disturbing ambivalence which inspired a combination of fear and veneration. Under closer consideration, we see that this ambivalence was linked, in fact, to the elements themselves used by the metalsmith for his work, elements which could serve to create very useful tools such as the plough, but also weapons which could cause death. Metallurgy was therefore perceived as a superhuman art and its techniques, as new discoveries seemingly introduced by magic into society. From whence came the common attitude that metalsmiths were foreign, ambiguous figures gifted with supernatural powers. They were respected, but also regarded with suspicion and distrust, and isolated because of their very capabilities. Given their nomadic status, these itinerant craftsmen enjoyed no protection from tribal bonds, but nevertheless they were inviolable precisely because of the exceptional character and usefulness of their ability to manipulate fire and metals, from which they forged marvelous and indispensable objects.

These comparisons help shed new light on the figure of Cain and at least part of his tribulations. The etymology of his name, which signifies "metalsmith," is no longer an isolated detail. Apart from his descendant, Tubal Cain, whom biblical commentators later make into the true creator of metallurgy, we note in the Old Testament a definite historical link between Cain and the Kenite tribe whose name is related to our hero's. This was a nomadic or semi-nomadic tribe devoted to itinerant metallurgy, whose historical existence outside the Bible seems certain. These nomads were specialized in metal working, music, and divination, and were looked upon with the greatest respect, but also with fear because of their magical abilities. Even if relations between the Israelites and Kenites were friendly, it is worth noting that in Gen. 15:19 the Kenites were said to be listed among the peoples who inhabited Canaan, the same population that would be divested of its land by God, in order to create the Promised Land of Israel. From all appearances, this would seem to be another indirect criticism of Cain, who is shown as the forefather of a people who unjustly occupy the land assigned to the chosen people.

In this context, we more clearly understand both the episode of the "sign" whereby God marks Cain and the Lord's intervention intended to punish the guilty man by banishment, though at the same time making him a protected and untouchable person. The famous mark, of which we know very little, appears in this case to be more a guarantee of inviolability and protection than a mark of infamy. It once again refers back to the example of the itinerant metalsmiths in need of protection.

Two approaches to the reading of the biblical tale of Cain and Abel may be proposed. First of all, a more traditional one, by reading a moral dimension into the story which condemns and banishes the jealous murderer, implying that his descendants are also to be judged negatively. The Bible's preference for pastoral life is explained, ideologically speaking, by the concept according to which Israel's founding fathers were shepherds and that their nomadic way of life in the desert was a

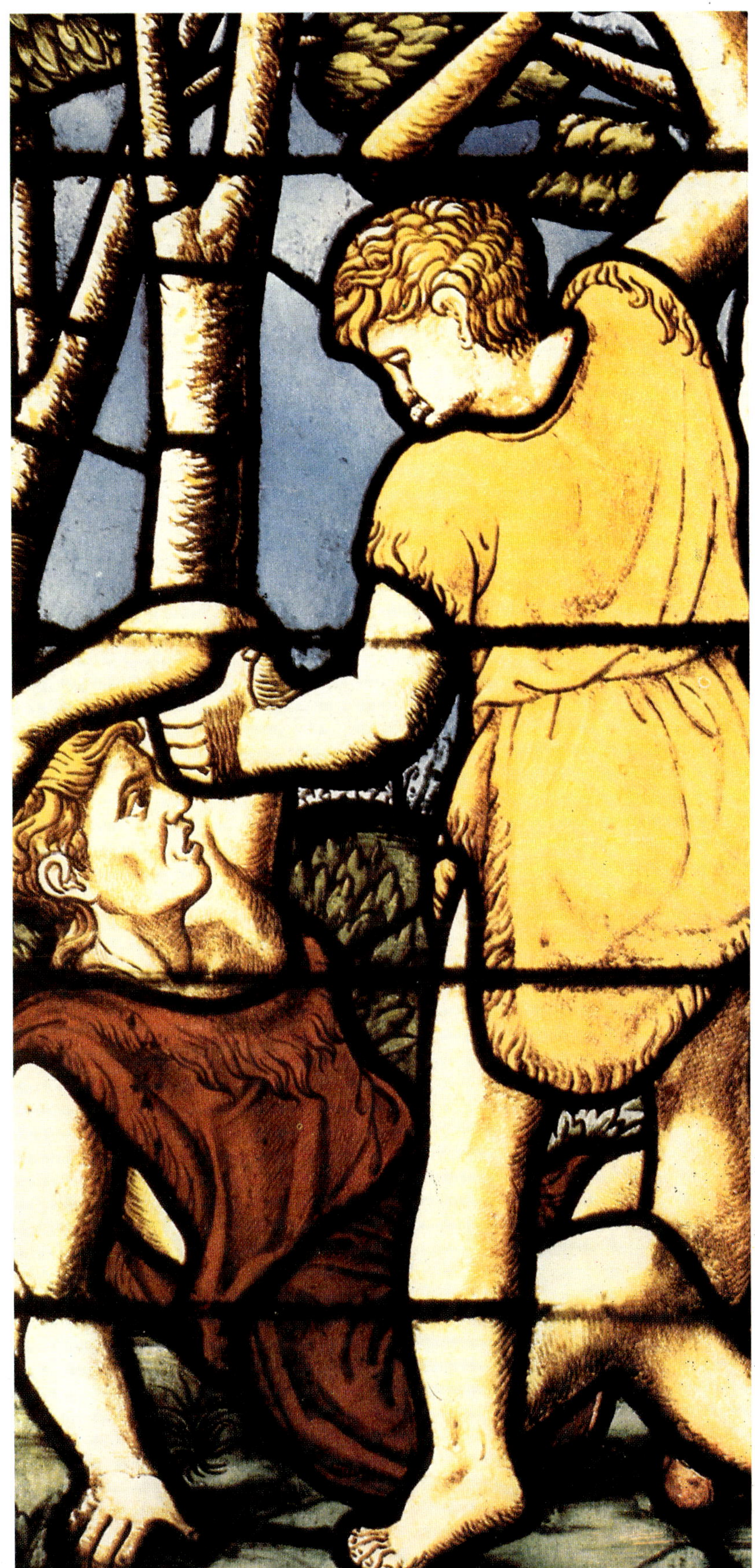

Stained glass, *Cain and Abel*

A comparative study of the history of religions may provide some insight into Cain's strange destiny.

purer existence, far from the moral degeneration of sedentary life in the city. In addition, it is suggested that the shepherd relies completely on God for the fruits of his labor, whereas the farmer, who also depends upon his own resources, is not so completely dependent upon divine Providence.

However, a second historical approach also exists which may serve to interpret the episodes. Cain is then considered a character comparable to the culture heroes in many mythologies, creators and disseminators of technical innovations of great economic and social value. In addition to Cain's role as founder of the first city, very ancient traditions considered our protagonist the eponym and forefather of all metalsmiths. The social standing enjoyed by these artisans, as attested in a number of cultures, was remarkably high, and though not belonging to any tribal groups, metalsmiths were at the same time feared and respected because of their impressive powers and almost magical abilities. The "sign" God places on Cain is more clearly understandable if we consider that the primitive metalsmith, not belonging to any well-defined social group and leading an itinerant existence, was constantly exposed to the risks of aggression. In order to counteract this, convention declared him inviolable, untouchable in virtue of his formidable powers and, objectively, the indispensable nature of his work.

In this dual perspective, the story of Cain returns an ambivalent personage to us: alongside the vile fratricide, epitome of sin and evil, we discover another Cain, a positive hero, mythic creator of the art of metallurgy and its techniques. Originally this second Cain must surely not have had a negative moral connotation. Most likely the partial merging of his personality with the criminal Cain was simply in answer to narrative requirements and editorial devices which today can only be grasped in their broad outlines. Moreover, the theme of brotherly rivalry belongs to universal folklore, as well as the association between fratricide and the founding of a city; the most famous example probably being that of Remus and Romulus and the origins of Rome.

In conclusion, it would seem that in the narrative of Cain and Abel, the biblical editors took advantage of a popular tale at hand, bending it to the necessities of their own didactic and moral objectives. They achieved this through a reworking of the story which, nevertheless, at times even today reveals other underlying literary strata and a far more ancient tale. Although the figure of Cain as "epitome of evil" certainly does not emerge rehabilitated, we do see quite clearly, at any rate, how the other Cain, innocent popular hero from a remote prehistoric time, lent his name and part of his personality to the terrible fratracide, thus becoming accomplice despite himself to a primordial crime to which originally he was completely foreign.

NOAH

The Second Founding of the Human Race

It was the final cry from the last man.
For a long time over the rising water his hands
sustained Sarah pursued by the waves.
But when he had lost his vital strength,
the world was invaded by sky and sea.
And the rainbow shone for now
everything was complete.

ALFRED DE VIGNY, *The Flood*

Following the dramatic adventures of Cain and Abel, numerous other children are born to Adam and Eve and among them Seth, a son who will take the place of the slain Abel. Seth in turn has a son, Enos ("man"). At this point in history, relates the Old Testament, men begin "to invoke the name of the Lord." This statement will signal the end of the "prehistoric" period of humanity, when relations with God existed but apparently were not yet adequately codified, and announce our entry into the actual "historical" phase of humanity, when men fully discover the Divine, his name, and his cult. We also find echoes in the Bible of an alternative and more widespread tradition according to which Moses was the first person to whom God's name was revealed, a revelation which would have taken place during the celebrated theophany on Mount Sinai. For our purposes, the details concerning the invocation of God serve to help situate the various patriarchs, whether anterior or posterior to the Flood, in the context of religious orthodoxy.

Before the Flood, men lived under unique and exceptional conditions. Still not long after the age

Kessel, ***Noah's Ark***
Noah and his family take two of each species of animal, including birds and reptiles, into the Ark with them as well as everything necessary for their sustenance.

of Eden, these distant ancestors boasted of extremely long lives, as witnessed by the extraordinary case of the proverbial Methuselah, who lived to be 969 years old. Among these mythical figures, one of the most outstanding was Enoch, who escaped from death, the common lot of all men, when the Lord took him away to be by his side forever (as will also be the case of Elijah, whom we will consider in a later chapter). As a result, Enoch is considered one of the greatest figures in Hebrew tradition and various works considered as Apocrypha are notably attributed to him. After him, Lamech, son of the aged Methuselah, becomes father to Noah, hero of the Flood. Noah in turn, at the venerable age of 500 years has three sons, Shem, Ham, and Japheth, who will be identified with the origin of the different races and languages of the earth.

We may justifiably ask ourselves why the biblical editors attributed such long existences and exceptional fertility in advanced age to these legendary characters. There are perhaps two responses, one of a theological nature, and the other of a strictly historical character. From a theological point of view, a theory existed associating human longevity to the concept of retribution: a long life signified God's benediction and grace (according to an anthropocentric perspective which placed human life at the center of all values). The progressive shortening of longevity would then have coincided with the spreading of evil in the world, and the ineluctable moral degeneration of mankind, who could only recover this ancient privilege in the messianic era. Moreover, it has been pointed out that the numbers of years attributed to these archaic figures often had a symbolic significance, as in the cases of Noah and Abraham, based as they were on the sexagesimal system. From a historical perspective, however, the very long lives attributed to these figures were a fundamental factor aimed at emphasizing the exceptional character of the epoch in which they lived, which was unique, absolutely extraordinary, typical of a fabulous and mythical time; and which would be eradicated forever by the great Flood, a prelude to mankind's entry into present reality. The Bible alludes to this moral degradation in very obscure terms, making use of hermetic terminology referring to unions between "sons of God" (types of demi-gods or heroes, depending upon the tradition) and mortal women. This type of scenario cannot help evoking those found in Greek mythology, and in particular, the theogony of Hesiod. At this time, therefore, the earth was still populated by a race of giants (recalling the Titans in Greek mythology), who lived without the slightest notion of discipline or rule, indulging in rampant polygamy. It was a chaotic and wild epoch, vacillating between the residual golden age of Eden (long life, prodigious capacities, the possibility of being taken up into the heavens by God), and the most unacceptable barbarism in the eyes of the Hebrew society, the society which collected and compiled these stories.

Underlying this narrative of the first legendary patriarchs, we find many critical elements directed against specific mythological traditions held by Semitic cultures close to the Hebrews. In the beliefs of Syrian and Palestinian peoples a very important role was played by heroic figures placed in a mythical dimension. These were originally

J. Cossiers, *The Flood*

For "many days and many nights" floodwaters sweep the earth, destroying all forms of life. Giant tides merge with the torrential rains to create the most formidable cataclysm in all earth's history.

mortal kings, princes or famous warriors from very distant historical times to whom exceptional feats were ascribed, as well as good works performed in the interests of humanity. The reference to "giants" of the primordial epoch may be more clearly understood if we note that in using this term, the biblical editors were seeking to reduce to the status of common mortals those personages who, given their colossal proportions, Syro-Palestinian mythology considered as semi-divine. The early patriarchs, on the other hand, are presented as fully human figures with their qualities and defects, struggling in a simple and primitive world. Sedentary life, the division of society into various professions, and urban civilization, are not, according to the Bible, a gift or revelation from God (as is often the case in mythologies of other peoples), but are the result of man's own conquests and inventions. On the basis of the fabulous characteristics attributed to the age of the patriarchs, one perceives, as mentioned previously, one of the key values of biblicial ethics according to which retribution for the righteous is realized solely on earth, and is expressed through the long life and many descendants granted by Yahweh to those who obey his moral commandments. Here, as well as elsewhere, eschatological doctrine remains well out of the picture, the dimension of the hereafter, as far as it concerns common mortals, is not of the slightest interest to the biblical editors and remains explictly outside Yahweh's concerns.

As previously mentioned, this primordial epoch is considered a period of progressive moral degeneration, and this forces the Lord to intervene. At first, he limits himself to reducing human life to 120 years, but then he resolves to destroy humanity altogether and create new conditions for its regeneration. But what was the cause of this decadence? As we have seen, the text speaks of "sons of God" who, after having created women, discover feminine beauty, and begin to take wives indiscriminately and without limit. Most probably this is an allusion to an extremely ancient myth concerning semi-divine (or assimilated) beings that was borrowed, it would seem, from Canaanite traditions. In any case, the Lord decides to shorten the duration of existence, and even comes to regret having created Man at all, whom he decides to eradicate from the face of the earth along with all the other living creatures. Only Noah, among all men, finds grace in his eyes and will be spared, for he is destined to found humanity anew.

We are never told whether Noah has done anything in particular to deserve such a privilege, that is, salvation. We know only that he represents an exception to his contemporaries in that he is honest, just, without weaknesses, and that he "walks with God" (therefore is of perfect moral conduct). On the other hand, in the world around him there is nothing but moral decadence, corruption, and violence.

Two versions of the story of the Flood exist (both in turn having collected and combined several other sources or stories); one is more concise and vivid (J), and the other is lengthier and more elaborate, though not as graphically narrated

(P). There are some differences between their episodes, but the similarities largely prevail.

Among the differences we may note for example:

J	P
God decides to destroy mankind and all other living creatures.	God decides to destroy mankind only.
The description of the ark is missing.	A detailed description of the ark is given.
Noah takes seven couples from the "clean" animals and one couple from the "unclean" animals.	Noah takes two of each species of animal.
The episode of the raven and the dove is related.	The episode of the raven and the dove is missing.

The date of the beginning of the Flood is also different, as well as its duration, and various other details (such as the precise origin of the Deluge, the stages of flooding, etc.). Nevertheless, a global reading of the story allows us to follow a reasonably linear narrative, thanks to its editing, which sought to give an organic form to the collection of disparate traditions, reworking them with impressive concern for formal symmetry. The story of the great Flood may thus be resumed in these terms.

God first manifests himself to Noah, who has just turned 600 years old, and reveals his awful intentions to him: an immense natural catastrophe will destroy all forms of life on earth. Only Noah will be saved, under the condition that he scrupulously follows the Divine commands. He must build an ark — described in the minutest detail as to building materials, shape, and measurements — that should also have a roof and three decks divided into small areas. It is interesting to note that the Hebrew term used here to refer to the ark is the same one used to designate the basket where Moses was placed before being abandoned on the Nile. The agreement between Noah and God stipulates that

Michelangelo, *The Flood*

Because of Man's continued moral degeneration, God decides to eradicate humanity and all other living creatures from the face of the earth. Only Noah is spared and is destined to save the animal kingdom and found humanity anew.

Michelangelo, *The Flood* *(detail)*

Other Near Eastern mythologies also narrate the destruction of the world by a divine flood, but the biblical tale is motivated by a specific theological purpose. Man falls into sin a second time and is again regenerated to fulfill God's plans.

Noah and his wife, along with their sons and daughters-in-law will be saved from the Flood. They will take two of each species of animal, including birds and reptiles, into the ark with them as well as everything necessary for their sustenance (no doubt this pertains mainly to vegetables).

Noah scrupulously obeys God's commands though he only has seven days before the Deluge will be upon them. Everything comes to pass as God has foretold it, and during many days and many nights (the duration varies depending on the source) floodwaters sweep the earth destroying all forms of life, while the curious boat resists against the swirling torrents. Giant tides which, according to ancient cosmological conceptions surrounded the earth, merge with the torrential rains to create the most formidable cataclysm in all the earth's history.

At last, a strong wind rises over the apocalyptic scene where death reigns everywhere; the waters begin to recede progressively, and little by little land reappears. According to one of the two versions of the story, after seven months the ark ran aground on Mount Ararat, but other sources affirm that Noah set a raven free and it returned to the ark because there was no dry land where it could rest. Noah then despatched a dove, and the same thing occurred. However, set free a second time, the dove came back to the ark with an olive leaf in its beak; and then let go a third time, the bird did not return at all, a sign that the earth was finally dry! God again manifests himself to Noah, inviting him to leave the ark and to allow the human and animal passengers alike to emerge. Their task is now to spread over the earth and re-populate it. Noah builds an altar and makes a burnt offering to God, a great sacrifice of birds and animals in thanks for his deliverance. The fragrance of the sacrifice rises up to God, and he shows that he appreciates Noah's offering. Never again, he resolves, will unrestrained fury be directed against man. The cycles of nature will forever be restored to him, the alternating seasons, the succession of day and night, the normal rhythm of the earth.

Here, we are confronted with a veritable second Creation: as with Adam, Noah is also another "first Man," who benefits from God's protection and is decreed superior to all other living creatures. The Lord concludes a solemn covenant with the Flood's captain and, as a sign of this peace, sets a rainbow in the sky as a reminder to all men of his promise that never again will the waters and clouds be unleashed in a fatal threat against humanity.

Noah, the second founding father of mankind, is joined by his three sons who will be the originators of the different human races: Shem, Ham, and Japheth, and God blesses them and tells them to be fruitful and to multiply. Thus concludes the story of the Flood which, we note, presents remarkable analogies with narratives notably of Mesopotamian origin, and to which we will return later. Before that, let us look at the final events of Noah's life as narrated in Genesis. Noah becomes a farmer and plants a vineyard, the discovery of wine production apparently being attributed to him. One day he drinks too much, and falls asleep naked; his son Ham, the father of Canaan, happens to see Noah in his tent in this drunken condition. He runs to tell his brothers, who enter the tent backwards and cover their father with a garment, being careful to avert their faces from him. When Noah awakes and learns what has happened, he curses his son, and all his descendants, who have seen his nakedness and who evidently (the biblical text is not at all explicit about this) made fun of him. Canaan, therefore, in virtue of this curse will be made a slave to all the other brothers. Noah's reaction should not surprise us too much since, according to conceptions of ancient Hebrew society, it was perfectly normal for the wrongs of a father to be borne by his sons. This episode may, moreover, be read and interpretated from different angles and on several levels. Our focus here is the story's principal objective, which attempts to justify the dominion of the Hebrew people (embodied by Shem) and perhaps of the Philistines (represented by Japheth) over Canaan and the populations which descend from it. The importance of wine and the vineyard in this event should also be understood as an implicit criticism of Canaanite civilization which engaged in widespread cultivation of the vine and where use of wine, for ritual purposes or not, played an active role in everday life. The Bible wishes to warn against excesses that confuse the mind and lead to perilous or erroneous moral conduct.

Noah lives for another three hundred and fifty years after the Flood, and dies at the age of 950 years. As the second Adam, he has now accomplished his delicate mission and humanity may once again resume its difficult course in history.

* * *

In the mythologies of many peoples, particularly of the Near East, the theme of a great flood which eradicates almost all humanity, which is then regenerated by a few individuals singled out and saved by a divinity, is well documented. The same may be said of folk literature which represents a rich convergence of characters and themes from ancient mythologies. For our purposes here, it is useful to note that the biblical narrative was largely dependent on stories which circulated orally in Mesopotamia and of which we know the existence thanks to a few surviving cuneiform texts. It is important therefore to take a look at some of these stories and at the other "Noahs" from Sumerian and Accadian traditions. This will enable us to examine some of the formal and functional affinities they share with the tradition preserved in the Old Testament, though naturally, the biblical tradition will still retain its originality by virtue of its strictly monotheistic theological position.

We note a similar structure in all the Mesopotamian stories: humanity's conduct is condemned by the gods who decide to annihilate all men by a natural cataclysm. One god, however, is more compassionate and favorable to mankind and at least succeeds in warning one man, distinguished for his piety, of the impending disaster. Thanks to the counsel of the benevolent god, this person is saved and thus enables humanity to continue its course in history. The details of the typical story are also similar to the story in the Old Testament (for example, the description of the preparations, the construction of the ark, and the episode of the bird set free which does not return, and also the sacrifice giving thanks after the calamity has passed). What differs between the biblical account and the Mesopotamian versions is, above all, the fact that in the Bible, Man's sole interlocutor is Yahweh, who plays the dual role of instigator of the Flood and savior of the human race. Moreover, in the Old Testament the reasons for divine wrath are strictly moral (in other words, mankind's sinful behavior), whereas in the Mesopotamian story it is not really a question of sin, but rather impatience with humanity's boisterousness and rebellious behavior which disturbs the tranquillity of the gods. It is almost as if the extra-biblical tales are more concerned with a demographic problem than a moral one, the gods wishing to limit human presence on earth because it has grown too disruptive. Another important difference between the two traditions, as we will see, is the fact that the heroes of the floods will not share the same fate.

The most ancient story on the theme of the Deluge is a text written in Sumerian dating back to about 2000 B. C. Humanity is threatened by divine anger, but the ancient text has only come down to us partially,

Mosaic, *The Crow and the Dove Are Set Free*

Contrary to his Mesopotamian "counterparts," Noah is not rewarded with immortality. Spared from the Deluge, he is to be the first link of a new chain in the story of the Covenant and the conquest of the Promised Land.

Medieval Miniature, *Noah and the Ark*

The biblical text gives a minute description of the Ark's building materials, its shape and measurements. It has a roof and three decks and stalls for all the animals.

and we do not know the reasons for the gods' displeasure. We do know, however, that the god Enki and the goddess Nintu warn a man, Ziusudra, a legendary king whose name means "life of prolonged days," of the impending catastrophe. Ziusudra then builds a boat and in this way is able to save mankind and the animal kingdom. He offers a great sacrifice to thank the gods and, thus making peace with the them, they accord him a life resembling their own, that is, immortal.

Assyro-Babylonian literature provides us with two other stories concerning the Flood from a more recent epoch, whose heroes are respectively, Atra-Khasis ("the very intelligent one") and Uta-Napishi ("I have found my life"). The first story opens at the time of the Origins, before the existence of Man. The gods are obliged to do all work necessary for their survival themselves (dig irrigation canals, cultivate the land). Exhausted by this labor, they decide to create men to relieve them of these thankless tasks. But humanity begins to proliferate rapidly and its constant noise disturbs the divinities' sleep. The gods intervene by sending a series of calamities to induce men to keep quiet. First a plague, then famine and drought, but all in vain, partly because an astute god, Enki ("Ea" in Accadian) sides with mankind. Enki repeatedly helps limit the gods' destruction by suggesting to those under his protection the most appropriate behavior and rituals to follow to quell the gods' anger. Finally, however, the pantheon of deities decides on more drastic action and plans the total destruction of humanity by a great flood. The Mesopotamian "Noah" here is a certain Atra-Khasis who, thanks again to the advice of the good Enki, is able to escape death. Following the cataclysm, he performs what will be the first sacrifice ever offered to the gods, and a new humanity, created by Enki and Nintu, then re-populate the earth.

The famous myth of Gilgamesh contains another narrative of the Flood. The hero of this adventure, a mythical Sumerian king, concentrates his entire existence on the search for eternal life. During his wanderings, he encounters the very ancient Uta-Napishi, hero of the Flood, whom he questions about the secret of his longevity. Uta-Napishi reveals to Gilgamesh that the gods had wanted to privilege both him and his wife by giving them an existence without end. He then relates what had come to pass a long time ago, an adventure which does not present many structural variants from those we have already encountered up to now: the creation of Man, his faults toward the gods (but not of a moral nature); a cataclysm sent by the gods to destroy him; salvation granted to only one individual (thanks to the advice of a benevolent god, here also Enki/Ea), and the birth of another humanity. In this version as well, we note numerous narrative details also found in the biblical story, thus demonstrating beyond a doubt the Old Testament's dependence on the mythical narrative traditions of Mesopotamia.

We should nevertheless note here that contrary to the biblical Noah, the representative head of a genealogical line, the Sumero-Accadian tradition shows the hero of the Flood rewarded with eternal life, though there is no implication that he abandons the human world nor gives up his role as "father" to humanity. The gods will see to it that humanity

Michelangelo, ***Noah's Sacrifice***

After the Deluge, Noah offers a great sacrifice and this so pleases God that he resolves never again to unleash such destruction against Man. The cycles of nature are forever restored, the alternating seasons, the succession of day and night, the normal rhythm of the earth.

survives by creating mankind over again, but we do not see, as in the Bible, a direct "genetic" relation between the hero of the Flood and this new generation. This feature, however, is fundamental to the biblical version whereby Noah re-populates the world through his own descendants. This is clearly understandable if we stop a moment to consider the objectives of the editors of the Old Testament and the specific theological orientation that motivated them, that is, to show how in the context of his relationship with God, Man falls into sin a second time (after Adam) and is again regenerated in order to fulfill the divine promises concerning the chosen people and the Promised Land.

A feature shared by all of these tales — which testifies to the indisputable mythological origin of the biblical narrative — is the purifying value ascribed to the Flood, and by the fact that it serves to close a primordial epoch in order to open another period, that of historical reality. In Mesopotamia this difference between epochs is made even more obvious by a comparison between "before" and "after": before the Flood, there is a period during which Man does not yet exist, the gods are forced to work, and sickness and famine are unknown. After the Deluge, we find ourselves in a historically real situation characterized by the establishment of a formal relationship between gods and men through the intermediary of the sacrifice, and man's subordinate role forcing him to work for the gods and making him subject to a mortal destiny. There will be only one exception to this, precisely the hero of the Flood, who receives immortality as a reward but who, for this reason, is set apart from his fellow men, those who are obliged to accept death as an intrinsic expression of their human condition. Regarding the biblical Noah, such a superhuman promotion was impossible for the biblical editors of the sacred text to envisage since the principle of procreation — upon which all the biblical genealogies are based — necessarily had to be preserved, and because he who was delivered from the Flood would be called upon to become the first link in a new chain that would lead Israel to its destiny and to its land, Canaan, in accordance with Yahweh's unfathomable plans.

François Boucher, ***Noah's Sacrifice***

Noah, the hero of the "second Creation," benefits, like Adam before him, from God's protection and is decreed superior to all living creatures. As a sign of this new Covenant, the Lord sets a rainbow in the sky as a guarantee that never again will the waters and clouds be unleashed against humanity.

ABRAHAM

The Father of Believers

Sometimes the Chaldean was the man who had discovered God.
God, in his joy, kissed his fingertips exclaiming,
"Until today, no man has ever called me
Lord or Almighty; this is how I will be called from now on."

THOMAS MANN, *Joseph and His Brothers*

After the Deluge destroys the first men of earliest humanity, Noah's descendants multiply and re-populate the earth, thus giving birth to a new phase in human history. These "new" men, however, who still share a common language, commit a great sin of pride in the eyes of God by deciding to build a tower from the city of Babel up to the sky. In answer to this, the Lord suddenly creates complete chaos in their speech making their one language a cacophony of incomprehensible tongues. When men are thus made to realize their limitations, the Lord then scatters them to the four corners of the earth to fulfill his ineffable works.

At this point, the biblical narrative turns its attention to generations born after the Flood and gives their genealogy. Beginning with Shem, one of Noah's sons together with Ham and Japheth, it goes on to Terah, a native of Ur in Chaldea (central Mesopotamia). We are told that Terah later moves to Harran (in northern Mesopotamia) where he dies, the father of three sons, one of whom is Abraham.

This is how the first great Patriarch abruptly and unexpectedly appears on the scene, a man destined to become the exemplary ancestor of the Hebrew nation, father to all, artisan and pillar not only of the first covenant agreement with God in the Old Testament but also of the new one, bound to the person of Jesus Christ and sanctioned by the New Testament. Ancient tradition bestowed the title of "patriarch" (in Hebrew, "father") on the great heads of families, though at the same time stressing at various periods and in different ways, that the title belonged first of all to Abraham, Isaac, and Jacob, the true founders of the dynasty of Judah. Modern exegesis, however, makes broader use of the term and understands it to include the ten post-flood patriarchs, the three traditional patriarchs and, in addition, all the tribal eponyms as well as Joseph and his brothers.

Abraham's original name is *Abram*, which means "exalted is the (divine) Father," but Yahweh changes his name to Abraham, which keeps the same meaning, but can be interpreted as an assonance of the expression *Ab-hamon* and understood as "father of the multitude," thus indicating all the more clearly Abraham's destiny as forefather not only of the Hebrew nation, but also of other countries and kings.

The story of Abraham's call begins while he is still living in Haran and, as we have mentioned, is introduced immediately, without the slightest preamble. The Lord speaks to Abraham and asks him to leave without delay for an unknown country with only his faith in God and the promise of a land and descendants as his possessions. Abraham takes his wife Sarai (who is barren and therefore has no children with Abraham), his nephew Lot, together with their belongings and servants, and sets off on the road to Canaan. When they eventually reach this land, Abraham finds local populations already settled there and has no other alternative but to encamp with them, wandering from Shechem to Bethel, and then to the Negev. In the context of the Book of Genesis, these were sites of ancient Canaanite sanctuaries where Abraham — as the narrative points out — does not go to worship local divinities, but rather his own one God.

Although Abraham's situation is far from encouraging (he is without children, in a foreign country with limited prospects), God clearly confirms to him that Canaan is the Promised Land intended for his descendants. How the Lord's promise will be fulfilled and the chronological development of these events will be the theme of Abraham's story, a man characterized by heroic faith and blind obedience to God, in complete acceptance of his divine commands. As we will see, Yahweh's plans will materialize through a series of very loosely connected episodes and mysterious channels.

First of all, Abraham is forced to leave Palestine because of famine there, and this leads him to Egypt where he is victim to a curious misfortune. Fearing for his life because of the jealousy his wife's beauty will undoubtedly provoke, he poses as Sarai's brother instead. This obliges him to silently watch as his own wife goes to live in the house of the pharaoh and enters his harem, at the same time, accepting provisions and good treatment in exchange. But God sends a series of scourges upon the Egyptian sovereign who, when he discovers the true relationship between Abraham and Sarai as man and wife, expels them from the land. Parallels to this story also appear in subsequent passages of the Book of Genesis with such protagonists as, for example, Abimelech, the king of Gerar, dealing with Abraham and Sarai; or their son, Isaac and his wife Rebekah. The biblical editors' moral condemnation of Abraham's behavior is obvious even if the patriarch was acting out of extreme necessity. Behind this episode we glimpse traces of an ancient legal custom that existed in the

Bruegel, ***The Tower of Babel***

After the Deluge, Noah's descendants re-populate the earth, but they commit a great sin of pride in the eyes of the Lord by trying to build a tower from Babel up to the sky. God creates chaos in their speech, making their one language a cacophony of incomprehensible tongues.

Near East whereby marriage between brother and sister allowed for the entrusting or "lending" of the woman to another party, on a temporary or permanent basis, subsequent to a favorable commercial transaction.

Upon his return to the land of Canaan, more precisely Bethel, Abraham soon begins to realize that co-existence with his nephew, Lot, and his herdsmen might not be so easy. Because of this friction, the two clans decide to separate peacefully and, while Abraham stays where he is, Lot and his people take the lower Jordan valley, an extremely fertile area, where they encamp near the city of Sodom. Almost as if to "reconsecrate" him after his experience in Egypt, God then reconfirms to Abraham that the land of Canaan is truly the future homeland of the chosen people, and on the basis of this, the patriarch settles right there, near Hebron, by the oak of Mamre where he builds an altar to Yahweh.

His nephew Lot, in the meantime, is involuntarily drawn into the wars raging between local kings and the oriental sovereigns of the great powers of the time. The biblical narrative seems to be on rather weak historical footing here, and is perhaps alluding to punitive expeditions for the control of commercial routes between Syria and the Red Sea. In any event, Lot is taken prisoner while Sodom is sacked. Abraham's swift intervention against the invaders' coalition enables him to free Lot and return the plunder to the king of Sodom, from whom he refuses to accept any reward.

The events which follow are not directly linked to the rest of the narrative, but nevertheless do have their significance. After his victory over the enemy coalition, Abraham is approached by Melchizedek, the priest-king of Salem (Jerusalem) who offers him bread and wine and blesses him in the name of "the Highest God" (El Elyon, an ancient Canaanite divinity, here considered as the manifestation of Yahweh). Abraham pays the man a tithe on the plunder, the episode reflecting a much later historical reality when the kings of Israel were forced to pay this tax to the sanctuary at Jerusalem. Theological exegesis exercised its imagination on Melchizedek, seeing in him the archetype of the Davidic Messiah king and making him into a supernatural figure, even a forerunner of Christ or a parallel to him.

After all of these vicissitudes, Abraham is already quite old and considering the divine promise of boundless descendants, "as many as the stars in the sky," he probably doubts in his heart that this will ever really come to pass. But Yahweh repeats his promise to him once again and, as a sign of this covenant, has him perform a solemn and mysterious ancient ceremony: a heifer, a goat, a ram, a turtle-dove and a pigeon are killed, split in two and the two halves are placed one facing the other. According to this ritual, known in a number of ancient cultures, the "signataries" of the pact walked between the pieces of the slain animals and invoked the same fate for themselves as the victims if ever they break the agreement. After this ritual, God predicts to Abraham that his people will initially be oppressed in a foreign land, but repeats his promise that in the end his descendants will take possession of the land of Canaan.

Beyond Abraham's personal case (and Jacob's too, as will be seen), it is worth highlighting here the particular importance ancient societies in the Near East attached to progeny in general. The theme of the

M. De Vos, *Abraham at Hebron*
Abraham, after many years of wandering, finally settles near Hebron and establishes a foothold in Canaan. He is later buried in Hebron by the side of his wife Sarah.

childless father who, by divine grace is miraculously blessed with an unhoped for child, is abundantly illustrated in all literatures, both ancient and modern. In the East, in particular, children represented the possibility of living on through them, since no clear eschatological hope for a blissful eternal life existed. Moreover, children were responsible for keeping the memory of the deceased father alive, for maintaining his tomb, and providing the funeral offerings, food and water, believed to be indispensable in a hereafter where, in place of food, drink, and fresh air, only dust, mire, and putrefaction prevailed. In exchange for this care, even if only a symbolic guarantee of subsistence, it was believed the dead would try to contain their antagonism towards the living and, on occasion, might even be moved to perform good works such as offering protection, foretelling the future, or curing sickness. For these reasons, anyone who found himself childless was understandably desperate to do all in his power to obtain this priceless gift from the divinity.

This therefore was Abraham's situation, made all the more critical by the fact that far greater hopes were also built upon his role as "father of a multitude," and that not even the feeblest beginnings of such a line of descendants was yet to be seen. At this point, believing that no child will ever be born to them, Sarai gives Abraham one of her personal slaves, an Egyptian woman named Hagar (the rabbinical tradition even considered her to be the Pharaoh's daughter or a princess in his harem). As a result of this union, Hagar becomes pregnant, but her attitude then completely changes and she no longer shows the slightest respect for her mistress. Reprimanded and driven away, Hagar then has a divine vision announcing that she will give birth to a son, Ishmael, and also many other children after him, and enjoy a long line of descendants. This convinces Hagar to return to her mistress and remain in her service. In the Bible, Ishmael is considered the forefather of the desert Arabs, proud nomads, fiercely independent, bellicose rebels to all authority. Ishmael's name, which means "listen, God!" is also an allusion to the events surrounding his birth when God, at least in part, answered Abraham's prayers.

When Abraham is 99 years old, God again appears to him and changes his name to emphasize even more strongly his role as founder and head of a long line of descendants, "a multitude of men." During this solemn occasion Yahweh gives very specific, even unconditional, details of his covenant with Abraham. Circumcision will be the visible sign in all men of this agreement, to which all male children will be subjected eight days after birth, an obligation also applicable to foreigners residing in Israel. In ancient times, this was an initiation rite leading to marriage — later practiced a short time after birth — which originally took place at the time two people were engaged. The rite announced, among other things, the establishment of a very strong family bond and blood relationship between those submitting to it and belonging to different families. This ritual was adopted by the Hebrew people not only as a token sign of an agreement with the Divine, but also, and above all, as an ethnic and cultural means of identification in a world consisting of populations who, though having at one time practiced circumcision, were in the process of abandoning it. Therefore Abraham, thirteen year-old Ishmael, and all the other men in his household submit to circumcision in obedience to the Lord's command. God then confirms once again to the incredulous and aged Abraham that within a year he and his wife will have a son named Isaac, through whom the Covenant will be renewed, and that his son in turn, will be blessed with many descendants. Sarai's name is also changed, as was Abraham's, and becomes "Sarah" which is, as was her husband's second name, a variation of the first, and in her case retains the same meaning of "princess," or "sovereign" though also serves to foretell Sarah's destiny to become the mother of a king.

Despite this, the by now very aged couple cannot help feeling skeptical about the possibility of having children. An amazing event, however, then renews their hope. The biblical text relates the details through the literary device of a "divine visit." One day as the aged Abraham is sitting before his tent at Mamre in the heat of the day, three strangers appear before him. He kindly welcomes them and hurries off to tell Sarah, so that she may prepare the food and drink normally offered to visitors. In fact, these people are no other than Yahweh and two angels. After accepting Abraham's hospitality, they then announce that the elderly and barren Sarah will conceive a child. A tender and comical note: the woman cannot help letting out a chuckle at this idea, and God will quickly reprimand her.

At this point in the Book of Genesis, the biblical compilers insert the story of the two cities of Sodom and Gomorrah, infamous capitals of sin and evil, which the Lord intends to destroy as punishment. Learning of God's intentions, Abraham generously intercedes in defense of the righteous who might also be living in these wicked cities, and manages to obtain from the Lord a promise of clemency for those not living in sinfulness. Moreover, it happens that at the time, Abraham's nephew, Lot, and all of his family are also staying in Sodom. When the two angels of the Lord arrive in the city, Lot himself offers them hospitality and, as it turns out, even attempts to protect his guests against the blind lust of the Sodomites and their unnatural sexual practices. The fate of this population is by now sealed and the reasons are obvious. Beyond a purely moral condemnation, God's wrath is also motivated by the licentious practices identified with the Canaanites and against which he reacts. Moreover, homosexuality and sodomy are seen as the direct negation of the principle of fertility and procreation which forms the basis of the divine plan for Abraham (who will be blessed with a long line of descendants to occupy the Promised Land). Acting on God's advice, Lot and his family flee the city before the divine wrath is unleashed, having been warned that they must not, under any circumstances, stop to look back. Lot's wife, however, disobeys the divine command and as they run away from the doomed city, turns to look behind her. She is immediately transformed into a statue of salt, an episode interpreted as the severe punishment for an act of disbelief. Then from the sky "brimstone and fire" rain down mercilessly over Sodom, reducing the entire city to a heap of smoking ruins. In an annex to the

Marc Chagall, *Abraham and the Three Angels*

Abraham and his wife, by now quite old, believe they will die childless when three strangers visit them. The couple kindly welcome the visitors who are, in reality, Yahweh and two angels who have come to announce to them the birth of Isaac.

Jan Victors, ***Abraham and the Three Angels***

The theme of a divine visit announcing a birth is frequent in the Bible. Besides the divine Announcement to Mary, we will see that Samson is also the object of a similar prophecy.

story, the Book of Genesis then relates the tale of the stealthiness of Lot's two daughters who sleep with their drunken father and become pregnant, giving birth to the ancestors of the Moabites and the Ammonites. This episode is based upon a popular aetiological tale that deals with incestuous behavior, morally condemnable, but partially justified by the necessity of ensuring the continuity of the family line.

Concerning the events in Sodom, Abraham had demonstrated his generosity and greatness of vision by daring to criticize God's plans, interceding in favor of the righteous who would have paid for faults they had not committed. The time had come for the divine promise to be fulfilled, and the much awaited child to be born. Thus Sarah finds herself miraculously pregnant and will have a son called Isaac, a name meaning "He (God or the child himself) has laughed," an allusion to the time when God's announcement of her son's prodigious arrival had given Sarah "a good laugh."

> God has made laughter for me.
> Now everyone who hears, will laugh over me!

The little Isaac is born and circumcised, and after some two or three years, according to the custom of the time, is weaned. It is now the moment for Hagar and Isaac's half-brother, Ishmael, to be removed from the scene since in God's plans Abraham must have only one heir. However, divine Providence looks after Hagar and her son who are given protection and settled in the Paran desert, where Ismael will become the founder of a great nation.

After a brief parenthetical episode regarding a dispute between Abraham and Abimelech, the king of Gerar, over the possession of a well in Beersheba (an episode which will give rise to this place-name), we then come to a dramatic and decisive turning point in Abraham's life. For, God decides to put Abraham's faith to test in a most awful way. This God, so benevolent and just, who has granted the miracle of paternity to Abraham at the age of one hundred years, now asks him to give up what is most precious to him in all the world: Isaac, the son of the Promise. According to the divine command, Abraham must go to the land of Moriah, climb up to a mountain top, and there sacrifice the child in an offering to the Lord. Without any indication in the text of a reaction from the aged father before the enormity of God's demand, Abraham follows the divine instructions to the letter in an absolute and blind obedience which can only be born out of immense faith. When Isaac is bound and placed on the altar, Abraham raises the sacrificial knife to perform the final dreadful act but the Lord stops his hand. The angel of Yahweh can now say, "I know you fear God," and the cruel command is abolished. A ram is taken and sacrificed in Isaac's place, and the Lord's promise of descendants and the Promised Land is renewed. This tale, of profound historical and religious implications, is most likely connected to the founding of a Yahvist sanctuary near Shechem, according to one tradition, or according to another, on the Mountain of Yahweh in Moriah. The episode should also be considered in relation to a custom — practiced in the ancient Syro-Palestinian region — whereby first-born sons were sacrificed to the divinity in thanks or to obtain special favors. The practice of this rite was particularly widespread in Phoenicia and Carthage, though it probably originated in Canaan and was not unknown to Hebrew society itself either. The episode of Isaac, delivered by God and replaced by a ram, suggests that the barbarous custom had been eased and softened by the sacrifice of an animal which would represent, in the eyes of the divinity, the

(*opposite page, below*)

Mariano Salvador de Maella, ***Hagar and Ismael in the Desert***

After Isaac's birth, Ismael and his mother, a slave of Egyptian ancestry, are moved away from Abraham. Divine protection, however, permits them to survive in the desert which later becomes the territory of Ismael, ancestor of the desert nomads.

Guercino, ***Lot and His Daughters***

After Lot's wife is turned into a statue because she looks back at Sodom (shown in the background of the painting), Lot's daughters seduce their drunken father and thus become the ancestors of the Moabites and Ammonites, two neighboring enemy populations of Israel.

first-born child in a family. This then is the story's historical background whose symbolism is later magnified and enriched in theological exegesis, even influencing Christian liturgy, where the figure of Isaac prefigures at times the innocent and patient victim who is later sacrificed, just as was Jesus Christ.

After these events, Abraham and his family move to Beersheba. The years pass and Sarah, at the age of 127 years, dies in Hebron. After the rites of mourning over his wife's body are carried out in accordance with Canaanite traditions, Abraham arranges for a tomb for his wife and realizes how friendly the local people are towards a foreigner whose grave they willingly accept on their territory. The patriarch asks if he might buy the cave at Machpelah, facing Mamre, located on the land of a Hittite, a certain Ephron. After simple negotiations, Abraham obtains what he desires and buys the cave with the surrounding land and trees, and there Sarah is buried.

Abraham is advancing in years and concerns himself with finding a wife for his son Isaac. In view of this, and not wanting a local Canaanite woman for a daughter-in-law (a detail that undoubtedly reflects a later xenophobic ideology) he sends his most trusted servant off to Haran in northern Mesopotamia, their homeland, after making a solemn vow to choose a young woman willing to share in the family's fortunes and come to Canaan. The servant thus departs and arranges for a young woman named Rebekah, a daughter of Abraham's brother, Nahor, to be designated — with her fullest consent, moreover — to marry Isaac. In this episode Rebekah's brother, a man named Laban, also makes his appearance and distinguishes himself by his greediness. He will play an even greater role in the adventures of Isaac and Jacob. The servant and the fiancée leave for Canaan, with

Caravaggio, ***The Sacrifice of Isaac***

This event is a turning point in Abraham's life. When God decides to test his faith in a most awful way, Abraham does not hesitate to raise the sacrifical knife to cut the throat of Isaac, the son whom he so greatly desired. However, the Lord's angel stops his hand and in Isaac's place a ram is sacrificed.

Medieval miniature,
The Sacrifice of Isaac

In the Syro-Palestinian region, in Phoenicia from where it later spread to Carthage, the first-born son was sacrificed to the divinity to show thanks or to obtain special favors. The episode of Isaac, spared by God and replaced by a ram, suggests the original custom had been eased by the immolation of an animal.

the blessings of the entire family. After a very long journey, they finally arrive in the Negev where Isaac lives and the two young people meet for the first time. Their love for each other is instant and intense, so much so that by Rebekah's side Isaac is able to find consolation for the still recent loss of his mother.

Abraham the Patriarch has now reached the venerable age of 175 years. He has lived a rich and intense life, surely not without pain and suffering, but also full of great happiness, a life of faith dedicated completely to God and to the joy of seeing his divine promises fulfilled. It is thus in great serenity that Abraham sees the end of his days, and "dies in the happiness of old age, satisfied and fulfilled; to be re-united with his ancestors." His sons, Isaac and Ismael, the latter naturally having returned for the sad occasion, see to it that he is given a sepulcre in the cave at Machpelah near Hebron, where Sarah is also buried. Abraham's earthly destiny has been accomplished and the mission is now passed on to Isaac, who will represent the next link in a long chain of personages responsible for the fulfillment of the divine promise.

The Bible's story of Abraham is a complex and substantially late compilation based on diverse and heterogeneous material in which many diverse sources can be identified. These various stories were most probably based upon very ancient oral traditions that suggest the existence of an essentially true historical foundation. Abraham and Lot are presented not as nomadic Bedouins travelling by camel, but as semi-nomadic people on donkeys wandering in the wake of their grazing flocks. This is a historically plausible environment and reflects a real period during which, before the establishment of a system of tribes, the ancestors of Israel lived as semi-nomadic shepherds and herdsmen organized in family clans. Progressively, these clans tended to become sedentary (a very long process which took place from the beginning of the second millennium to the end of the thirteenth century B. C.). The "sons of Abraham" could have belonged precisely to one of these clans connected with the sacred center of Mamre/Hebron. From a historiographic point of view, on the other hand, the story of Abraham cannot serve to reconstruct "the Origins" but rather should be considered as material reflecting the condition of the Hebrews in monarchical times and in part also during the Exile, when the narrative was reworked and actually committed to writing.

From a theological perspective, with Abraham the history of redemption truly begins. God plays a personal role in the adventures of mankind, he predetermines events and influences them, thus involving in his inscrutable plans not only the chosen people, but all of humanity. Abraham's personality and qualities are the antithesis of the arrogance and pride of the first men who lived in great sinfulness, and his life serves to remind us of the immense value God places in the total abandonment of the self to unquestioning faith. Abraham's principal merit is to have taken God on his word when he was called, putting everything into question including his own existence, without hesitation, even when circumstances seemed anything but encouraging, even hostile. For these reasons, Abraham is considered the "Father of believers" by the faithful, circumcised or not, of the three great monotheistic religions: Judaism, Christianity and Islam.

(opposite page, below)

Nicolas Poussin,
Rebekah at the Well

Abraham sends his most trusted servant to Haran, his homeland, to find a bride for Isaac. When the servant returns with Isaac's future bride Rebekah, the two young people meet for the first time in the Negev and their love for each other is instant and intense.

ISAAC

The Son of the Promise

"The patriarch Isaac... did not stand out from the tumult of the crowd for any other reason if not that his tranquil soul questioned itself and this made him pleasing to God"

ATHANASIUS, *Lettera XXII* (352 B. C.)

Medieval miniature, *Abraham, Isaac, and Jacob*
Isaac seems to represent a transitional character between his father Abraham and Jacob, his son, two much more striking personalities.

When Isaac is compared with the figure of his father, Abraham, he definitely appears to us a much less vivid and striking character, his existence less rich in important episodes in which he plays a leading role. The biblical text, it is true, tends to include the story of Isaac's life in the saga of Abraham and his sons. Only after Abraham's death does our hero become a leading figure for a short while, though never without completely ridding us of the impression that he represents a transitional character between the first great Patriarch, his father, and Jacob-Israel, his son.

Indeed, a strange destiny is Isaac's: he starts out by being an absent though desperately awaited hero, the miraculous son of the Promise, only to later be attributed a very modest role as perpetuator of the family line, where he is of very secondary importance compared to his father and his more prestigious descendants. This makes it difficult, from a narrative point of view, to present, without forcing the text, an autonomous story of the adventures of Isaac and to lift this character out of the broader narrative that, in fact, relates the trials and tribulations of the two generations between which his life unfolds.

The miraculous and marvelous circumstances surrounding the birth of Isaac have already been presented. Genesis, as mentioned, gives many details

of Isaac while narrating the adventures of Abraham: from the interminable waiting for the almost unhoped for child, to the prodigious birth of "the son of laughter" (according to the etymology of Isaac's name); to the dramatic test of Abraham's faith and his son's deliverance from the sacrificial altar by God. We have also been told of Isaac's marriage to Rebekah, a young woman of Aramean stock from northern Mesopotamia, and of the great love that binds them. With the death of Abraham, Isaac temporarily comes to the forefront when, as in his father's story, he discovers that his wife Rebekah is barren. This time, however, the situation is made much less dramatic with the intervention of Yahweh who helps Rebekah. In fact, she finds herself soon pregnant with twins, the future Esau and Jacob, who even in their mother's womb already seem to be at odds with each other. Divine prophecy has foretold, in fact, that the two sons will father two rival peoples, and that one will be oppressed by the other.

The circumstances of the twins' birth and their physical features will confirm this prediction. Esau, the first born, has a rough complexion and bristly red-hair (his name means precisely, "hairy") which are features expressed in Hebrew by a play on the words *seir* ("hair") and *edom* ("red"), and are terms which also refer to the region his descendants, the Edomites (later conquered by David) will eventually settle. As for Jacob, he is born clutching his brother's heel, which will give rise to the popular etymology of his name as "heel" related to the verb "to deceive" (although, in fact, the true significance of his name is "may (God) protect."

The two brothers are complete opposites in their personalities as well as in their physical features. Esau is an avid hunter who loves the steppe, while Jacob prefers the tranquility of the camp and pastoral life. Their father, Isaac, who has a great appetite for wild game, is partial to the first born who brings him all of these good things in abundance (it has been presumed, justifiably, that Esau was also acting out of religious motivations: the rites of sacred hunting were not unknown to the ancient populations in Jordan or southern Arabia). Rebekah, however, prefers the peaceful Jacob. Divine plans have already decided that the rights of the first born, which imply various social and religious privileges, will be granted to the second-born Jacob. This will come about in an episode in which Jacob shows himself to be anything but admirable. Esau returns exhausted and famished from hunting and finds Jacob busily preparing soup. Jacob takes advantage of the situation and asks his brother for the rights that come with the status of the first born in exchange for food. The rather naive and impulsive Esau, not hesitating a moment, gives up everything in exchange for a little lentil soup and some water. The ruse, or blackmail if you will, committed by Jacob is partially justified in the biblical text by the extenuating circumstances represented by the limited intelligence and sensibility of Esau, who accorded such seemingly little importance to his rights as the first born, or in other words, the undeserving courseness of his character. Moreover, this is not the first time we see God use human weakness to realize his plans, which raises the eternal issue, expressed in different forms throughout the Bible, of the relationship between predestination and free will.

Rembrandt, *Abraham and His Son*

Isaac is born when his mother and father are already very old. His name, moreover, means "He [God or the child himself] has laughed," since Sarah, his mother, found the divine announcement of this unhoped for pregnancy a "good laugh."

The constant conflict between the two brothers, one which we will see develop further on, represents in fact quite a complex historical and traditional background. We have already mentioned before that Esau is also the forefather of the Edomites, a population at odds with the Israelites represented by Jacob. Moreover, the two brothers embody two different cultural models and their confrontation should be interpreted precisely as an echo of the antagonism that distinguishes a civilization based on hunting, from a semi-nomadic civilization engaged in sheep farming with all their respective socio-economic and ideological aspects. Also worth remembering is that the theme of conflicting forms of civilization (hunting/sheep farming or sheep farming/agriculture) was always very common in all ancient Near Eastern literature. We will only mention here the well-known Sumerian compositions such as the *disputes* or *dialogues*, also referred to in the chapter on Cain and Abel, in which anonymous authors stage a scene with two characters (generally divine), who must defend their preferred cultural model, thus demonstrating their adroitness and dialectical ability. The outcome of such "disputes" was generally conciliatory for, even if one of the orators was declared the winner, recognition was also given to the other participant (and the activity he represented and defended) and to its validity and social usefulness. Finally we should also note that in the oral and written traditions of many peoples, the universal struggle between brothers (often twins, Remus and Romulus come to mind) is a familiar theme, with the victory of the younger brother over the elder related in a wide range of situations and events. These interpretative keys help us to

Donatello, ***Abraham and Isaac***

A strange destiny is Isaac's. From an absent but desperately awaited hero, miraculous son of the Promise, he is later attributed a very modest role as perpetrator of the family line, father of Jacob and Esau.

brother. Abimelech eventually discovers the truth, however, but decides to protect the couple. Meanwhile Isaac, as a colonist, takes up agriculture and soon amasses a fortune in grain, livestock and slaves which provokes the Philistines' jealousy. Abimelech therefore forces him to leave Gerar, and Isaac finds himself constantly confronted with the hostility of the local people over the possession and use of various wells, which will each be named after the events related to these conflicts. Finally Isaac makes his way to Beersheba and there he is witness to another divine apparition and builds an altar. King Abimelech joins him there and, impressed by the wealth and power of his God, invites him to conclude a treaty of alliance and brotherhood with him, sanctioned by an oath and a common meal. The last detail included in this story concerns Esau's marriage to two Hittite women, and his parents' strong disapproval of this decision, being opposed as they are to exogamic marriages. This detail seems to reflect a documented custom whereby the Edomites, originally hunters, would usually take wives outside their own clans. The Bible presents, as a family conflict between parents and their son, what is actually a cultural difference between two peoples: one, Israel, strongly attached to the principle of endogamy (no foreign wives), and the other, Edom, accustomed at least originally to the practice of exogamy.

Continuing in the fulfillment of his unfathomable plans, Yahweh prepares another unfortunate surprise for Esau, already having been tricked out of his birthright by his younger brother. Isaac, by now very old and almost completely blind, feels the end of his life approaching. He calls for his favorite son, Esau, and asks him to go out hunting and prepare a meal of succulent venison so that he might enjoy this pleasure one last time. After which, feeling that death is near, he intends to give his final blessing to the first born. Evidently Isaac is unaware that Esau has sold his privileges as first

see the conflict between Esau and Jacob as a story based on an ancient mythological motif that probably circulated widely in oral form, which biblical editors reworked from a literary point of view and used in a theological perspective.

After these events, the Book of Genesis relates the only episode in which Isaac truly appears as the hero; an episode, in fact, partially drawn from previous events in his father's life. Forced to flee famine, Isaac and his family go to Gerar, to the house of Abimelech the Philistine king, and from there intend to carry on to Egypt. However, the Lord intervenes and encourages Isaac to stay in Gerar, and again solemnly renews the promise also made to his father, Abraham, that he will be given a line of descendants and a land. Just as in his father's story, Isaac also fears that the beauty of his wife, Rebekah, may put him in a dangerous situation and he therefore pretends to be her

Relief, Antwerp Museum, ***The Sacrifice of Isaac***

Isaac, the sacrificial victim, is bound and placed on the altar. Abraham raises the sacrifical knife but the Lord stops his hand just in time.

born to his younger brother, for he wishes to transfer all the rights in his possession to his eldest son by way of a special testimonial blessing.

Esau leaves to go hunting, but his mother, who has been eavesdropping on the entire conversation, convinces Jacob to go in his brother's place to receive the paternal benediction. This would officially sanction his possession of the rights which he has already stolen from Esau. Rebekah prepares a meal of kid meat from their own herd and has Jacob put on the fine robe for such occasions (that is, a ritual or priestly garment) which belongs to his brother. To avoid Jacob's smooth skin giving away his true identity, she covers his arms and neck with kid-skin. Jacob goes to his father who, though very surprised at how quickly Esau has caught his prey, thinks he recognizes the feel of Esau's rough skin though Jacob's voice, telling lie after lie as he pretends to be his brother, is not at all convincing. After having finished his meal, Isaac embraces Jacob and the smell of Esau's clothing reassures him of the identity of his son. The elderly father then officially gives his blessing to his son, invoking for him divine favor, abundance, and prosperity, dominion over his own brothers and over all the inhabitants of the land.

As soon as Jacob, the supplanter, leaves his father's tent, the unfortunate Esau comes back with the desired game. His astounded father begins to tremble uncontrollably, but knows very well that the benediction already granted Esau's younger brother can neither be revoked nor annulled. Esau, who finds himself once again the victim of his brother's cunning, pleads for the paternal benediction as well. Isaac must tell him that instead his destiny will be to live in a poor and arid land where he must survive by the sword and serve his brother as a slave. With his heart full of pain and hatred, Esau devises a plan to avenge himself and even considers killing Jacob after his father's death. Rebekah realizes his intentions and in order to avoid a murderous dispute between the two sons, urges Jacob to leave immediately for Haran, and to stay with her brother Laban, as long as is necessary for the episode to be forgotten or Esau's desire for vengeance to be calmed. Isaac approves of his wife's idea too, and also hopes the voyage might give Jacob the opportunity of choosing

Carlo Maratti, ***Rebekah and Eleazar at the Spring***

Though the text does not explicitly name him, Eleazar is generally recognized as the aged servant Abraham sends to Mesopotamia to find a wife for Isaac. The first person he meets is Rebekah who offers water to the foreigner and thus wins his confidence.

M. De Visch, ***The Death of Jacob***

On his deathbed, Jacob pronounces a solemn blessing in favor of Joseph and legally adopts Joseph's two sons. He then foretells the unique destiny of each of the Twelve Tribes of Israel. After his death, he is embalmed according to Egyptian custom and buried in the family tomb in Machpelah.

a non-Canaanite wife from among the daughters of his brother-in-law, Laban the Aramean, just as his grandfather Abraham had done. Jacob leaves with his father's blessing while Esau, in an effort to satisfy his parents wishes, takes another wife, this time from Ishmael's clan. In his choice, the principle of endogamy is theoretically respected, but we know very well that Ishmael and his descendants have not been included as direct heirs of the Promise. Poor Esau has failed again. This episode will explain the ethnic mixing between the Edomites, of whom Esau is the ancestral patriarch, and the Arab peoples.

Jacob then finds himself at the center of many adventures. He meets his uncle Laban but argues with him, nevertheless eventually marrying his two daughters, Leah and Rachel, after a series of events which we will come to shortly. For now, we will skip over these events and take up our story, after Jacob has become Israel and a foremost patriarch, at the moment when he returns to Mamre, the place where Abraham had lived, and where his father Isaac still resides. For, almost as if on tip-toe, Isaac now leaves his earthly existence. He will be piously buried there in Mamre, in the family tomb, by his two sons reunited in their grief.

Thus Isaac leaves the scene, a character as fundamental as he is retiring, more a witness than a protagonist, sometimes even an involuntary and powerless spectator to events orchestrated by God's supreme will. Nevertheless he is a Patriarch in the fullest sense of the word, affectionate, adored by his sons and his wife, a figure the biblical text tacitly exalts for his humility and faith, but sacrifices somewhat to the practical and narrative requirements of the plot's development.

This evaluation all in half-tones of the character of Isaac is also echoed in the analysis of this figure provided by Christian and Judaic exegesis. Isaac is considered a character rich in allegories and, despite the limited depth of the personage, tradition has often bestowed upon him privileges even greater than those accorded to his father, Abraham, or his son, Jacob. Archetype of the paschal lamb and the Messiah sacrificed on the cross (in both cases, the offerer is the victim's own father), Isaac is perceived as the man who believes without falling prey to human passions, a man of perfect virtues, the fruit of a divine gift. His life is marked by three fundamental events: his miraculous birth, his deliverance from sacrifice, and his marriage bond with Rebekah (who tends to be identified with Wisdom). Theologians have speculated for centuries about this "trinity" in the search for allegorical interpretations sometimes quite persuasive, and at other times highly improbable. Certainly Isaac is a unique character who has paradoxically inspired minds and imaginations by the linear quality of his life's parable, a hero who has served, in Judaism and in Christianity, as the symbol of the most important historical manifestations of Man's faith in God.

JACOB

The Biblical Ulysses

All his life he fought the battles of virtue.

FILONE D'ALESSANDRIA, *Of Joseph*

Jacob is another figure whose story unfolds through the narrative of his father's life or in the stories of his own sons (mainly Joseph's). Compared to his father Isaac, however, Jacob is by far a more striking character, an active protagonist of great stature and autonomy, who always finds himself at the heart of the action. Just for memory's sake let us quickly review the background of Jacob's story: the circumstances surrounding his birth; the conflict with his brother Esau, and the destiny which prepared him even before birth to become the most exemplary representative of the people of Israel, after whom he will be named. After stealing the rights of the eldest son from his brother Esau and then tricking his father into bestowing upon him the irrevocable paternal blessing, Jacob is sent away for fear that his brother might murder him out of vengeance. Jacob goes to stay with his maternal uncle in northern Mesopotamia where his parents also hope he will choose a wife from his own kin instead of marrying a local foreign woman. During his journey, Jacob stops overnight at a spot, later to become the city of Bethel, where he falls asleep using a stone as a head-rest. There he has a dream. He sees a sloping staircase (quite similar to the Mesopotamian ziggurats which served as models for the Tower of Babel) that leads from the ground right up to the heavens and upon which the Lord's angels come and go. Yahweh himself then appears to Jacob as the God of Abraham and Isaac and reiterates his ancient promise of "a multitude of descendants" and the conquest of the Promised Land. Yahweh's blessing and protection will never abandon Jacob as long as all to be fulfilled has not come to pass. Jacob awakes, frightened and yet intrigued with the secret knowledge that this spot is a sacred place. In fact, he is now convinced that it is the "house of God" (from where the place-name "Bethel" comes from) and the gate to heaven. He takes the stone which had served as his head-rest and carves a sacred pillar from it, then anoints it with oil. Rebaptizing the site "Bethel" he pronounces a vow: in thanks for God's protection, he will see to it that this sacred place becomes a true home for the Lord (that is, a permanent temple and not an open sanctuary) and promises to give one-tenth of all he possesses as an offering.

This episode, which will later be taken up in quite a different and more detailed version, reflects a very complex editorial history and is clearly intended to relate how the important center of worship, the sanctuary of Bethel, came to be founded while at the same time alluding to widespread religious practices of the Syro-Palestinian world. Jacob's dream, which comes to him in clearly sacred surroundings, may be associated with a rite of incubation which was practiced in numerous places of worship in the Near Eastern and classical world. This rite was based upon the belief that sleeping in a holy place brought prophetic dreams or beneficial manifestations of the divinity (Yahweh himself did not hesitate to appear in dreams to those with whom he wished to communicate). The erecting of a sacred pillar, as Jacob had done after his dream, is a classic act of worship in Semitic religions and is motivated by the hope that the divinity may reside or appear in these steles. The rite of anointing the top of the stone represented the consecration of a previously profane object.

Jacob then sets off again on his journey and finally reaches his destination, his uncle Laban's village. There he sees three flocks of sheep pressed around a well which is covered by a heavy stone. Jacob asks the busy shepherds tending their thirsty animals what the name of the village is and if they know Laban. They tell him they do in fact know his uncle and that he is in Haran. As they are speaking, Jacob sees a strikingly beautiful shepherdess approaching who turns out to be none other than Laban's own daughter accompanying her father's herd. Jacob is deeply moved and unable to hold back his tears, he embraces the young woman. Informed of Jacob's arrival, Laban warmly welcomes Jacob and tells him to be his guest. After some time, Jacob enters into Laban's service.

Thus begins the touching story of Jacob's two marriages and his relationship, with all its ups and downs, with his uncle Laban. To demonstrate his generosity, Laban insists on remunerating Jacob for his services and asks him how much he wishes to be paid. Jacob, who has loved Laban's daughter, Rachel, from the first time he set eyes on her, asks for the young girl's hand in exchange for his promise to serve his uncle faithfully for seven years (the number seven here representing a symbolic value). Laban has no objections and consents to Jacob's proposal. Laban however also has another daughter besides Rachel, the elder Leah, who is as dull and unattractive as Rachel is vivacious and beautiful, so much so that Laban is secretly tempted to play a very cruel joke on his much in love nephew.

Sustained by his love for Rachel, the seven years Jacob spends in his uncle's service seem to fly by ("seven years... were but a few days in his eyes, so great was his love for her"). After the completion

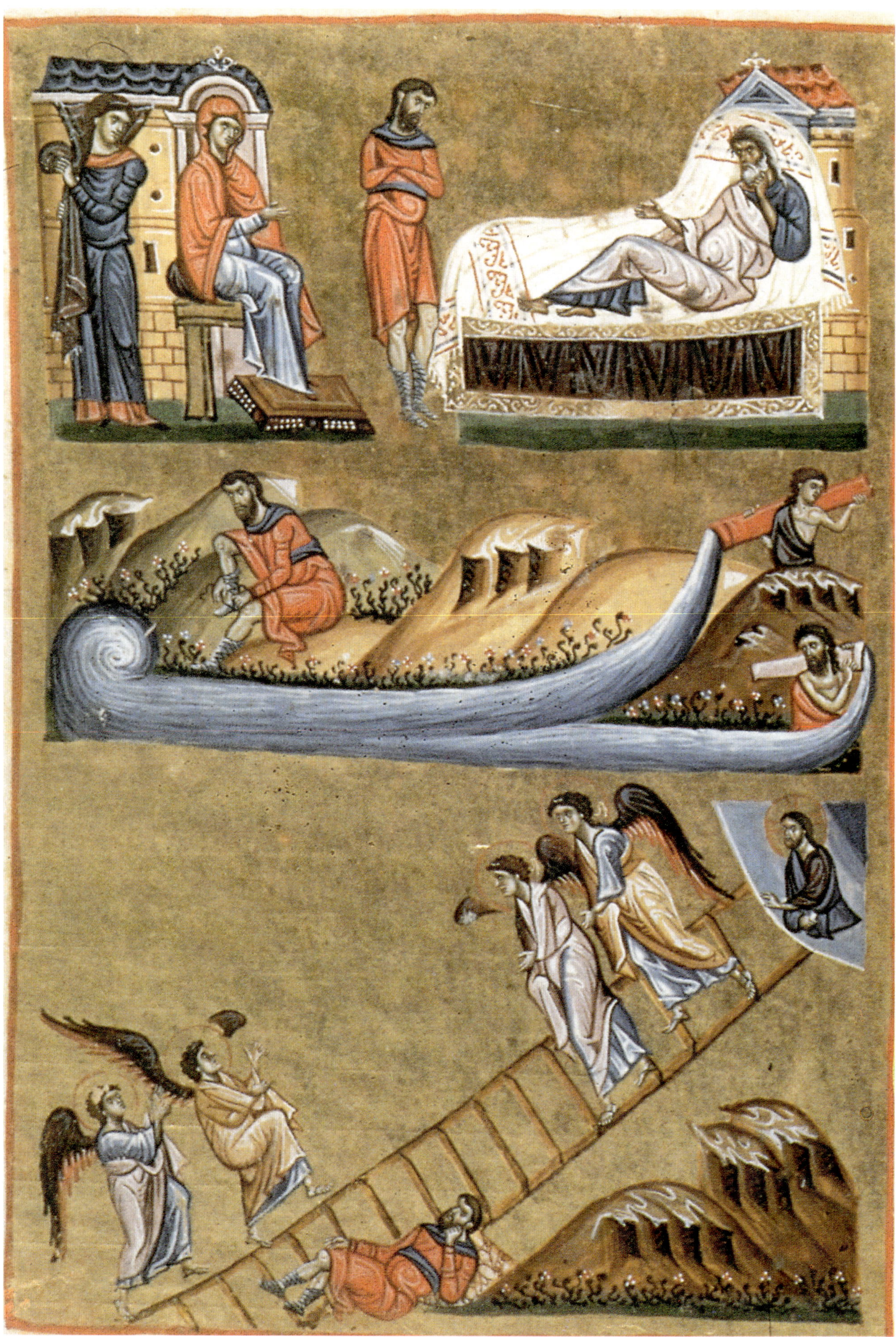

Marc Chagall, ***Jacob's Dream***

On his way to his uncle Laban's house in Mesopotamia, Jacob stops overnight in Bethel and falls asleep, using a stone for a head-rest. In a dream he sees a sloping staircase rising from the earth to the sky, along which the Lord's angels walk.

of this period he goes to his uncle to see their agreement honored. However, now it is Jacob, the one who had so cleverly deceived his brother Esau and his father Isaac, who sees himself victim of an extremely cruel deception. Laban gives a wedding feast in his nephew's honor and afterwards Jacob retires to his tent with his young bride. But how great is his astonishment and dismay the next morning to discover the homely Leah by his side instead of the ravishing Rachel! The ancient custom forbidding the groom to set eyes on his bride before their wedding night, and whose fiancée is therefore brought to him heavily veiled, has made the substitution possible. Beside himself with rage, Jacob immediately demands an explanation. His uncle impassively justifies himself: local custom prohibits marrying a younger daughter before an elder (in reality, Jewish law also forbade a man to marry two sisters, but evidently this interdict was enforced at a later period). So Jacob has no other choice but to go back into his uncle's service for another seven years in order to finally win the hand of his beloved Rachel. Another seven years of faithful service and his dream finally comes true, he marries the woman whom he loves and has always loved more than any other. Even after having fulfilled his obligations, he nevertheless remains an additional seven years in the service of his uncle and father-in-law, for a total of over twenty years. In passing, we might mention that the relationship between Laban and Jacob is a faithful reflection of the standard contractual terms concerning adoption in use during the period in Syro-Mesopotamian society and which have come down to us in the form of cuneiform texts dealing with legal matters of the epoch.

As to be expected, in his married life Jacob shows a marked preference for his second wife Rachel, first in his heart, and Leah finds herself slightly neglected by her husband. The Lord favors Leah precisely for this reason, and sees that she is blessed with great fertility whereas Rachel remains for a long while barren. The Book of Genesis then relates the story surrounding the births of Jacob's sons conceived not only with his two legitimate wives, but also with his slaves. The purpose of this passage, in the minds of the biblical editors, is to trace the descent of the historical Twelve Tribes of Israel to the seed of the Patriarchs. Today scholars agree that this represented a projection into the past of a situation that would only actually exist long after Israel's settlement in Canaan was largely accomplished. What is particularly noteworthy here is the editors' desire to establish a connection between themselves and this legendary epoch by tracing the establishment of the Tribes of Israel back to Jacob, an objective which is successfully achieved, though not without some very obvious incoherencies. For example, to come to the number twelve, the editors include a woman, Dinah. After this appearance, however, she is never mentioned again and is subsequently replaced by Benjamin, while the tribe of Levi, which supplies the class of priests, will be replaced by Joseph's two adopted sons Ephraim and Manasseh. It is revealing that this narrative, more than any other, shows such painstaking concern for the etymology of Jacob's sons' names, conscientiously backing up each one of them with a precise event.

Leah, the apparently neglected spouse, gives birth nevertheless to four children. The first child is Reuben, whose name suggests that God "saw her humiliation" (in fact, the meaning of the name is uncertain, it could mean "Look, it's a boy!"); a second son, Simeon ("granted") is given this name because "(God) heard" his mother's pleas; the third, Levi, thus called because Jacob "bound himself" to Leah, mother by now of three of his heirs (this name may also mean "secluded" since this son will be dedicated to God). The fourth son, Judah (a name

(*opposite page*)

Medieval miniature, ***Jacob's Dream***

God promises Jacob a "multitude of descendants" and the conquest of the Promised Land. From his stone head-rest Jacob carves a sacred pillar and vows to build a permanent temple to Yahweh, which he does some years later.

De Nollet, *Jacob and Esau*

Jacob, who more than once has taken advantage of his brother's naivety, meets Esau again after his exile and many vicissitudes. Jacob fears the worst, but Esau, who has peaceful intentions, runs to his brother to embrace him.

perhaps associated with "ravine") may have thus been baptized because Leah "gave praise" to God.

By this time Rachel can no longer contain her jealousy of her sister's prodigious fertility and demands that Jacob give her a son. Jacob protests that he is not responsible for her sterility. Out of desperation, Rachel offers her servant Bilhah to Jacob in the hope that a son will be born of their union. The servant does in fact give birth to a son named Dan, since through him God has "rendered justice" to the barren mother; then, to a second son named Naphtali, as a testimony of how Rachel "had fought" or more precisely "had gotten even" with her sister Leah. (In fact, this is a geographic location and its exact meaning is unknown.)

Engaged in this frenetic fertility contest with her sister, Leah in the meantime seems to have become sterile and decides to use the same solution Rachel had resorted to previously, encouraging the union of her husband (who plays the role here of the submissive husband manipulated by his two wives) with her maid servant Zilpah. From this union two more sons are born to Leah, Gad ("luck") because fortune has shone on Leah, and Asher, the "happy one" according to popular etymology, because all the women will "congratulate" the mother.

But the tale of Jacob's descendants is still by no means over. Leah's eldest son Reuben finds some mandrakes in a field (traditionally considered a potent aphrodisiac with powers of fecundity) and takes them to his mother. However Rachel, who has still evidently not lost all hope of having her own child, asks her sister for the plants and in exchange promises that Jacob will spend the night with Leah. As a result of this union Leah gives birth to a fifth child named Issachar since, it is said, he is a "salary" from God. Leah's generous womb, however, does not stop there for she then gives birth to two more sons: the sixth, Zabulon ("little prince") is a symbol of the "respect and honor" the grateful Jacob feels toward such a fecund mother and finally the seventh child, a girl named Dinah, the only one for whom an etymology is not given, most likely because of her sex (though it has been suggested her name may be associated with "trial" or "sentence").

But Rachel, in this whirlwind of pregnancies and births, still lives with the sorrow of the barren woman. Without even one child she can truly call her own, God has pity on Rachel and finally blesses her with a child, granted only one, but a son who will become the greatest hero of the following generation, Joseph, thus called because the Lord "alleviates" Rachel's disgrace by "adding" ("may God add another") one more child to Jacob's numerous progeny, the twelfth and final heir.

Now strong with his wives and numerous children, Jacob informs Laban that he wishes to return to Canaan and claims the compensation due for his services which have, moreover, helped his father-in-law to considerably increase his own personal fortune as well. Faced with his uncle's hesitation, the astute Jacob quickly proposes the following arrangement: from their common flocks and herds Jacob will take only the black sheep and the spotted or streaked goats. Black sheep and spotted or streaked goats are, in fact, extremely rare in the Orient and, in addition, this would be an easy way for Laban to control the operation. Believing he has struck a good deal, Laban accepts Jacob's proposal. All the animals corresponding to the characteristics described by Jacob are driven to one side and those Laban will keep for himself, to the other. Laban then orders his herdsmen to keep careful watch over the two flocks so that they remain well apart. But Jacob, whom we already know is extremely clever, is also an expert on the laws of nature and well-versed in magic. He gathers some branches and whittles white marks into them and then, placing these near the drinking trough, arranges for Laban's black goats to mate near the branches. Under the influence of the streaked markings, all the kids born from these goats are spotted or streaked. As for the ewes, he makes sure that at the moment of their coupling, Laban's black goats are in sight so that by sympathetic magic these ewes conceive black sheep. Having encouraged mating between the healthiest and strongest animals of the herds, he eventually finds himself in possession of a prize stock of animals all corresponding to the original characteristics of the agreement. Jacob then gathers his animals together and prepares to take leave, having respected his agreement with Laban to the letter. He is now a prosperous man not only in herds and flocks, but also in servants and slaves.

But Laban and his clan are not at all satisfied with the way things have turned out and feel cheated by Jacob. Seeing their mounting hostility, he sends for Leah and Rachel and complains about the situation. By not telling them the whole story, Jacob presents a false and purposely dishonest version of what has actually happened. He hides the fact that he resorted to contrivances to obtain what he wanted, claiming that his animals were born with these markings thanks to the special favor of the God of Bethel who has now also commanded him to depart for his homeland. Here, of course, a theological interpretation allows us to consider various levels of reality since we have Man's will on one level superimposed by the reality of divine plans on another. Jacob's two wives, who say they feel more like strangers in their own house anyway, have no objections to fleeing with Jacob. Before their departure, however, Rachel stealthily removes her father's *teraphim* and takes it with her. The *teraphim* was a collection of ancestral idols, central to domestic worship, representing the family's ancestors who kept watch over the house and who were believed to ensure protection of the members of the family.

Jacob's family, with all of their belongings, slip past Laban's watch and leave Haran. After crossing the Euphrates, they continue toward Galaad and along the way stop to rest. Their furtive departure discovered, Laban and his men set out after them. However, when they eventually catch up with Jacob's party, God appears to the Aramean in a dream and commands him not to harm Jacob. Laban, however, goes to confront his son-in-law and reproaches him for having left in secrecy, indignant that he was not allowed to say good-bye to his daughters or give the family a proper farewell feast. Also, he complains the *teraphim* is missing. Jacob explains that he had been afraid of Laban's anger and resentment and then, unaware of what Rachel has done, he adds that Laban is free to search the camp for the idols, assuring him that when they are found the thief will be put to death. Laban searches the entire encampment in vain. When he enters Rachel's tent he finds her sitting on a camel saddle (where she has hidden the idols) and when she excuses herself for not getting up saying that she is menstruating ("women's problems"), he does not insist.

Jacob is furious with Laban who cannot find anything to justify his accusations. He reminds his father-in-law of his long years of service, his diligence and dedication, in short, the important contributions Jacob has made to the growth of his uncle's fortune. And in return what does he get? Only ingratitude and injustice from Laban. The argument between the two men becomes increasingly heated and when they are just about to come to blows, the situation begins to calm down, both men becoming more and more reasonable. Finally Laban even proposes to conclude a family peace pact and erect a stele right on the spot as an eternal reminder of their good faith. As a symbolic gesture of peace, Jacob and Laban mark the ground with a pile of stones and share a meal together on them. Jacob solemnly promises to love and respect Leah and Rachel and to take no other wives. This episode, as happens frequently in the Old Testament, serves as an opportunity to explain a place-name by relating it to a specific event and is aimed not only at justifying the pact that puts an end to the quarrel between two families, but also shows how the territorial borders were determined between Laban's people (the Arameans) and Jacob's (the Israelites). The stele and the pile of stones are referred to as "witnesses" in the text, not only of the agreement between Jacob and Laban, but also more specifically as symbols marking the two parties' respective territories. The "gods" of the two parties are called upon to see that the covenant is kept: the god of Abraham, meaning Yahweh, and the god of Nakhor, the ancient patriarch, his ancestor, apparently another manifestation of the god of Israel. A solemn sacrifice and a communal feast finally conclude the pact. The next day, the two groups prepare to go their separate ways and Jacob resumes his journey to the land of Canaan, during which he will have an encounter with an angel of God. This episode will offer the biblical editors yet another explanation of a place-name.

As Jacob approaches his destination, he decides the time has come to make peace with his brother Esau who lives nearby in the region of Edom. Jacob sends his men to give news to his brother of his whereabouts and to carry his greetings to Esau with a message of hope that their relations may be renewed. However, Jacob learns that Esau is already moving towards the encampment with four hundred men. Panic-stricken and fearing the worst, Jacob divides his group into two companies hoping that in case of an attack at least one of the two will survive. As he waits for his brother, he fervently invokes the Lord, reminding him of his promise of protection and pleading to be saved. Suddenly Jacob has an idea. He herds a large number of his animals together and has them advance slowly at regular intervals in his brother's direction. The herdsmen are told to offer Esau the animals as a gift. Jacob will follow in person behind the caravan in the hope that the sight of the animals will placate

his brother's anger and when they finally come face to face, Esau's desire for vengeance will have vanished.

That night Jacob undergoes a strange experience which even the biblical text does not completely elucidate. As a result, however, a new name will be bestowed on the patriarch who from then on will be called "Israel." In the middle of the night, Jacob accompanies his wives and children to the Jabbok river and has them cross at the ford to the other side. Alone, Jacob wrestles until dawn with a mysterious personage. During the struggle, neither opponent manages to defeat the other until the stranger finally strikes Jacob in the hip and injured, the patriarch gives up. Jacob then begins to realize that his adversary is a supernatural being and he pleads for the being's grace and blessing. Jacob's opponent, who refuses to reveal his identity though whom we imagine is God in person, even if the biblical text does not explicitly tell us this, solemnly declares that the patriarch will no longer be called Jacob, but rather "Israel," since he "struggled with Elohim (God) as with a human being and won." The name "Israel" is thus given a popular etymology here even though the name really means "that God be strong." Two details underline the aetiological character of the episode: Jacob baptizes the place of their combat "Penuel" ("faced with God") to commemorate his encounter and struggle with the Lord. Secondly, in memory of Jacob's injury from his adversary's blow, the Israelites establish the custom of abstaining from eating that portion of the animal which contains the sciatic nerve. The narrative, as we see, leaves many aspects unexplained and seems to be purposely shrouded in ambiguity. The changing of Jacob's name suggests a vague historical event, perhaps the ancient merging of two clans or groups, one of which was headed by Jacob and the other by a certain Israel.

Though Jacob's mysterious opponent in the story is of course a divine angel or God himself, there are good reasons to believe that originally this personage represented a divine pagan entity. Some scholars have seen in him the Jabbok river god who marked the limits between Jacob's territory and Esau's, or Esau's own personal god. In any case, the episode seems to be related in some way to an attempt to halt Jacob's advance, a struggle from which he emerges injured but not defeated, an outcome which serves to legitimize his territorial rights as well as his possession of the special rights of the first-born son. The ancient traditions were later combined and reworked and the Lord, or one of his angels, was given the role of the patriarch's adversary.

A short while later Esau and his men are seen approaching. Jacob and his clan await their fate, Jacob trembling and trying to protect his wives and children. When his brother draws near, Jacob, desperate, throws himself to the ground in his path. But Esau runs to him, takes him by the arms and embraces him. Both weep, deeply moved (Jacob, probably as much out of relief as out of joy). Esau looks up and wonders who all the people are gathered around them and Jacob presents his wives and children and then reminds Esau that the preceding caravan had been intended as a gift, a homage to him. At first Esau refuses, saying that he is already rich enough, but under his brother's insistence he eventually accepts. When it comes time to resume their journey, Esau suggests they join together and go in his direction, but Jacob (who is still not completely convinced of his brother's intentions) prefers to remain independent, and so the two brothers part. This episode should also be understood in terms of the underlying desire of the biblical editors to establish a connection between the two populations represented by the twin brothers. Though reconciled, the brothers separate and while Esau returns to Edom, Jacob and his people move on to Succoth (meaning "huts") in the Jordan valley, where they construct shelters for themselves and their herds. The caravan later resumes its journey and continues on to Shechem, in Canaan, where Jacob buys a field from the local prince Hamor and builds an altar which he baptizes "El, God of Israel."

At this point in the narrative, the Book of Genesis relates the story of how Jacob's daughter Dinah and wife Leah are attacked, and the events which ensue. This chapter combines a family tale with various ancient traditions concerning relations between the Israelites and the people of Shechem, two peoples incapable of living together peacefully. It essentially represents an example of the Israelites' failure to conquer Canaan. Dinah is kidnapped and raped by a certain Shechem, the son of Hamor, prince of the land. "Shechem" is most likely an eponym for the local population. Despite his behavior, Shechem is truly in love with Dinah and declares that he wishes to marry her. His father, Hamor, goes to see Jacob to negotiate a marriage agreement for his son. However, the patriarch's sons, who arrive during the discussion, are indignant and oppose the union of their abducted sister with Shechem. Confronted with their hostility, Hamor even proposes an alliance between their two peoples and offers hospitality to the Israelites with the right to take wives from among the local women. But Dinah's brothers have no intention of forgiving Hamor and they set very harsh conditions in exchange for their agreement. Shechem must agree, with all the other male inhabitants of the city, to submit to circumcision (the real reason for demanding this is to temporarily weaken their adversaries). Hamor and Shechem accept these conditions and tell their people what must be done, explaining that the Israelites have honest intentions and that a situation of peaceful co-existence will thus be established between their peoples. In addition, they announce, the two populations will put all their property together and become but one united people. A few days later, when the Shechemites are still recovering from the general circumcision, Simeon and Levi with their men take the city by surprise and kill all the male inhabitants, including the prince and his son, and then go to recover their sister Dinah. The massacre is followed by a sacking of the city during which the Israelites help themselves to all the livestock. Jacob strongly disapproves of his sons' actions and also fears the violent reaction from the inhabitants of the entire region. In any event, it is now too late to do anything to remedy the situation.

After these dramatic events, the Book of Genesis proposes another story, this time related to Bethel, concerning the honoring of a promise which Jacob had once made. The Lord tells Jacob to go to Bethel

(opposite page)

Donato Creti, *Jacob Fights the Angel*

Following his combat with an angel on the banks of the Jabbok river, Jacob is re-baptized Israel most likely to show to what degree his destiny may be associated with that of his people.

Claude Gellée called Le Lorrain, *Jacob, Laban, and His Daughters*

The Book of Genesis relates with great mastery the touching story of Jacob's two marriages with Leah and Rachel, his uncle Laban's two daughters. From these unions the ancestors of the Twelve Tribes of Israel are born.

with his people and build an altar to God. This was the spot where, fearing his brother's vengeance, Jacob had invoked the Lord's protection. The patriarch obediently prepares to leave, and orders his people to destroy all idolatrous foreign gods and such objects of worship (in the form of statues, most probably), including Laban's famous *teraphim* stolen by Rachel. Also to be considered in this category are all magic amulets, which are symbols and instruments of pagan idolatry. All of the objects are then buried under an oak tree near Shechem.

Jacob and his people travel unhindered by the local population since God has instilled great fear in them. Upon reaching Bethel, Jacob builds an altar and baptizes it El-Bethel. He then buries Rebekah's nurse, who has just died, under an oak tree. Without the slightest worry about being redundant, the biblical editors then repeat the story of how Jacob's name is changed to Israel and God's promise of a land for his descendants is reiterated. They then again relate how a stone stele is erected by Jacob and a sacrifice is offered out of thankfulness.

We then learn, without any opening remarks, that Rachel is pregnant and that near Ephrath, on the journey home, she goes into labor. There are difficulties during childbirth and Rachel knows she will not survive. She gives birth to the child and, before she dies, she is told it is a boy. Rachel says the child's name should be Ben-oni, "son of my suffering," a name which Jacob prefers to change to "Benjamin" ("my right hand") because this name expresses "force" and "protection" and is not so sad. The name Benjamin may also have a geographical significance ("son of the South") and as such it could designate an ancient semi-nomadic clan mentioned in Mesopotamian and Syrian cuneiform writings. Beyond the birth of a human being, the biblical text is chiefly concerned with relating the story of the tribe named after Benjamin and the connection between it and the clans of Jacob and Joseph.

Rachel dies quietly and is buried along the way to Bethlehem. On her grave Jacob places a tombstone which, according to the biblical editor, still stands at the time of the writing. We find it somewhat surprising that the text gives no indication of Jacob's feelings or reactions when he thus loses his beloved wife, for whom he has suffered and struggled so greatly. However, the narrative's purpose is not to delve into the hearts of its heroes, but rather to trace the fulfillment of God's greater plans; even if this means at times eclipsing, even rather brusquely, men's personal dramas. The patriarch now passes through Migdal-Eder where the incestuous union between his eldest son Reuben and his father's concubine Bilhah, mother of Reuben's half-brothers Dan and Naphtali, is related. Jacob learns of his son's act and though we are not told what his immediate reaction is, it is evident that this event will eventually provoke the loss of Reuben's birthright. Genesis then gives us a general table of the "sons of Jacob" who, since they differ slightly from those mentioned before, we feel might be worth summarizing here:

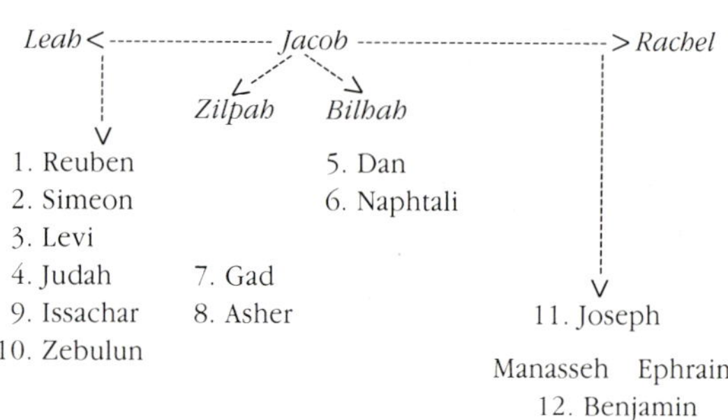

After these events, Jacob finally reaches Mamre-Hebron and is with his father Isaac when he dies. With the help of his brother Esau, he sees to his father's burial and decides to settle there in "the land where my father lived." With this note the Bible then seems to officially close Jacob's story. For, right after this episode Joseph's biography follows: the son who will become the supreme hero of the final events of the Book of Genesis. Of Jacob we will still receive some news indirectly through the adventures relating to Joseph, the child whom Jacob loved above all others. We will come back to the details concerning the patriarch in his last years, but for now we must leave him since the most significant episodes of his life have now come to an end. Because of famine, Jacob finds himself, by divine inspiration, in Egypt where he joins his son Joseph and his clan. Settled in Egypt, Jacob becomes very wealthy and sees the number of his descendants increase considerably. He spends the last seventeen years of his life in the land of the Nile and dies there after having pronounced his solemn blessing in favor of Joseph and having legally adopted Joseph's two sons, Ephraim and Manasseh (who thus become full-fledged members of the Twelve Tribes, on an equal footing with Jacob's other sons), and also after having foretold the unique destiny of each of the tribes. On his deathbed, Jacob expresses his desire to be buried in Canaan. After his death, his sons, abiding by his wishes, bury him in the family sepulchre at Machpelah. An impressive funerary caravan accompanies the patriarch's body, embalmed according to Egyptian custom, to its final resting place.

The story of Jacob's life has come down to us in a complex and stratified compilation based upon a historical foundation dating back to very ancient times. Historically, this represented the merging of two clans, the "Sons of Jacob" and the "Sons of Israel," both associated with the city of Shechem, that then combined their respective traditions concerning the single figure of the patriarch Jacob-Israel. The two wives, Leah ("cow") and Rachel ("ewe") are transparent symbols of two different and opposing cultural models: sedentary livestock breeders on the one hand, and semi-nomadic shepherds on the other. These were two functions which nourished the roots of Hebrew civilization above and beyond any particular historical factor. Moreover, while the story of Jacob and Esau alludes to Israel's contacts with hunting peoples (Esau) or proto-Aramean clans (Laban), the events which follow then go back to the occupation of Palestine, with its difficulties and setbacks, and to an earlier period when the Hebrew people first began to adopt a sedentary way of life and settle in the area around Shechem.

From the narrative point of view, Jacob is definitely a fuller and more human character than the first patriarchs. He possesses many important virtues without being exempt of weaknesses and his personality as a clever and cunning "supplanter" is shown on many

Guercino, *Jacob Blesses Joseph's Sons*

The last seventeen years of Jacob's life are spent in Egypt where he dies after having pronounced a solemn blessing in favor of Joseph and Joseph's sons, Ephraim and Manasseh. They thus become ancestors of the Twelve Tribes on an equal footing with Jacob's legitimate sons.

occasions. God does not spare Jacob from traps or ambushes either and his misfortunes should often be read as true expressions of the law of "an eye for an eye" for his dishonest dealings with Esau and Laban. Though a diligent, hard worker full of gentleness, he has absolutely no scruples when it comes to matters of money; a passionate man, extremely attached to his family, he is also easy prey to his instincts and shows partialities that are at times difficult to comprehend (not so much in his love for Rachel, but for his sons, as in the case of Joseph and Benjamin). A vigorous figure bursting with life, Jacob is rich in human qualities, capable of acts of greatness but also of shameful deviousness. Perhaps it is precisely this profound humanity, buoyed by his unerring faith in God, that makes this patriarch so likeable and inspires in us a feeling of solidarity with him, apart from any theological appreciation. These qualities, plus his perfect respect for God's will and precepts, will earn Jacob the privilege of embodying the ideal man in rabbinical tradition, which prefers to minimize his human weaknesses and extol his religious virtues.

Perhaps more realistic in its evaluation of a man, whom it nevertheless considers a fundamental link in the grandiose story of redemption orchestrated by God, Christian exegesis celebrates this patriarch with fewer honors. The Lord, however, has repeated to Jacob the ancient promise made to Abraham and Isaac. With the journey into Egypt, the moment of the Exodus is gradually forming — an event which will represent one of the greatest moments in the history of the Hebrew people.

JOSEPH

The First Israelite on Egyptian Soil

"Little one," said Joseph, "little one," he said and lifted Benjamin up so their heads were close. "Do not speak, all of that is not so great nor so far from us, and my glory is not all so grand, the essential thing is that we are again twelve."

THOMAS MANN, *Joseph the Provider*

With Joseph, the Book of Genesis introduces us to a figure of great scope, of extreme interest from a human, literary, historical, as well as ethnographic point of view. His adventure unfolds principally on Egyptian soil and the biblical editors, in gathering and compiling the various narrative traditions, show impressive knowledge of the reality they describe. Though the entire story was committed to writing at a much later date than the events it relates and does not pretend to be a precise historical reconstruction, it nonetheless contains interesting and often plausible elements. Joseph's name was not unfamiliar in Egyptian texts and many of the details in his story are based on solid fact, though they are perhaps a more accurate reflection of the period in which they were written rather than the presumed epoch of the events themselves, a much more archaic time. From a literary point of view, we note that Genesis abandons the type of narrative defined as the "saga" to adopt a novelistic tone, an easier style, richer in descriptive detail and more attentive to the psychology of its characters. This is a form that comes alive by the use of popular themes common to many ancient and modern literatures. The sapiential and didactic aims evident throughout the narrative in no way undermine literary mastery which succeeds in creating a story that is exciting, moving, and dramatic.

As we recall, Joseph is the first of two sons by Rachel, Jacob's favorite wife, for whom this birth is the crowning blessing of long and patient years of waiting and which puts her on an equal footing with her sister Leah, a much more prolific mother. We later find adolescent Joseph a shepherd in the footsteps of his brothers, though he is envied and detested by them because of his gifts and the fact that he is their father's favorite. Jacob even gives Joseph a special robe to wear, a "coat of many colors" that resembles a royal garment and symbolizes Joseph's superiority and ambitions of predominance. Though ostracized by his brothers and the victim of their jealousy, Joseph is apparently unaffected by the situation and does not even bother mentioning his brothers' meanness to his father.

One night Joseph has two dreams, one inspired by an agricultural theme and the other by an astral one. He openly relates these dreams to his brothers though, considering their already strong fear and hatred of Joseph's presumed ambitions, the significance of these dreams could only cause great consternation. In the first dream — the oneiric dimension is often present in Joseph's story, gifted

Velazquez, *Joseph's Tunic*

An extremely dramatic moment: Jacob is told the news of the presumed death of his favorite son Joseph, who, in fact, has been sold into slavery by his jealous brothers.

interpreter of dreams himself — Joseph and his brothers are binding sheaves in the fields and suddenly his brothers' sheaves bow down before Joseph's. In the second dream, it is the sun, moon, and eleven stars that bow to Joseph. In both cases the symbolism is transparent and clearly suggests Joseph's supremacy over his brothers, not only in relation to his individual destiny, but also in terms of the tribes of which each brother is the leader and eponym.

Such an incident, as could only be expected, only further sharpens the brothers' bitter resentment against Joseph and finally leads to the dramatic turn of events which will completely change the course of their lives. We should note in passing that Joseph's entire adventure is exempt from those divine apparitions which have until now so characterized the stories of the other patriarchs (the last theophany goes back to Jacob when he was faced with the decision whether to leave for Egypt or not). Here, however, God acts without direct intervention, with no consideration for men's calculations nor their intentions, even less for their social rules (such as the birthright of the elder son), but he uses their ideas, their emotions and actions to accomplish his own plans just as an adroit stage director perfectly orchestrates a theatrical performance.

Sent to help his brothers pasturing their herds, Joseph sets off for Dothan or Shechem (depending on the tradition). But his brothers are already plotting to rid themselves, once and for all, of this young family upstart whose presence, they all agree, is becoming just a bit too intrusive and unwieldy. Having been persuaded against bloodshed by Reuben's intervention, they push Joseph into a dry well and, when a caravan of Ishmaelite traders appear bound for Egypt, urged by Judah, they sell their younger brother into slavery for twenty pieces of silver. The eldest brother, Reuben, who in fact had secretly planned to take Joseph back to their father, is now panicked at the thought of how Jacob will react when he finds out what has happened. The only thing left to do is to make their father believe that Joseph is dead, devoured by a wild animal. The brothers stain Joseph's tunic with goat's blood and take it back to Jacob who, at the sight of it, collapses in grief and inconsolable mourning over his beloved son.

Meanwhile, Joseph's destiny is unfolding in the land of the Nile. The Arab traders in turn sell Joseph to an eminent personage at the pharoah's court, a certain Potiphar (an Egyptian name that means "a [man] whom the King has gratified"), a high official and "captain of the guards" of the pharoah, a title that indicates very important responsibilities as military chief and the sovereign's ambassador. But the young Israelite slave, assisted by God, soon distinguishes himself as an extremely capable administrator and rises steadily in his master's esteem. Having become Potiphar's personal slave, Joseph is then named chief steward of the residence and is entrusted with the management and control not only of his master's household, and but also of all his farming property as well. The Egyptian's confidence is so

Guercino, ***Joseph Resists Potiphar's Wife***

In Egypt, Joseph's extraordinary destiny unfolds. Slave, then prisoner, he finally becomes the pharoah's all-powerful vizier. When he rejects the advances of his master Potiphar's wife, this episode brings about his imprisonment.

great that Joseph is not even asked to account for his administration.

The episode that follows finds numerous parallels in the folk and literary narrative traditions of many cultures. This shows the unsuccessful attempt of the master's wife to seduce an innocent man and the false accusations by the woman (we may recall the Egyptian story, *Tale of Two Brothers* or, from the Greek world, the cases of Hippolytus, Bellerophon, Peleus, and Phoenix, among many others). The young Joseph, whom we know is a handsome man, involuntarily attracts the attention of Potiphar's wife who tries time and again in vain to seduce him. The loyal staff member refuses to betray his master, so trusting and generous, and rejects the woman's advances on religious and moral grounds. One day, however, Joseph finds himself alone in the house with Potiphar's wife and the covetous woman rips part of his clothing, pretends that he has tried to rape her, and cries to the servants for help, well aware that they will make excellent witnesses against him. When Potiphar comes home and receives the news, he is beside himself with anger and humiliation and imprisons the slave whom, he believes, has so vilely betrayed his trust.

Even in prison God sees to it that Joseph's exceptional talents are quickly noticed, until finally the head of the prison even appoints Joseph to be keeper of the prison, entrusting him with its day to day management and the responsibility of watching over the other prisoners. Among his wards are two important court functionaries, the pharoah's head cupbearer and his chief baker, both imprisoned on the order of the king himself in a form of "house arrest" for faults unspecified in the text. Joseph is assigned to the service of these two illustrious prisoners and gains their esteem as a gifted interpreter of dreams. The two dignitaries have both, in fact, had very puzzling dreams which they are trying to explain. The head cupbearer has dreamt of a vine with three leaves that bears flowers and fruit. He squeezes the fruit into a chalice and offers the cup to the pharoah to drink. In the chief baker's dream, the man sees himself carrying three breadbaskets on his head, one of which contains various foods destined for the pharoah, but birds swoop down and devour them instead. Joseph interprets their dreams for them. For the head cupbearer, the message is a favorable one. In less than three days the pharoah will "lift his (the cupbearer's) head," meaning that the prisoner will be pardoned and restored to his functions in the pharoah's service. It is a fatal omen, however, for the head baker who will also have his "head lifted" by the pharoah, in the sense that he will be hanged and his body left to be eaten by the birds. Jacob's interpretation is based on the double meaning of the expression to "raise" and to "lift" which, in the first case, means to render homage to someone, and in the second, to be hanged or beheaded. Joseph reminds the cupbearer not to forget him and his accurate interpretation once out of prison.

Everything comes to pass exactly as Joseph has foretold, but the fortunate cupbearer forgets all about the service Joseph once rendered. Nevertheless, events seem to be ripening in favor of our hero. A short while later the pharoah also has two dreams that none of the court experts (magicians, prophets, priests) are able to interpret satisfactorily. In the first dream, the sovereign sees seven healthy fat cows come out of the Nile and go to graze, but then seven other cows, emaciated and ugly, appear and devour the first. In the second dream, seven ears of wheat sprout from a single stalk, large and full, but immediately after that seven dry thin spikes appear that swallow the first. Troubled by these dreams and by the magicians' inability to explain them, the pharoah finally decides to follow the advice of his head cupbearer who, in the meantime, has remembered the young prison keeper and his impressive gift for interpreting dreams. Brought before the pharoah, Joseph willingly reveals the key to the Pharoah's dreams, though first pointing out that it is God who gives him the tools necessary to reveal their deep significance.

After listening to the pharoah's description, Joseph tells him that the two dreams concern a single event: the seven fat cows and the seven full ears of wheat indicate seven years of plenty in Egypt, not only for cattle breeding but also for harvest yields; the seven thin cows and the seven dry ears, however, signify seven years of severe famine which will again be followed by a period of abundance. Given the imminence of these events (indicated by the double dream), it is urgent that the pharoah find a wise and intelligent man to administer the country. For, during the period of abundance, one-fifth of all the grain will have to be rigorously put aside in order to face the ensuing famine.

Joseph's interpretation of the two dreams and his practical recommendations for dealing with the scourge that threatens Egypt greatly impress the pharoah who, without hesitating a moment longer, appoints the young Israelite his vizier, that is, the person who in virtue of his powers and prestige, holds the second highest position in the country, just below the Pharoah himself. The sovereign bestows upon Joseph the symbols of his power (a signet, a fine linen tunic, and a gold necklace), has him mount a chariot that follows immediately after his own, and parades through the capital with his new vizier. The Egyptians give Joseph a tremendous ovation. Potiphar's former slave has now become the pharoah's most powerful minister and, with this change of fortune, Joseph is told he must also change his name. The Egyptian "Zaphnath-Paanea" is chosen for him, which perhaps signifies "the man who knows things." He also receives for a wife a certain Asenath, daughter of the high priest of Heliopolis, the worship center of the sun god Re, and through this marriage thus becomes related to this influential priestly family.

The young vizier gets to work immediately and with great zeal. He travels the country far and wide seeing that large quantities of food are collected and stored as provisions against the famine. During this period his wife Asenath bears him two sons destined to become eponyms of two of the Twelve Tribes of Israel. The first is Manasseh, whose name is explained by the fact that he has made his father "forget" all his suffering and his father's house in Canaan; the second, Ephraim, because God has made Joseph "fecund" in a foreign land. We note, nevertheless, that in the biblical text Manasseh and Ephraim are not considered of Egyptian ancestry, an origin which, moreover, the Semitic etymology of their names denies, and which may only be explained by the geographical setting of Joseph's adventures.

After the years of plenty, a terrible famine descends upon the land. The Egyptians, in great suffering, turn to Joseph who opens the granaries to them and, because Egypt is not the only famine-stricken nation, this attracts peoples from the "four corners of the earth." It also happens that the land of Canaan is among these starving lands and Jacob finds it only natural to send ten of his sons to Egypt to obtain food supplies. Only Benjamin, the youngest son, is kept at home by his father who lives in constant fear of losing him as he once lost Joseph.

Once in Egypt, the ten brothers are bound to meet Joseph as he is responsible for overseeing all operations at the granaries. They bow down before him, not for an instant imagining the true identity of the pharoah's powerful vizier. Joseph, however, recognizes them instantly but manages to control his sudden turmoil and acts as if this is just another normal transaction. He treats them a little roughly after that and then, asking where they come from, cannot help yielding to a surge of vengeance when he remembers his brothers' cruelty to him so long ago. He accuses them of being spies who have come to Egypt to explore the territory for obscure motives. This accusation, not only appropriate to the critical situation of the moment, also has a certain historical validity. Asian bedouin populations, in fact, were constantly infiltrating the Nile delta inside the borders of the Egyptian kingdom, a flux that posed serious problems to Egyptian sovereigns. The ten brothers declare their innocence and explain their family's difficult situation, but the inflexible vizier will not listen. He decides to keep one of them as a hostage and to send the others back to their homeland with their supplies of food. To free their brother held hostage, they must bring the youngest brother, Benjamin, before him. Knowing how Jacob loves Benjamin, Joseph's brothers are consumed with grief at the thought of having to bring their younger brother to Egypt. In any case, Simeon is designated by lot to remain with Joseph while the others, laden with their stocks, prepare to make the journey home. Before their departure, Joseph orders that the payment received for their purchases be returned to them as a gift. During their trip back, the brothers discover the money in one of their bags and are completely baffled by the vizier's disconcerting behavior. They begin to realize that an unfathomable force is hidden behind these events, something that must surely come from God.

When they are with Jacob once again, they relate everything that has happened down to the last detail.

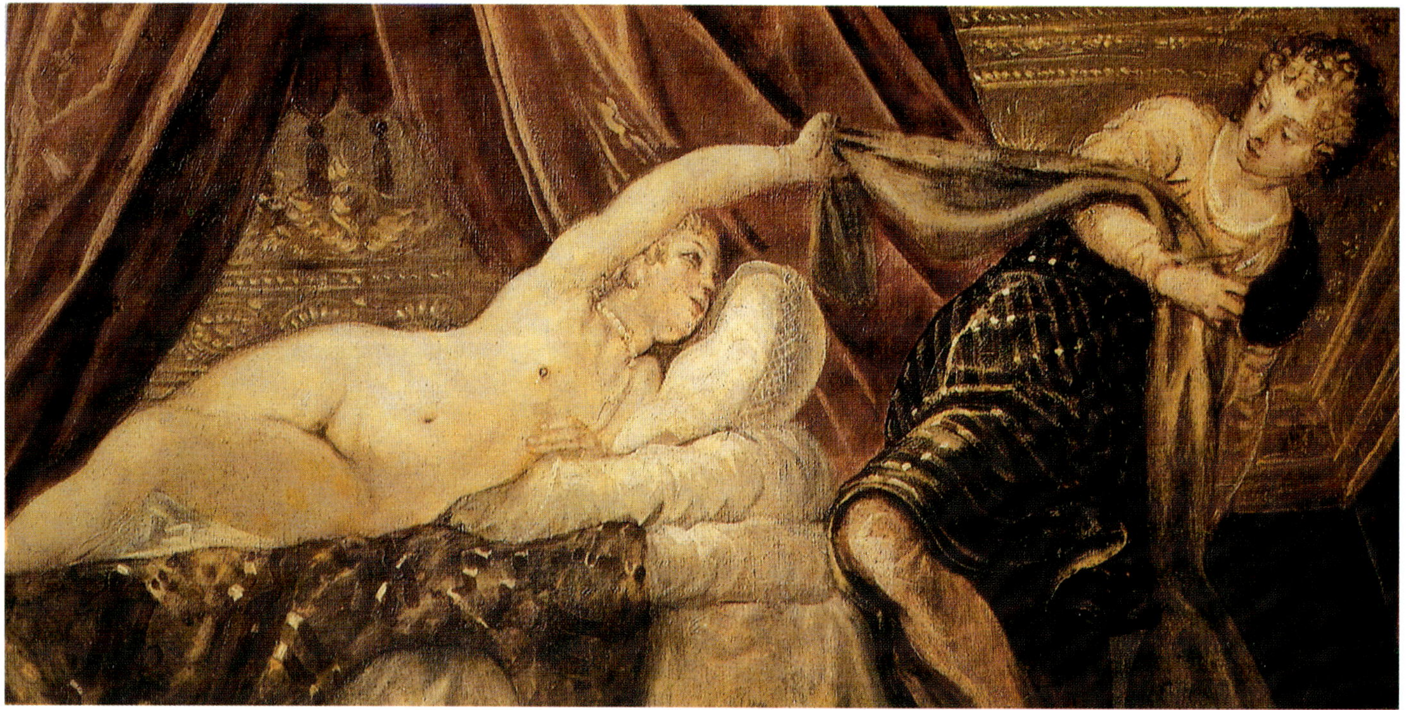

Tintoretto, *Joseph and Potiphar's Wife*

Though Joseph's story is not a historical reconstruction, it does contain some plausible elements and Joseph's name, in fact, is mentioned in Egyptian texts. However, just as in Moses' case, it is virtually impossible to separate history from fiction.

The old patriarch is deeply stricken by the events. Joseph is forever lost to him and now Simeon is hostage in Egypt, and what is more, Benjamin is being forced to abandon him. His first reaction is to object to Benjamin's departure despite Reuben's reassurances. But famine continues in the land and finally there is no other alternative but to return to Egypt for more food supplies. The problem of Benjamin comes up again, but Jacob still opposes his leaving. However, the entire family insists so strongly, particularly Judah who offers to be personally responsible for his younger brother, that the patriarch, heartsick, is forced to accept. A new caravan is therefore outfitted and Jacob watches as his sons set off, blessing them and having suggested they take double the sum of money and a selection of typical local products to offer in homage to the pharaoh's powerful vizier.

Upon their arrival in Egypt, Joseph's brothers again present themselves before the vizier who orders that they be taken to his residence for a meal. This initiative worries the guests who are suspicious about being received in the vizier's house. They fear the worst and are afraid of being accused of not having paid for the previous supplies, the money still being in their possession. But Joseph's major-domo reassures them: the money returned to them was an act of divine grace, and as for their brother Simeon, he would be joining them immediately. They freshen themselves and rest from their journey while waiting for Joseph who, as soon as he appears, is offered the gifts from Canaan. Joseph asks for news of their aging father and is particularly kind to Benjamin, who could have been his own son. At first sight of Benjamin, in fact, Joseph had been so moved that he had left the room to weep in secret. From the story, we understand that Benjamin was born after Joseph's disappearance and he is therefore introduced to Joseph as Jacob's youngest son. Having regained his composure and spent some time chatting with them, Joseph takes his leave, as local custom forbids him to take his meals in the company of foreigners (a detail confirmed by Herodotus in the second book of his *Histories* devoted to Egypt). However, he makes sure that the very best from his kitchen is served to his brothers and that the most generous portions go to Benjamin, all in an atmosphere of joyful serenity.

Meanwhile, Joseph orders that his brothers' bags be filled with grain and, again, that the money in payment for it be placed inside. He also has his own precious silver cup added to Benjamin's belongings. After his brothers have left the country to return to Canaan, Joseph orders his men to pursue them and bring them back under the pretext that they have stolen the host's precious cup. His brothers protest and claim their innocence declaring that whoever has stolen the cup will be put to death. Joseph takes them on their word and, searching their bags, he finds the cup hidden in Benjamin's bags. The brothers are dumbstruck and give themselves up to Joseph who, beginning to let them in on his secret, tells them that the guilty one will not, in fact, be executed but instead must remain in Egypt as his slave. The others are free to return home. But Judah speaks on behalf of his brothers and expresses their terrible fear. He tells Joseph of their father's special attachment to his youngest son and how their father, with heavy heart and against his will, had allowed Benjamin to be brought to Egypt. The aging Jacob would never survive his youngest son being taken away from him. Joseph's decision, if he insisted upon it, would be the same as a death sentence for their father. Judah then proposes that he remain as a slave himself, instead of Benjamin, whom he begs the vizier to allow to return to his father. Joseph, before this moving scene, can continue his play-acting no longer and the vizier asks to be left alone with his brothers. He then reveals his true identity and with tremendous emotion they all recognize him; their sobbing is so great that it carries out into the street and eventually even the pharoah is informed of the event. Joseph's brothers are anxious, however, that he will want to seek vengeance for their cruelty to him. But Joseph reassures them that he no longer harbors the slightest feelings of bitterness. His long journey from the well where he had been hidden to the position of second highest official in Egypt, administrator of all the crown's property, had been willed and directed by God. God alone was the true artisan of the story and his brothers had been nothing more than unconscious instruments. The time had now come for them to go to Jacob and let the aging patriarch know that his son Joseph was alive, honored, and wealthy, and that if he desired, his son was waiting in Egypt for him, and all of their people, to come to settle. Joseph's words are met with joy and embracing and, as Joseph gives a special hug to Benjamin, his brothers look on dazed and still unable to believe their good fortune.

The pharoah in person, having learned of the arrival of Joseph's brothers, welcomes them and insists they bring their father, families, and all of their possessions back to Egypt, even passing a special decree for the circumstance. His nation is prepared to offer them hospitality, food, and work, to welcome them honorably. Joseph's brothers once again set off on the road to Canaan, richly outfitted by Joseph who has been extremely generous to all of them, particularly to Benjamin. When they reach home, they give Jacob the incredible news: Joseph is alive, he is the pharoah's powerful vizier! At first the old patriarch dares not believe his sons' discovery. What if they were all only victims of a terrible ruse? But when his sons repeat what Joseph has declared to them word for word, and Jacob sees with his own eyes the chariots his son has sent to carry him to Egypt, he cannot deny the truth any longer. "My son Joseph is alive, I will see him before I die..."

Thus Jacob-Israel departs for the land of the Nile, tracing the same route, but in the opposite direction, that the Israelites will follow at the epic moment of the great Exodus. Before leaving, Jacob goes on a pilgrimage of thanks to Beersheba where he honors the God of his forefathers with sacrifices and receives the last theophany, or divine appearance, in the history of the Patriarchs. The Lord manifests himself to Jacob and exhorts him to set out on his journey in confidence. Israel will give birth to a great people and, with the help of God, they will return to the land of Canaan. After this prophecy, in accordance with God's will, the Israelites and their families depart for Egypt.

Judah arrives first and receives instructions from Joseph concerning the practical details of the peoples' settlement and is advised on the usages and etiquette of this land, certainly very hospitable, but nevertheless foreign to them. Joseph is too impatient to wait for the others to arrive in the city and goes out to receive his father along the way; the meeting of the two heroes is a beautiful and intense moment. The pharoah, who has already expressed his favorable attitude towards the new immigrants, receives Joseph, Jacob (who blesses the sovereign), and a small group of new arrivals and officially extends his invitation to settle in his land. He bestows upon them the responsibility of overseeing all the royal herds and flocks.

Joseph, after having settled his relatives in the eastern part of the Nile delta, at Goshen, is confronted with grave administrative and economic problems caused by the famine which, once again, ravages the lands of Canaan and Egypt. As vizier, he sells the reserves of stored

Medieval miniature, *Joseph and the Egyptians*

Joseph is the last hero in the Book of Genesis. With the Book of Exodus a new man, born and brought up in Egypt appears: Moses, who must lead the people of Israel out of Egypt and finally conquer the land of Canaan.

Stained glass, Bruges Military Chapel, *Joseph and His Brothers*

It is interesting to see how art has constantly brought the biblical tales up to date, from the Middle Ages to contemporary times, from Donatello to Chagall, demonstrating the continued relevance and universal impact of these themes.

grain and receives monies which are deposited into the coffers of the king. But the starving populations are very soon out of food and money and turn to Joseph in desperation. Everyone receives quantities of bare subsistence and, in exchange, Joseph accepts cattle and other animals in payment which results in the amassing of an incredible hoard of animals of every imaginable type (horses, asses, oxen, sheep). After a year, however, the inhabitants have again exhausted their stocks and have nothing left to offer this time in exchange for food except their own person or their land, in need of cultivation. Joseph buys their lands on behalf of the pharoah and arranges to transfer inhabitants to wherever they might be most useful. Only the priests are allowed to keep their properties. To the former landowners, who have given up their land for food, Joseph distributes sowing seeds under the condition that when harvest time comes, they pay one-fifth of their crops to the pharoah.

The years pass, the Israelites in Egypt multiply, and Jacob, feeling that death is near, sends for Joseph and expresses his wish to be buried with his forefathers in Canaan. Joseph promises him that this will be done. After which, Joseph has Manasseh and Ephraim draw near, his two sons born of the union with his Egyptian wife. On his deathbed, Jacob adopts them as his own children and thus enables them to enter as full-fledged members into the circle of the twelve tribal heads. Jacob blesses them and foretells their future destinies. Ephraim, the younger of the two, blessed by Jacob with his right hand, will enjoy a glorious future and will become the ancestor of a large and strong tribe, whereas Manasseh, blessed with the left hand, despite his status as the elder, will have a less fortunate destiny, his tribe remaining forever inferior to Ephraim's in all respects. Joseph tries to intervene in favor of the rights of the elder son, but in vain. The episode very significantly reflects the figure of Jacob as "the supplanter," and serves to demonstrate once again that God reserves the right to upset human rules and customs to accomplish his own objectives. In addition, Jacob's act also alludes to a widespread practice of legal adoption documented in ancient Near Eastern civilizations.

The aged patriarch's last act is to pronounce a series of benedictions, which are in fact types of oracles in the form of aphorisms, that recall the main characteristics of the tribes of Israel and foretell, in broad outlines, their future destinies. Reuben, generous and exhuberant, Jacob's eldest son, because he is guilty of incest will be deprived of primacy; Simeon and Levi, both with violent characters, will see their tribes dispersed over all of Israel's territory (Simeon will disappear rapidly, absorbed by Judah, while Levi will constitute the clergy). Judah, with the heart of a young lion, will be bestowed with vigor and supremacy which, for a long time, will make his the leading tribe; Zabulon will live by the sea, whereas Issachar will yield to the influence of the feeble and refined Canaanite culture to which his tribe will be subjected. Jacob then announces that Dan will receive the role of Judge; Gad's combative nature will oblige his tribe to defend itself from the pillages of nomads; Asher's qualities will lead him to settle in a rich region where delicious bread is made. Then the beauty of Naphtali is evoked. As for Joseph, particularly blessed, he will benefit from great fecundity by divine grace and become founder of a powerful dominating tribe. Benjamin, finally, will be ferocious, a shrewd and skillful wolf-like warrior. We will note in passing that the aim of the biblical writers is to exalt Judah in particular who, as a mysterious personage with messianic features (who prefigures David), will dominate all the peoples and enjoy literally "heavenly" conditions of well-being.

After reminding them of his wish to be buried in Machpelah in his forefathers' tomb, Jacob dies peacefully. Joseph has his father's body embalmed and performs a great mourning ceremony. After which, an impressive funeral procession accompanies Jacob's remains to Canaan where he is buried in accordance with his last wishes. Back in Egypt, Joseph's brothers suddenly panic at the idea that now that Jacob is no more, Joseph may want to wreak vengeance on them for his past suffering. But Joseph has absolutely no intention of changing his attitude and even less of raising himself to the position of God, who alone may judge and condemn. The biblical editors very clearly show that Joseph's purpose has now been fulfilled and the time has come for him to leave the scene. Now God must be left the freedom to best manage, according to his perfect plans, the journey of the chosen people to their salvation. Of course Joseph continues to generously watch over his family and enjoys a long and happy old age during which he sees his grandchildren and great-grandchildren grow. At 110 years (a number that, in Egyptian tradition, represents the ideal age for death) and feeling his end near, Joseph sends for his brothers and, with them all gathered around him, he reconfirms God's promise to one day lead them out of Egypt, to the Promised Land, as foretold to Abraham, Isaac, and Jacob. When Joseph dies, his body is embalmed and placed in a sarcophagus according to Egyptian custom.

Thus with Joseph, the story of the Patriarchs draws to a close, culminating in a figure who represents the highest embodiment of human values though, at the same time, is also clearly only an instrument, among many others, in the realization and triumph of God's plans. His role is fundamental since the adventure in which he is the hero leads Israel (his father and his people) to Egypt, the land which future generations will leave, under the guidance of Moses and Joshua, on the journey to the Promised Land. Despite this, Joseph finds himself eliminated from the holy story in many respects since it is not upon him, but rather upon Judah, that primacy over the tribes is bestowed. Nevertheless, apart from any theological evaluation, his story truly remains a literary and psychological masterpiece, the exceptional work which inspired Thomas Mann in his famous tetralogy based upon Jacob and Joseph.

In the context of vast geographical and cultural horizons, our character distinguishes himself by his human and moral qualities without becoming a stereotype but rather by revealing a complex many-faceted personality who bends in docile respect to divine will. Ready and willing to adapt himself completely to a new country, even accepting the changing of his name, Joseph nevertheless remains intimately bound to the mission that had already been invested in his forefather Abraham and flawlessly accomplishes the responsibility entrusted to him. From a historical point of view, we can affirm almost nothing of this entirely idealized figure, whose adventure contains only the Israelite conscience of a prolonged stay in Egypt. Certain tribal traditions drew upon this more or less historical conscience and transformed it into a common heritage, making the land of the Nile an indispensable point on the itinerary that finally leads to the definitive return to Canaan, the Promised Land so greatly desired.

With Joseph, the Book of Genesis comes to an end, to be followed by the Book of Exodus. A new man, born and brought up in Egypt appears on the horizon, a hero whose formidable task it will be to lead the people of Israel out of Egypt, a land now become hostile, and to reconquer, this time for eternity, the land of Canaan. The adventure of Moses, since he is the man we are talking about, from now on occupies the forefront of the rest of the Pentateuch and it is therefore to this key figure we will now turn our attention.

De Boullanger, *Joseph and His Brothers*

Joseph is the first biblical hero with true psychological depth. Most likely this explains why art and literature have drawn so heavily upon the tale in, notably, the famous tetralogy by Thomas Mann and in an infinite number of lesser works such as this painting.

MOSES

The Man Who Talked Face to Face with God

You made me, my God, powerful and lonesome.
Leave me to fall asleep in the earth.

ALFRED DE VIGNY, *Moses*

The Israelites, who settle in Egypt under the leadership of Joseph and Jacob, adapt and multiply so quickly that their numbers and affluence finally begin to worry the pharoah, a new sovereign who had never known Joseph. Because of this, the pharoah decides to take very harsh action against the Israelite colony: taxes, forced labor, and finally slavery. But despite this repression the population of Israel still continues to grow, to such a point that the pharoah commands Israelite midwives to put all newborn male babies to death. These women, however, refuse to enforce such cruel measures. Appealing to his subjects' feelings of nationalism, the pharoah then asks every Egyptian to personally see to it that all Hebrew infants are thrown into the Nile as soon as they are born.

This then is the dramatic backdrop of Moses' birth to Amram and Jochebed, his parents, who will also have another son, Aaron. The name of Moses will be forever associated with the deliverance of Israel from the yoke of Egyptian oppression and his mission of leading the Hebrew people to the Promised Land, though Moses himself will never set foot upon its soil. Here is one of the most formidable protagonists of the entire biblical adventure, a hero whose saga fills no less than four of the five books of the Pentateuch (Exodus, Leviticus, Numbers, and Deuteronomy) though moral and legislative passages in these works are also attached to his name and combined under it, essentially to give greater authority to the precepts they contain. Nor is it altogether insignificant that during the beginning of the Christian era the first five books of the Old Testament were attributed to Moses, reflecting a belief which Jesus and his Apostles also shared, as testified in the New Testament. Even if the most ancient traditions never explicitly affirm that the Pentateuch was entirely due to Moses, their constant reference to him nevertheless sufficiently demonstrates the role this figure played in the scope of the religious tradition which interests us here.

Born of a woman from the tribe of Levi who nurses him in secret until the age of three months, Moses, whose original name is unknown, is placed in a reed basket and abandoned to the waters of the Nile by his mother who knows she is exposing him to an "uncertain fate." But a handmaiden of the pharoah's daughter discovers him and takes him to her mistress who has pity on the child and, though he is a Hebrew, finds a nurse to take care of him. Luck has it that she calls upon the infant's own mother, who is then able to bring him up herself.

When Moses becomes a young man, he is given back to the pharoah's daughter who adopts him as her own son and gives him the name Moses. This is not an attested Hebrew name despite the popular etymology handed down to us by the Bible that associates it with the verb "to draw forth" in reference to Moses' rescue from the Nile. Moses, in fact, is an Egyptian term meaning "son" or "born" and because of this, appears in the names of numerous pharoahs such as Thut*mose*, Ah*mose*, etc. This fact supports the existence of a vague historical basis of the character, who probably did exist, though many events and episodes of different origins later crystallized around his name.

The young Moses is brought up at the pharoah's court, but he nevertheless cannot help being affected by the cruel oppression that weighs upon his Israelite brothers, to such a point that one day he reacts personally to the Egyptians' violence by killing one of their men. News of this crime travels quickly and Moses, sought after by the pharoah, escapes to Midian (perhaps in Arabia or most probably the Sinai peninsula, east of the Paran Desert). There, Moses is kindly taken in by a local priest to whom tradition has attributed various names (Jethro is the most well known among them) and marries one of this priest's daughters, a certain Zipporah, who gives Moses a son named Gershom. Meanwhile, oppression becomes more and more unbearable for the Israelites. Their cries of suffering and pleas for deliverance eventually find grace in the Lord's eyes who decides to intervene and wield his immense power to free his people. This is where the story of Moses' calling begins, for he is the one destined to realize the Lord's plans and become the obedient and faithful instrument of his divine purpose.

One day, while Moses is leading Jethro's herds in the desert, he comes to Mount Horeb and has a vision: the Lord appears to him in a burning bush and reveals that he is the God of his forefathers. He has decided, he tells Moses, to deliver the people of Israel from Egyptian bondage, to bring them out of that country, and to lead them to a land of milk and honey, Canaan, the Promised Land. To Moses is entrusted the mission of preparing and guiding this extraordinary Exodus from the country of the Nile. Moses then asks in whose name he should act and the Lord reveals his name in these terms: "I am that I am," in other words, I am the one who exists, life. According to the divine commands, Moses must first reveal his mission to the elders of

Nicolas Poussin, ***Moses Abandoned to the Nile***

The Israelite colony in Egypt, increasingly large and prosperous, is persecuted by the new pharoah. He orders midwives to put all newborn male babies to death, then asks his Egyptian subjects to throw all Israelite infants into the Nile at birth. This is the dramatic context into which Moses is born.

Israel, and then go before the pharoah to ask his permission to remain in the desert three days with the Hebrew people to offer a great sacrifice to the God of Israel. So that the pharoah will listen to him and believe what he says, God endows Moses with the special powers of a magician or wonder-worker such as the ability to change a rod into a serpent and vice versa, or to make his hand leprous and then to heal it again immediately, or even to transform the Nile's water into blood. Moses is not an eloquent man, quite the contrary, he is awkward with words, and this he confesses to the Lord. God then decides that his brother Aaron will be Moses' spokesman to make announcements to the people. Another version also exists of Moses' call and the revealing of God's name. According to this variant of priestly origin, the event takes place in Egypt itself, God's name is Yahweh and not El-Shaddai, and Aaron's function differs (he acts on behalf of the pharoah and not as spokesman for Moses).

Feeling irresistibly called to accomplish this immense task, Moses has no other choice but to take leave of his father-in-law Jethro, who blesses him, and to depart for Egypt with his family though God has foretold that Moses' future wonders will not suffice to move the pharoah's heart of stone. During the journey, in a mysterious episode, the circumcision of Moses' son is performed.

When Moses arrives in Egypt, he agrees on a plan of action with Aaron. Moses goes with his brother to see the pharoah and asks him to allow the Hebrew people to leave for the desert where he will celebrate a religious feast. But the pharoah pretends not to know of the Israelites' God and refuses to give permission; even worse, he decides to make the lives of the Israelite immigrants even more miserable by declaring that from now on workers must gather their own straw necessary for brick-making, though at the same time they will still be expected to produce the same quantity of bricks. This royal measure causes tremendous hardship for the Hebrew people and the Lord makes it known to Moses, to whom they complain of the unbearable oppression, that he is about to intervene in a grandiose and terrible way against the persecutors of God's people.

Thus begins the story of the famous plagues of Egypt sent against the obstinate pharoah who refuses to permit the Hebrew people's departure and greatly tests the Lord's patience. Before these terrible cataclysms are unleashed, Moses and Aaron try to persuade the sovereign to change his mind by a harmless demonstration of the divine powers with which God has endowed them. They magically transform their rod into a serpent but the Egyptian magicians, whose skill is famous and unchallenged in all the world, do the same. Although Moses' rod devours the other serpents, the pharoah still is not convinced by this show of power. This then is how, in a formidable crescendo, the most awesome catastrophes Man has ever witnessed are sent by God to descend upon Egypt, through Moses and Aaron.

1st Plague — *The Nile waters turn into blood*

Aaron's magic rod passes over the Nile and it becomes a river of blood. The reeking, undrinkable waters kill all the fish and create great hardship for the population. The Egyptian magicians, however, can accomplish a similar wonder and the pharoah refuses to change his mind. Meanwhile, the population find a way to draw enough drinkable water from their wells for as long as the curse lasts.

Johann Liss, *The Discovery of Moses*

Nursed in secret until the age of three months, Moses is placed in a reed basket and abandoned to the Nile where a handmaiden of the pharoah's daughter discovers him. The Egyptian princess finds a nurse for the child and when he is a young man, he is returned to the princess who adopts him and gives him the name Moses.

2nd Plague — *Frogs invade the land*

Aaron spreads his hand over all the rivers, canals, and pools of Egypt thus provoking a tremendous invasion of frogs. However, again, the Egyptian magicians are also able to match the feat. It is still necessary, however, to find a way of getting rid of the batrachians after these wonders have been performed, and the pharoah asks Moses to pray to his God so that the cataclysm will cease, promising in exchange to let Israel go into the desert and offer its sacrifice. However, once Moses has obtained the elimination of the frogs, the pharoah goes back on his word.

3rd Plague — *The invasion of mosquitoes*

Swarms of mosquitoes, created by magic from the dust on the ground touched by Aaron's rod, cover the land of Egypt. This time the Egyptian magicians are unable to imitate the wonder and they begin to fear that this is indeed a very powerful God. The pharoah, however, despite the magicians' doubts, remains firm and lets the mosquitoes devour men and beasts.

4th Plague — *The invasion of flies*

Swarms of flies cover all of Egypt though Goshen, where the Israelite colony has lived since the time of Jacob, is left untouched. Faced with this new calamity, the pharoah gives his permission to let Moses and his people go to sacrifice under the condition that they remain inside the borders of Egypt. Moses insists that the feast must take place in the desert and the pharoah agrees, if Moses can get rid of the terrible insects. This is done, but the pharoah again takes back his promise.

5th Plague — *The plague destroys all animals*

Horses, asses, camels, large and small beasts contract a mysterious type of plague; only the Israelites' animals remain healthy, while the Egyptian's cattle and other animals perish. But even faced with the magnitude of such a catastrophe, the pharoah remains inflexible.

6th Plague — *Boils*

Moses and Aaron, with the help of God, transform the ashes from ovens into a great ulcer that produces boils which spread over the country covering men and beasts with puss-filled wounds. The pharoah, obstinate, refuses to listen to those in his court who advise him to give in and remains firm in his position.

7th Plague — *Hail*

A violent storm of giant hailstones gathers, ready to break over Egypt. Moses and Aaron ask the pharoah once again to let their people go in order to halt the imminent catastrophe, but to no avail: the hail devastates all of Egypt. Men, beasts, and crops perish everywhere except in the land of Goshen. The pharoah, who then seems to have finally changed his mind, sends for Moses and asks him to stop the hail in exchange for the greatly desired permission. However, once the storm dies down the sovereign again goes back on his word and refuses to give his authorization.

8th Plague — *The invasion of locusts*

This time the disaster which Moses and Aaron bring about is an invasion of locusts. The royal ministers advise the pharoah to let the Israelites go, to avoid yet more suffering in the country, and to this the pharoah finally agrees, under the condition, however, that only the men are allowed to leave and that they leave their wives and children as hostages in Egypt. Such conditions being unacceptable to Israel, a skyful of voracious locusts descend upon Egypt destroying everything in their path. The pharoah repents, and with God's help Moses and Aaron see that the wind blows the locusts away towards the Red Sea. The conclusion of this episode remains, however, identical to the previous ones: once the danger past, the pharoah goes back on his word.

9th Plague — *Darkness everywhere*

For three days, light is obliterated and thick darkness descends everywhere over Egypt, except over Goshen. Such an event is so spectacular that it cannot leave the pharoah indifferent. He summons Moses and tells him the Israelites may go, but that they must leave their animals behind in Egypt. This condition is unacceptable to Moses but the pharoah is unwilling to concede anything further. Vexed, the pharoah tells Moses never to come before him again or he will run the risk of being put to death. Moses confirms that this is the last time they will meet and takes his leave, just as the final and most terrible plague is in the making, the one which will finally break the pharoah's resistance.

10th Plague — *Death of all the first born*

The last calamity, which will definitively change the pharoah's mind, is the massacre which God decides and announces to Moses of all the first born of men and beasts. The biblical text associates this terrible event to the establishment and observance of Passover, a feast whose origins are clearly bound to two different traditions from a social and chronological perspective, and to which we will return. All of the first born of the Egyptians and their slaves are killed by an angel exterminator sent by the Lord who spares only homes whose doors are marked by the blood of a lamb that has been sacrificed and eaten, with unleavened bread, by the Israelite families. Obeying the instructions the Lord has given to Moses, the people of Israel follow these terms to the letter and that night mourning and grievious suffering strike every Egyptian home, sparing not even the pharoah's own family. This time, the Egyptian sovereign, overcome with shock and grief, not only authorizes the departure of the Hebrews, but drives them away accusing the people of having caused him countless misfortunes. Thus, after four hundred and thirty years of existence in Egypt, six hundred thousand Israelites gather all their possessions and animals and begin their march out of Egypt, the Exodus. First they march towards Succoth, deciding not to take the shortest route which would cross Philistine territory (a detail rather out of place here since these people do not yet exist at the time of this story) and instead make their way towards the Red Sea.

We referred above to the establishment of Passover: this celebration appears to have originally been an ancient pastoral festival during which the sign of a

Medieval miniature, ***Scenes from the life of Moses***

Moses is an Egyptian name meaning "son" or "born" and appears in the names of many pharoahs such as Thut*mose*, Ah*mose*. Later, an infinite number of events and episodes from different origins crystallized around his name.

Medieval miniature, ***Moses and the Burning Bush***

On Mount Horeb, Moses has a vision. The Lord appears to him in the form of a burning bush and reveals his name, "I am that I am," that is, "I am life." This event is the prelude to the great Exodus which leads Moses to the threshold of the Promised Land.

sacrificed lamb was meant to chase away the malevolent powers of a demon responsible for destroying animals. To this feast another was later associated, that of the Feast of Unleavened Bread, which was apparently celebrated in an agricultural context (at wheat harvest) and during a period following the Israelites' establishment in Canaan. This second feast was incorporated into Passover only after the reforms of Joshua. The term "Passover" is of uncertain etymology, but the most plausible hypothesis is that it is a derivative of the verb meaning "to skip, to pass over" (that is, "to spare"). The ancient paschal blood ritual became the commemoration of the salvation willed by God who spared the families whose houses were marked with this sign. To this feast is also associated the rite of the redemption of the first born (of men as well as animals) who are saved from death, but whom God wishes to see dedicated to the divine in an unharmful way.

The people of Israel, well armed and with all their belongings, begin their march. God walks in front, in the form of a misty pillar like a cloud during the day, and at night, in the form of a pillar of fire. Moses sees to it that Joseph's bones are brought with them which will be a source of strength and support to his faith and will. The caravan stops and encamps at the border of the desert at Etham, the men composing it, however, are but passive actors in a scenario created and directed solely by God. The Lord has already predicted everything that will come to pass and knows the pharoah will go back on his decision and want to recapture the Israelites who represent an indispensable work force to him. In fact, here we see the pharoah now mounting his chariot and, at the head of his troops, leaving in pursuit of the Hebrews. The Hebrew people are seized with panic when they realize the pharoah is bearing down upon them with his chariot force and all blame Moses. Faced with death, they are filled with regret, even to the point of wanting to go back to Egyptian servitude. But Moses reassures his people and tells them not to fear, for God is with them. The Lord miraculously impedes the Egyptians from catching up with the caravan until it reaches the shores of the Red Sea. There Moses, invested with prodigious powers, separates its waters which, in one night, divide and create a dry passage between the two immense walls of the sea. The Israelites pass rapidly through, pursued by the Egyptians who, finding their chariot wheels slowed down by God, already have an ominous presentiment. As they had feared, the Egyptian troops are unable to return to safety before the waters close up again, and the swirling currents are upon them. That day, the people of Israel witness Yahweh's terrifying power with their own eyes and finally confirm their belief in their God and in his servant, Moses.

Safe and sound, Moses and his companions begin a solemn chant of victory and praise to the Lord who has accomplished such extraordinary wonders. The biblical text here naively combines the theme of this miraculous rescue with another, of a later period, that takes place upon their arrival in the land of Canaan (which they have as yet not reached) and of the construction of the Temple of Jerusalem.

Nevertheless, following the rejoicing comes the long crossing of the desert, a period of severe trials for the Israelites who often complain to Moses and rebel against God's will, tormented as they are by hunger, thirst, and the dangers of war. And yet this period is particularly sacred in biblical tradition since beyond the difficulties, suffering, and disloyalties, it represents a very special moment, that of the "engagement" of the chosen people to Yahweh, a time of promise in the simplicity of nomadic life, of intense passions, serious failings and immediate repentances, a time that eventually cements the pact between God and his believers forever.

At Marah, in the desert, the first problem arises: a severe shortage of water, but Moses uses his magic rod and they arrive at the oasis of Eylim, a fresh and well-irrigated place. After a certain lapse of time and another crossing in the desert, the people dramatically lack food and many begin to miss Egypt where, though they were slaves, there was food to eat. As happens frequently during the period of the Exodus, we witness a joint intervention of both God and Moses, the Lord's representative and spokesman. The people's hunger is satisfied thanks to abundant manna and quail God brings to them in the desert, even though the biblical text once again gives away its late editing and theological objectives by relating how the Lord regulates the supplies of food, making provisioning only possible six days of the week and providing a double ration for the seventh day, Saturday (*sabbat*), a day of rest devoted to the Lord. Manna, which popular etymology suggests derives from the Hebrew expression *man hu* or, "What is it?" is in fact a substance secreted by insects found on desert tamarisk trees. As for the quail, it is likely that they could have been found in large quantities in the desert when, blown by strong westerly winds, they "emigrated" there, though this phenomenon would be more common along the coast. As we see, here again composite elements of diverse origins have converged in this sacred tale and we, the readers, should best read them in the spirit suggested by the editors, while at the same time not losing sight of the historical aspects and problems underlying the narrative.

Before arriving in the Sinai where, through a series of encounters with God, Moses receives the divine Commandments and the other rules which form the Law, or *Torah*, the story presents a few minor episodes: Moses performs a miracle making water spring from a rock and then following this, the battle against the Amalekites, the outcome of which (positive for Israel) depends upon Moses' ability to keep his arms raised for a long period. After this episode, Moses meets his father-in-law Jethro (according to one version, Jethro brings Moses' wife Zephorah and their sons whom Moses had sent to stay in the paternal house), and the text stresses Jethro's position as priest of Yahweh. Finally, the creation of the institution of judges is treated, people to whom Moses delegates the power to settle less fundamental questions which he can no longer see to personally. It goes without saying that such an event is only conceivable in the context of a sedentary society where decentralization of powers guarantees a smoother functioning of civil society.

The episode on Mount Sinai that follows is a central and particularly significant moment not only of Moses' story, but even more so for the whole Bible and more generally for the religions that have drawn upon it. The tale of the Covenant between God and Moses and the resulting Ten Commandments constitutes one of the most sublime and dramatic points of the story of salvation, a moment whose intensity makes other aspects seem of secondary importance: the editors' repetitions, the overlapping of variants, the details that are of little importance or are frankly boring; Moses' innumerable comings and goings who, alone or with others, meets with God and then constantly returns to his people to pass on God's messages and commands. We will simply touch here on the most salient episodes and recall that if in Abraham's case the Covenant with God concerned only one individual to whom a specific promise was made, here on Mount Sinai, God makes a commitment to all the people, and gives them (as he did to the Patriarch long in the past) not only the law of circumcision, but more notably a vast set of sacred laws that will forever regulate relations between the divine sphere and the human sphere. The importance of the figure of Moses, even if he sometimes appears as a passive mediator, is indisputable if we stop to consider the universal scope of the events of which he is the hero and of which Mount Sinai (a place whose exact location is unknown, but could be in the south of the Sinai peninsula) is the theater.

The complex Sinai episode is structured in various phases: from the divine promise of an approaching covenant, to the preparation of the people who will be witness to the event in a condition of absolute purity, then to the theophany and the solemn proclamation of the Decalogue. The Israelites keep at a good distance from the Mount as they wait for God to manifest himself to them (contact with the Divinity could be fatal!). After a period of three days, in fact, a trumpet sounds and similar to an erupting volcano that produces fire, smoke and great blasts, Yahweh, with a thundering voice, appears to Moses who has

Marc Chagall, *The Crossing of the Red Sea*

Invested with prodigious powers, Moses divides the waters of the Red Sea creating a passage for the Israelites pursued by the Egyptians. The latter, unable to return to safety before the waters close up again, all perish. This miracle demonstrates Yahweh's terrible power and that of his servant Moses.

J. Borchmans, *Moses and the Ten Commandments*
Moses, in the Old Testament, is the figure of the legislator par excellence. In the various Books in which he is the hero, a great number of measures and laws are attributed to him which often date from much later periods.

climbed up the Mount alone. Then, the Lord conveys his Decalogue, conceived in the form of a series of brief sentences that have come down to us in two slightly different versions, a summary of God's basic moral and religious code. The most striking characteristic of these obligations is the demand expressed by Yahweh to receive exclusive worship, the indispensable condition to obtaining his favor and protection.

After the Decalogue, the Book of Exodus gives a series of instructions known as the "Code of the Covenant" which, though referring to anterior precepts, are not as closely bound to the revelation on Mount Sinai and even presuppose that Israel has been a sedentary community for quite some time. These are various rules based on custom that find parallels in other ancient Near Eastern legislations and concern civil and criminal law, worship, and social ethics — in short, subjects as varied as slavery, murder, assault and battery, animal theft, rape, rites and festival, and miscellaneous types of offences with their punishments and fines. Also elaborated are some obligations concerning entry into the Promised Land, among which emerges the necessity, several times underlined, of maintaining a specific religious and moral identity, and if not, of running the risk of having to deal with God's enmity.

Following this enumeration, Moses writes down the divine commands and, after a public reading of the Book of the Covenant, great sacrifices are celebrated. It is interesting to note in passing that a variant of the episode of Moses on Mount Sinai mentions Joshua for the first time by his side, as a helper to the great hero, a figure to whom we will return in detail and who is destined to receive Moses' heritage and preside over the settling of Israel in the Promised Land.

The following chapters of the Book of Exodus present another series of obligations which Yahweh is supposed to have given to Moses. These mainly concern the construction of a sanctuary with its different sections and the people dedicated to its worship. These passages contain many very ancient elements and other more recent ones, but the editors' obvious intent is to point out the divine origin of the institutions involved. Among the various subjects treated are the Ark of the Covenant (a portable wooden chest with bars that contains the stone tablets of the Law), the *mishkan*, the sacred tabernacle also called the "Tent of Meeting" or "Tent of Testimony," also portable, that follows the Israelites on their journeys, and finally, its sacred furnishings (altars, candelabras, and various small objects). This tent will be the special place for encounters between Yahweh and Moses, mediator between God and the people. Also mentioned is a description of the clothing priests must wear (Aaron and his sons), and the ceremony that must be followed for their consecration; after this, the subject of daily sacrifices is treated as well as how the altar for burnt offerings should be consecrated, the rite of libation and, finally, terms concerning Saturday as the day of rest (sabbatical rest) in memory of the work of divine Creation.

After this long list of precepts, the narrative is resumed with the famous episode of the golden calf. Moses has been on the Mount for quite some time in communion with God, and the people fear he will never return. They go to Aaron to ask him to build a visible God who can guide them. Aaron has the people melt all the gold they possess and makes it into the statue of a calf, the animal symbol of the Canaanite God, Baal. Aaron gives it over to the Israelites for worshipping and for the next day plans a great festival accompanied by sacrifices, banquets, singing and dancing in honor of the new god. But on Mount Sinai God warns Moses of what is happening and even tells him of his intention to wreak merciless vengeance upon the idol worshippers. Only Moses' intercession and appeal to the promise God made to the great patriarchs, manage to calm the divine wrath. Accompanied by Joshua, Moses descends the mountain carrying the two tablets of the Law dictated by God, and before the spectacle of the drunken crowd singing hymns in honor of the golden calf, he breaks the tablets of the Law, destroys the golden idol, reducing it to dust and dispersing the rest of it into the water which he makes the Israelites drink. He then asks Aaron for an explanation, but the latter can find no justification and only complains about the Israelites' natural inclination to wickedness. It is absolutely necessary to take extreme punitive action as the people are out of control. Moses gathers Yahweh's faithful servants, the Levites, around him and gives the order to put to death all of those who are against Yahweh, even if this means that brothers, neighbors or friends must kill each other. A terrifying massacre ensues during which three thousand people perish. It is then time to ask God's forgiveness and Moses goes up to Mount Sinai again to pray and personally intercede in favor of his people. Yahweh gives his forgiveness and commands they resume their march, though refusing to be present among them because of the grave sin they have committed.

At this point in the story we are presented with another version of the Covenant on Mount Sinai, a variation that most likely belonged to a different tradition than the first one. The editors insert it into the principal narrative by presenting it as a reiteration of the first Covenant interrupted by the episode of the golden calf.

Moses, upon divine order, carves two new stone steles and goes up to the Mount. There, Yahweh appears to him and solemnly announces his desire to renew the Covenant agreement with his people. He gives Moses a series of terms, some of which are related to the previous ones and particularly concern worship practices. The Israelites are considered as legally "married" to Yahweh and therefore the worship of any other divinity is equivalent to an act of "prostitution" or treason (a frequent theme in the Old Testament). Everything is faithfully transcribed by Moses who, after a long period of fasting, again descends the Mount with the new tablets of the Law. His face, transfigured by the mystic experience, emanates great rays of light (a feature that is central to many representations of Moses in art, notably the famous statue by Michelangelo). He addresses the people and reveals his experience to them after which he covers his face with a veil.

In the next chapters, the Book of Exodus relates how the terms previously specified by Yahweh are put into practice, and this results in a repeating, almost word for word, of everything expressed before concerning the construction of the sanctuary, its materials, decoration, and furnishings, its priests and their clothes, etc. The sacred Tabernacle is then built. When Moses takes possession of this sacred dwelling it is immediately filled with a divine cloud. The presence of the cloud tells the Israelites that they must stop, and its absence is the sign to resume their march. At night, however, a supernatural fire fills the Tabernacle.

With these details the Book of Exodus closes, having witnessed the Israelites' departure from Egypt and their undertaking of the long voyage to the Promised Land. It is followed by Leviticus, a book which is essentially legislative in nature, interrupted from time to time by the narrative of the Israelites' experience in the desert. In this Book, all the obligations which have been pronounced are put under Moses' authority, the supreme servant of Yahweh from whom Moses has received them.

The Lord then summons Moses into the Tent of Meeting and passes on to him a long series of measures concerning sacrifical ritual, the investiture ceremony of priests (terms which concern Aaron and his descendants), rules regarding the notions of "clean" and "unclean" of which the most complete expression is the grandiose collective rite of Atonement. Then comes the Law of Holiness, a text which goes back to perhaps the end of the monarchical period during

Nicolas Poussin, *The Fall of the Manna*

To feed the starving people in the desert, God and Moses intervene by sending manna and quails in abundance. Manna is a substance secreted by insects that live on the desert tamarisk tree.

which the concept of "saint" or "holy" was developed, a specific attribute of God, intimately bound to the notion of purity. This is a document that presupposes the existence of only one city Temple (that of Jerusalem) where all worship is centralized (with an interesting phenomenon of retrospective projection to the past concerning the portable sanctuary of the Tent in the desert). It also contains a liturgical calendar with moral and cultural prescripts and closes with divine benedictions or curses directed at those who observe or not the established terms. An appendix presents rules to be observed concerning the redemption of people, animals or objects devoted to the Lord.

Though the biblical editors relate all of these laws to the experience in the desert and place them under Moses' authority, they are in fact a body of terms from a much later period. This definitive codification was achieved during the construction of the second Temple, following the Babylonian Exile. Of interest here is the desire to bind all of these detailed regulations in the field of ethics and ritual to the figure of Moses, those regulations which are still applied in present-day Judaism. Christianity, however, does not recognize their strictly moral value, and considers them as a sort of "preparation" for the sacrifice instituted by and with Christ.

In the Book of Numbers, which follows Leviticus, the theme of the journey towards the Promised Land is taken up again (in Hebrew the title of this book is "In the Desert") but we also find numerous legislative or ritualistic digressions that interrupt the narrative, which make it difficult to summarize only the narrative portion of the Book. It begins by describing the structure Moses gives to the Israelite people in accordance with divine will: a theocratic community comprised of twelve tribes plus the Levites who are assigned ritual functions by the side of the priest Aaron and his descendants. Next, the march in the desert is related from Mount Sinai to the steppes of Moab, east of the Jordan, opposite Jericho, where a while later under the command of Joshua the crossing into Canaan will take place. Finally the preparatory stages of this crossing are described and various divine commands are given concerning entry into the Promised Land.

Everything begins as usual by a discussion between God and Moses in the Tent of Meeting. This time we are on the first day of the second month of the second year after the departure from Egypt and Yahweh commands Moses to perform a census of all the Israelites to count the number of adult men able to fight, in view of the approaching battles over the conquest of the land of Canaan. From the census taken of the different families belonging to the twelve tribes (more than 600,000 individuals), the Levites are excluded and are counted separately as their task is to serve and defend the sanctuary (the "Dwelling") and, generally, to be responsible for worship and the sacred furnishings in collaboration with the priests of Aaron's family. The order in which the different tribes will encamp and march is meticulously established, in concentric circles around the sanctuary, the heart of religious life and communication with God, and this order generally reflects an already smoothly running social organization. The Hebrew community, founded upon ethnic ties, is described as an army on a war footing, perfectly organized to confront external as well as internal problems, a unique body in which all members live in submission to the rules dictated by Yahweh.

A new legislative section is then inserted which describes various ethical and cultural obligations, most notably, the establishment of the system of Nazirites. The Nazirite (meaning "dedicated") is a person set aside for God for a certain period of time during which he may not cut or shave his hair, consume alcoholic drinks, touch any dead creature which would render him "unclean." Samson and the prophet Samuel whom we will speak about later, are famous Nazirites. Also mentioned in this passage are the offerings performed by the heads of the tribes after the building of the divine Dwelling, the sanctuary Tent, and the consecration of the Levites. Concerning this tribe, we note that the Old Testament presents two different traditions: according to one of them (the one mentioned in the Book of Numbers), the priests among Aaron's descendants have greater liturgical and charismatic prerogatives than the Levites (only the former, for example, may pronounce a blessing), whereas according to the other tradition (attested in Deuteronomy), the entire tribe of Levi is invested with the same functions. This situation apparently reflects a historical evolution difficult to explain in detail, but which certainly must have come about after settlement in Canaan. It appears that the Levites, after the abolition of outlying sanctuaries as a result of the centralizing of the cult in Jerusalem, were reduced to a subordinate position in relation to the priests of the Temple and were appointed to secondary functions without benefiting from the recognition of any religious authority. Whatever the case may be, we will content ourselves here with noting that the biblical editors, once again, insist upon placing the minutest details of their historical reconstruction under Moses' authority and presenting the perfect social and religious organization of the Hebrew community as a heritage handed down by Moses. The date of Passover and its first celebration after the event in Egypt is then fixed, the famous night of the Exodus, including the measures concerning purity that will regulate participation of the faithful in the festival. The text then repeats the terms of God's presence in the Tent, which indicates to the Israelites whether to march or to stop and in this way has God fix the pace of their progress (that should naturally be considered as the ideal advance of the chosen people) toward the Promised Land. The solemn moments of assembly, the liturgical summonings and also the stages of combat will moreover be announced by the sound of two silver trumpets sounded by the Levites.

After this digression, the Hebrew people finally leave the Sinai and in strict respect of their set marching order, enter the desert. The various stages of this journey are characterized by chronic crises of the people who find the deprivations inherent in this demanding life unbearable and who miss the abundance of food in Egypt. The text then repeats the episode of the manna and the quails according to a slightly different version. The people are tired of the food miraculously provided by God and demand to be

given meat. Moses himself, criticized from all sides, ends up reproaching the Lord in a rather irreverent tone for being held responsible for controlling the people, a task that has become too much for one man alone, a man who is exhausted and practically stripped of all independent will. For once Moses' human side shows through, a hero subjected to unbearable pressure, caught between God's desires on the one hand, and the reticences of a weak and rebellious people on the other. Yahweh then intervenes and invests seventy elders with his spirit who will have the duty of lightening Moses' burden by assuming part of his tasks and responsibilities. The divine investiture manifests itself through the prophetic capacities granted to designated persons, who come running to the Tent, as well as others who are in the camp. But God punishes the rebellious and impatient in an unusual way: to the imprudent ones who have been so demanding he sends a sickening quantity of meat, instead of manna, to rain down upon the people; quails, brought by the wind, fall in such abundance upon them that all are racked with nausea.

In the next episode Aaron and his sister Miriam, a prophetess, reproach Moses for having married an Ethiopian woman (this is obviously a variant from the tale of his marriage to the Egytian Zeporah). Deep down inside, both of them are envious of the supreme charisma of their brother, God's only interlocutor. The Lord then personally calls the three into the Tent of Meeting and confirms that though special powers may be granted to others besides Moses, his privileged servant, Moses is and remains his supreme interlocutor. The intimate communion that binds God and Moses has nothing to do with the faculties, even exceptional, invested in prophets and holy personnel. Faced with the Lord's will to punish his brother and sister, Moses intercedes in their favor and obtains from God that Miriam alone is punished by being afflicted by a type of temporary leprosy which forces her to live in quarantine.

Finally, the time comes to establish contact with the land of Canaan. Moses sends the heads of the tribes on a reconnaissance mission, among them is Hosea, the son of Nun, the man who will shortly become the great Joshua. Forty days later the sentries return reporting of the extraordinary richness and fertility of the land, but also of the presence of a strong and bellicose population residing there. All of the Israelite community rise up against Moses and Aaron in fear of the dangers of an attack that seems extremely difficult. Joshua and Caleb speak up insisting that divine help will accompany the people in this undertaking, but the people, angry and afraid, threaten to stone them to death. The Lord intervenes immediately, intent on exterminating the rebels but, once again, Moses' intercession saves his people from annihilation. God nevertheless decides that because of their constant disobedience, all of those people belonging to the generation of the Exodus, with the exception of Caleb and Joshua, will die in the desert without the privilege of setting foot in the Promised Land.

When Moses passes on this divine decision to the people, all are stunned, and once again rebelling against Yahweh's plans, attempt a desperate invasion of Canaan, bent on attacking and conquering the land before they die. But Moses and the holy Ark do not follow them and the unfortunate group are easy prey for the local population who massacre them. This episode serves to explain why instead of following a direct route, Israel marches on Canaan by making a detour through the Transjordan. It is generally felt that this tale could be based on the failure of a first military expedition attempted by the whole community.

View of the desert

The crossing of the desert, beyond the people's difficulties and disloyalties, represents a particularly holy moment in Israel's history, the "engagement" between the chosen people and Yahweh. This is a trial that cements the pact between God and his faithful, a time of promise in the simplicity and purity of nomadic life.

At this point, the narrative is interrupted again, this time by a passage which concerns the various sacrifices which should be offered to Yahweh and punishments for those who do not respect these sacred obligations. We then read of an episode of the rebellion of two members of the tribe of Reuben, Dathan and Abiram, and a member of the tribe of Levi, a certain Korah, who question Aaron's powers, an episode which echoes claims made and rejected by rival groups concerning their priestly functions. The Lord sees that they meet a tragic death when they are swallowed up by the earth and sent to Hell; then Yahweh confirms the investiture of Aaron and his descendants, with particular consideration for his son Eleazar, destined to receive his father's heritage. We will skip over a series of conditions mainly concerning sacerdotal functions here to get back to the story of the journey which confirms the spiritual and initiatory dimension of any undertaking led by Moses. God's community continues its progress against all odds, despite the revolts and trappings that punctuate daily life.

Israel reaches the Zin desert and stops at Kadesh. There, another shortage of food and water causes the people to rebel against Moses and Aaron. Yet again, with the help of divine power, Moses makes water spring from a rock, but at that moment, in an unexpected and rather obscure way, the Lord not only protests against his people, weak and

Botticelli, *The Punishment of Korah's Sons*

The Exodus is characterized by the repeated infidelities of the chosen people and Moses must constantly intervene to plead for mercy in the face of divine wrath. The rebellion of Dathan, Abiram, and Korah is nevertheless severely punished. The guilty men and their sons are swallowed up by the earth.

rebellious, but also turns on Moses and Aaron. God reproaches them for not always having trusted in him and declares that they will also be deprived of the joy of entering Canaan. Certainly, it is logical that the two representative heads of their line share their generation's destiny, dying before their destination is reached, but the Old Testament does not explain why on precisely this occasion God decides to exclude his two privileged interlocutors from the Promised Land. The biblical text, here and in a few other allusions, seems to suggest some failings of Moses and his brother toward the Lord, but it is difficult to believe that such a banal circumstance (of which, moreover, we have no other details) could have blotted out all the benefits of an entire lifetime of service and absolute devotion to God. In the absence of other elements, we are obliged to leave this problem unresolved and to accept it as an aspect of the narrative that remains obscure to us in terms of its motivations.

In any case, the Israelites' caravan leaves Kadesh and reaches Mount Hor. There, the Lord tells Aaron that his life is nearing its end and that the transfer of power to his son Eleazar must take place without delay. Aaron removes his holy garments and gives them to his son to wear. After which Aaron dies on Mount Hor and the entire community weeps and mourns over him.

Continuing their journey the Israelites, after a victory over the Canaanite king of Arad, head towards the Red Sea when their passage through Edom is refused by the king. The people again complain about the long detour which increases the already great fatigue of this interminable journey and God, as punishment, sends poisonous snakes among them, killing many. Moses then intercedes once more in favor of his people and, obeying God's instructions, he has a bronze snake forged which he places on a pole; the creature will have a beneficial effect just as the snake of the caduceus of Aesculapius, famous symbol of all those who practice medicine.

The text then relates the stages of the journey towards Transjordan, conquered from the Arnon to the Jabbok by a victory over the Amorite king Sihon. After this, Moses victoriously leads his men to Bashan where he defeats the local king, Og. The Hebrew people then encamp on the Moabite steppes, east of the Jordan. This is where the episode of the famous seer Balaam, son of Beor, takes place, a biblical personage also mentioned in an Aramaic inscription recently discovered in Deir Allah. The Moabite king Balak, faced with the Israelite threat, sends for Balaam asking the seer to bless Moab and send a curse upon the enemies. But Balaam recognizes Yahweh as the only true God, and Yahweh then manifests himself to Balaam and incites him to bless Israel. Inspired by God, the seer pronounces a series of oracles that predict the Hebrews' victory over Moab and over all the other local populations. This tale presents various interesting and unusual aspects such as the episode of Balaam's female donkey which the Lord has talk to her master to convince him to follow the divine will. As for Balaam, who quite certainly existed, he must have been a sage whose prophetic virtues were famous, just as his magic and divining powers, someone who was believed to be capable of influencing the real world and predicting it.

The Hebrew people then settle in Shittim at the borders of Moab where a new episode of moral transgression takes place. The men are seduced by the Moabite or Midianite women (depending on the tradition) and begin to worship the local God, Baal-Peor. Many of the guilty perish, victims of divine punishment. In this repression Eleazar's son, Phineas, distinguishes himself particularly by his zeal in getting the people to respect religious orthodoxy, as should be expected of the son of the high priest. Quite a large territory having been conquered, it becomes necessary to distribute the land: a new census is undertaken of the number of families and tribes (with, as in the previous census, a separate count of the Levites) in view of subdividing the land. Among the various episodes of this phase, we will note in particular Joshua's investiture by Eleazar as Moses' official successor since the great leader's life is destined to end as soon as the land of Canaan appears on the horizon.

After a new digression in the text devoted to liturgical problems and various legal obligations, a new phase of the conquest is related with the tale of the holy war won over the Midianites, a conflict that leads to the massacre of the enemy, the purification and distribution of the booty and final offerings to the Lord. Part of the area of the Transjordan thus conquered is given to half the tribe of Manasseh, who will have to combat further before settling there, and the other part of the land is granted to the tribes of Reuben and Gad who are able to settle the land peacefully. The Exodus is then resumed and God gives Moses the conditions for penetrating into Canaan, the borders of their new country, and the criteria for its future division. He confirms to Moses the Levites' special condition that they will not receive a specific territory (they will only possess a few cities) but who will occupy all of Israel transversely from a social and territorial point of view.

All of these details concerning the imminent entry into the Promised Land conclude the Book of Numbers which gives way to Deuteronomy (literally "Second Law"), a Book with a varied rhythm, drawn from several sources of different periods and characterized by remarkable originality in terms of its objectives and observations. It is essentially a code of religious and civil laws that are related, though not without some rather great differences, to obligations proclaimed by God in the desert. Inserted here, more or less smoothly, are three long speeches attributed to Moses just before his death and that deal essentially with the theme of respect for the Law and faithfulness to it, though they also evoke various episodes of the great saga of the Exodus. In addition, this Book also contains a few direct and indirect references to the last days of Moses, with a final canticle and series of benedictions pronounced by the great leader.

If normative aspects are of little assistance to us in the study of our personage, the speeches he pronounces, though largely reworked in terms of the "legislative" spirit of the text, are of particular interest in revealing the character of Moses. We will therefore turn to a discussion of them here and attempt to highlight their most significant aspects from our particular vantage point.

The first lengthy speech is a vast summary of the Hebrew peoples' adventures from the crucial period at Mount Sinai to their final arrival at the Massif of Pisgah on the Jordan. The speech is precisely dated in the text as being of the eleventh month of the fortieth year after the departure from Egypt. Moses recalls the events on Mount Horeb, the difficult march in the desert, the exploration of Canaan, the failed attempt to occupy it, and the resuming of the journey to the Red Sea; and then the victories over Sihon, king of Hesbon, and over Og, king of Bashan, with the resulting conquests of territory. All of these events are marked by the constant hesitations and fears of the Hebrew people, ceaselessly torn between faithfulness to Yahweh and their human failings. Moses speaks of the episode at Beth-Peor to remind the people of the principles of true wisdom: of obeying the divine revelations of Mount Horeb, avoiding all acts of idolatry, truly appreciating the special gift the Lord's presence at one's side represents, as guide and protector. Moses also mentions the Babylonian Exile (though this event has not yet happened) which will be the most severe punishment endured by the Hebrew people for its chronic infidelities, but despite this, the hope of redemption is left open and Moses foresees the prospect of the conversion of the Hebrew people and a return to its homeland after much suffering. One of the main themes of this passage is divine Providence and the Lord's choice of Israel as his privileged people, a choice which demands in exchange their absolute faith in Yahweh.

The second speech by Moses contains the presentation of the Code of Deuteronomy, a legislative work composed of the Decalogue followed by a series of precepts on religious and civil life. While referring to the theophany on Mount Horeb, Moses once again sets out the principles of the first Decalogue with a few slight variations from the Book of Exodus version, but introduced within the context of a set of ethics based upon the same inspiring principles such as faithfulness and obedience to God, fear of Yahweh, and eternal remembrance of the experiences during the Exodus which are at the very foundation and essence of the Law. These constitute a heritage which should be handed down from father to son for generations to come. True justice is nothing more than the applying of God's precepts, an absolute obligation of the people of Israel, chosen by God from among all peoples, based on a free choice and a spontaneous promise made to Israel's founding fathers, the glorious patriarchs of the earliest times. A large part of the speech consists of a warning to Israel for the future: yes, God has given and will give Israel the force to accomplish all that it must do; the desert was a very difficult but successful trial and now the land of Canaan will offer many temptations difficult to resist. The sin of pride for the victories won also threatens the chosen people. They must never forget that credit for any conquest goes not to themselves, but to God. Moses reminds the people of his personal role as intercessor on Mount Horeb and of the many other occasions when he intervened and appealed to God to save his people. Therefore, in the future they must be attentive not to "circumcise" only the flesh, but also the heart and to live the Law as an interior reality. Now, in this supreme moment of entering the Promised Land the time had come to choose between a life of divine blessing or an accursed existence, all depending upon their conduct.

This second speech is interrupted by the presentation of the Code of Deuteronomy, a collection of laws that only partially coincide with those of the Code of the Covenant mentioned above and which all deal with the notion of the uniqueness of God's sanctuary. Historically speaking, these laws were perhaps meant to replace previous legislation and refer to a code of laws "found" by Joshua (according to Kings 2:23) in the Temple and were at the basis of its religious reform. Other than the principle of the uniqueness of the sanctuary, other matters are treated such as sacrifices, idolatry, the notion of "clean" and "unclean," the tithes, sabbatical years; and other themes again such as the main festivals, cultural interdicts, the future establishment of the monarchy and various other moral, social and cultural precepts. After this, we are brought back to Moses' speech which continues on the theme of divine blessings and curses, a mention of the prospect of war and exile, the latter described as similar to a return to the bondage already experienced in Egypt.

In the third speech, of particular note is the mention of a Covenant between God and Israel which is supposed to have been reiterated in Moab (a detail that has never been mentioned before) and whose obvious purpose is to imbue the new precepts announced with holiness. We also find another prediction of exile, which will be a consequence of the people's breaking of the Covenant with God, though, adds Moses, Israel will finally return to its land and be converted again, forevermore. It is perhaps worthwhile noting the difference between the Covenant and the Law, the Covenant representing a choice desired by God, who stands guarantor for it, whereas the Law being a set of precepts that the other party, the people of Israel, must scrupulously respect if they want the Covenant to be upheld.

Finally, we come to the last events in the life of Moses, who is now 120 years old (the total of three generations) but who is still vigorous and in excellent health. He will not die of old age therefore, but rather because this is God's express wish. Moses reminds his people that because God has decided to punish him, he will not cross the Jordan with them, and that Joshua will take his place. After having written down all the terms received from God, Moses entrusts this to the priests: every seven years, during the Festival of the Tabernacles, there will be a ritual reading of the Law, placed next to the Ark of the Covenant.

Now time is running out, Canaan is on the horizon and God tells Moses that his death is imminent. He calls Moses and Joshua into the Tent of Meeting and predicts the future disloyalties of the chosen people in the Promised Land. Concerning this, Yahweh in person teaches them a canticle as a testimony of all they are told on this occasion. After this, Israel gathers to hear what Moses will announce to them. He then recites the famous Canticle of Moses, an ancient poem, perhaps a chant of collective lamentation composed after the Babylonian Exile. This hymn of praise to the Lord exalts the perfection of God's creation and his providence so little rewarded by the people who will be judged for their faults and severely punished by a long series of sufferings, cataclysms, and torments. But God will eventually take pity on the people of Israel and deliver them from their enemies, they will not be vanquished but will be washed of their faults forever by divine vengeance.

Moses then takes leave of his people, exhorting them to obey the Law, the source of all life. God tells Moses to climb to the heights of Mount Nebo, opposite Jericho, to contemplate the land of Canaan. There, on its peak, death awaits him and the benediction pronounced in chapter 33 of Deuteronomy is in fact his last act. This speech consists of a collection of poetic sayings, perhaps an ancient psalm of a warrior nature concerning the different tribes of Israel, a text that recalls the spiritual testament pronounced long ago by Jacob.

Thus ends the earthly adventure of Moses. From Mount Nebo, he can gaze upon the great land from which he has been excluded and filled with this vision, he closes his eyes forever. He is buried in the valley facing Beth-Peor in a tomb whose location, according to the Bible, has never been revealed. Moses is honored and mourned for many days and no other man will equal him in all of the Hebrew people's history: "And there arose not a prophet since in Israel like Moses, whom the Lord knew face to face, in all the signs and the wonders which the Lord sent him to do in the land of Egypt... And in all that mighty hand, and in all the great terror which Moses showed in the sight of all Israel." (Deut. 34:10-12).

If we had to describe Moses in just one word, we would certainly have to choose his quality as supreme "mediator" in terms of the Covenant that God establishes with Israel. He is responsible for making the Covenant known to the people and for watching over it; he gives it its authority as a "receptacle" that receives everything holy, important, irreplaceable in the tradition and religious and social organization of the Hebrew people. He is a paramount figure in the history of ancient Israel, prophet, the chosen one among the chosen, wise father and inflexible judge, an unfailingly obedient instrument of God's will. Through him the divine plan of redemption develops and is realized since God entrusts his will and his Law (the *Torah*) to Moses, its trustee. From a historiographical point of view, we should remember that a historical core must certainly have existed at the root of the figure of Moses, who most likely actually lived, even if his life must have been very different from the vast and composite dimension proposed by the biblical text. We might imagine an ancient Semite chieftain brought up in Egypt and at the pharoah's court, who distinguishes himself by his exceptional charisma and political and military qualities. His true identity is lost to us in the complex tradition that aims more at glorifying the undertakings of the Lord than at proposing any real historical reconstitution, and does not hesitate to blend various typical features from popular traditions into the tale such as the theme of "miraculous" birth, abandonment of a child to the waters, and so forth, features which underline the analogies between Moses and diverse mythical and historical characters, such as the Mesopotamian king Sargon or of Romulus and Remus in Latin tradition.

Moses' popularity has from all times been immense in post-biblical tradition and in all monotheistic religions. In Judaism, great hopes of deliverance are concentrated in him and in Christianity too, Moses is closely associated with the coming of the Messiah. The New Testament consequently gives him a principal role and recognizes him as the guardian and vehicle of the Law which Christ does not propose to abolish, but only to bring to its most perfect expression. The Gospels, to confirm the unprecedented greatness of the figure, make Moses, accompanied by Elijah, the privileged witness of the Transfiguration of Jesus and show him establishing the new Covenant with God and thus being the one who will announce the coming of God's Son to earth.

Tintoretto, ***The Bronze Serpent***

To punish the complaining people, God sends poisonous snakes among them, but Moses intercedes once again and obeying God's counsel, has a bronze snake forged and placed on a pole. The serpent is considered, notably on the caduceus of Aesculapius, symbol of those who practice medicine, to have healing effects.

JOSHUA

The Ideal Conqueror

In the march toward the Promised Land,
Joshua advanced pensive and pale,
because he was already the one chosen of the Almighty.

ALFRED DE VIGNY, *Moses*

Joshua, whose original name is Hoshea ("salvation"), is the son of Nun and belongs to the valorous tribe of Ephraim. It is Moses who changes his name to Joshua ("Yahweh, saved!"), a name that by a minor phonetic simplification becomes "Jesus." The changing of a person's name usually implied a rebirth, a transformation of his character. In Joshua's case, however, this does not signal any drastic change in his personality, but rather announces the solemn investiture and acceptation of immense responsibilities for which the most intimate communion with God, to which the name Joshua testifies, is an indispensable condition. It is not by chance therefore, that his name is changed at the dawn of an extremely dangerous and decisive mission. A handpicked group of men (of which Joshua is a member) is about to explore the land of Canaan to evaluate the ways and means of invading it.

Certainly less renowned than his inimitable predecessor, Moses, who led the chosen people out of Egypt and gave them the divine Law, Joshua nevertheless has an equally important role to play. For, it is his task to complete the mission begun by Moses and open the door to the Promised Land, making Israel's settlement possible after long and bloody struggles waged in the name of Yahweh.

In addition to the information contained in the Book of Joshua, other details concerning this hero are scattered here and there throughout the biblical text and despite their terseness help us to further define his character. Moses, whom Joshua succeeds, most certainly discerns exceptional qualities of courage and moral integrity in him when he chooses Joshua to head an expedition, in fact successful, against the Amalekites (nomadic raiders from the north of the Arabian peninsula). During the adventure-filled days in the desert, the gifted young Israelite becomes Moses' right-hand man and is notably called to serve inside the "Tent of Testimony;" he is also at Moses' side on Mount Sinai when the legislator receives the tablets of the Law from God. It is Moses who personally presents Joshua to the people and appoints him Israel's leader to the Promised Land for Moses knows he himself will never set foot upon its soil.

Joshua is forty years old when he is chosen to take part in the select expedition sent by Moses to explore the land of Canaan, and it is on this occasion that his name is changed. During those difficult days, with the support of Caleb, Joshua fervently defends the idea of the conquest of the Promised Land, a conquest he is convinced is possible with the help of God's immense power. His firmness vanquishes the reticence and defeatism of the majority of his people who fear they are undertaking a fatal expedition. Joshua and Caleb, after tearing their clothes in a sign of mourning and great suffering, pronounce a passionate and decisive speech. Yes, it is true, they say, the land of Canaan is densely inhabited by warlike peoples in fortified cities, but with the aid of Yahweh and his miracles it is certain the conquest is possible and, in any case, it must be attempted with all their faith. These words provoke the people's violent opposition who, panic-stricken and fearing for their lives, are about to stone the two orators when God's spirit suddenly appears to them, his presence filling the Tent, and manifesting his support of the two courageous men.

Joshua's determination and great faith earn him the privilege of leading his people on the conquest of the Promised Land. His strong moral qualities, military gifts, loyalty to the tradition's religious values, devotion and self-abnegation at Moses' side all contribute to making him the great leader's successor, a destiny Moses expresses memorably in a few words:

> Be determined and confident; you are the one who will lead these people to occupy the land that the Lord promised to their ancestors. The Lord himself will lead you and be with you, so do not lose courage or be afraid.
>
> (*Deut.* 31:7-8)

Just before dying, Moses, obeying God's will, places his hands upon Joshua and transfers his authority to him during a ceremony sanctified by the presence of the high priest Eleazar and all the people. Moses, knowing that he will not be allowed to enter the Promised Land, thus chooses as his successor a modest but valorous man, pious and determined, and gives him instructions for completing the task already begun under his leadership. When on Mount Nebo Moses draws his last breath, Joshua succeeds him in every respect, turning all of his attention to the tremendous task before him: the conquest of a country for his people who, until then, have wandered in the desert.

View of the Jordan

Moses, at 120 years of age, is called away by God before his people cross the Jordan into the Promised Land. His successor, Joshua, will be responsible for accomplishing this next step in the history of Israel.

After he receives Moses' investiture, God speaks directly to Joshua and commands him to cross the Jordan river at the point where his people are encamped and, without further delay, to embark on the great adventure. The recurring theme in this dialogue between the Lord and the chosen people's new leader is the firmness and absolute loyalty Joshua must show in the execution of the divine instructions, not only in his moral behavior but also in his conducting of the war, which entails very harsh treatment of enemy cities and their populations. Though seeing oneself as a simple executor might not be considered a sign of genius or exceptional intelligence, this recognition in Joshua nevertheless greatly enhances his stature, a man of faith and strong character whose humility, it must be emphasized, most certainly hides other qualities sacrificed in the name of the objective to be achieved.

Strengthened by God's presence, Joshua prepares for the conquest and adds to his own troops the two tribes (those of Reuben and Gad) and the half-tribe (that of Manasseh) already settled in territories that they have conquered on the right bank of the Jordan. Together, all of Israel might affront the great adventure shoulder to shoulder, as one people.

After the people swear a solemn oath of loyalty to Joshua, as they had once done for Moses, the operation begins by dispatching two spies into the neighboring city of Jericho. Here the episode of Rahab takes place, the prostitute who, having learned of Yahweh's miracles and convinced of the imminent victory of Joshua and his people, saves the lives of their two envoys whom she receives and hides. In exchange, Rahab and her household are promised to be spared by the Israelites when the city is taken (a small scarlet rope will identify her house). It is interesting to note that in rabbinical literature Rahab, the prostitute, is accorded such great importance that she becomes Joshua's wife and the mother of eight prophets (including Jeremiah and Huldah), and an ancestor of Jesus. As for Christian exegesis, she is made the symbol of the Gentiles who welcome Christ's message.

When the spies return to the Israelite encampment with their precious information, the campaign is launched with the people's crossing of the Jordan river. Foretold in a prophetic speech by Joshua, a miraculous event comes to pass: the river parts, forming two high walls permitting the crossing of

Medieval miniature, *Joshua Taking Jericho*
The conquest of the Promised Land is a long epic saga that begins with the capture of Jericho which sets the pattern of the relationship between God and Joshua. The former suggests a military tactic to the latter who scrupulously obeys divine orders thus ensuring the success of his troops.

the Israelites on foot, followed by the holy Ark. As soon as all have reached the other side, the waters close up again. This prodigious crossing is, of course, one of the elements that reinforces the parallel between Joshua and Moses, reminding us of Moses' crossing of the Red Sea by a similar miracle.

The event is commemorated by the erection of a monument on the new soil, at Gilgal, to the east of Jericho. This monument is symbolically built of twelve stones taken from the river and carried by twelve men, each representing one of the tribes. The site is to later become a place of worship and pilgrimage in memory of the chosen people's entry into Canaan and the miraculous crossing of the Jordan, and will also play a significant role in later Hebrew tradition. With the completion of this first stage, solemn religious ceremonies are performed, notably a general circumcision of all those who were born during the crossing of the desert and therefore have not been subjected to this rite. The highlight of the holy period is indisputably the celebration of Passover (*Pessah* or "passage" [of the Jordan]) on the fourteenth day of the month of Nisan (the first month of the year, in spring) when the new land's products are consumed (unleavened bread and grilled wheat). This meal is highly symbolic as it signifies the end of nomadic life with its manna, and the subsequent dependence upon food produced by sedentary peoples who live by cultivating the land. Near Jericho, the holiness of the occasion and the site where it takes place is further heightened when Joshua receives another divine vision: an angel of the Lord, with sword drawn, presents himself as the leader of God's army and commands Joshua to sanctify the spot.

It is from Gilgal that the invasion truly gets underway, first towards the west with the conquering of Jericho, then to the south, and finally northward, eventually bringing about the conquest of the entire country, with the taking of numerous cities and the massacres of their populations.

The story of the conquest of the Promised Land, though often related in a tone that in no way differs from the theological style of priestly inspiration, is in fact a long saga of epic dimensions, beginning with the taking of Jericho, an event to be considered as emblematic of successive actions and a model of how the relationship between God and Joshua will be structured. The Lord explains the strategy to be used to conquer the impregnable citadel of Jericho, Joshua follows his instructions to the letter, and everything comes to pass exactly according to divine predictions. Since the city is protected by great walls, a supernatural intervention is necessary to allow the Israelites to achieve their objective. They surround Jericho, and on the seventh day, march around the walls while seven priests, followed by the Ark and all the people, sound the *shofar*, a long trumpet made of sheep's horn usually used as a warning or to announce some kind of solemn event. At its sounding, a powerful cry rises up from the Hebrew people and the invincible walls crumble to the ground, allowing them to penetrate the city, raze it, and kill all of its inhabitants; women, children, and animals included. Only the prostitute Rahab and her family are spared as had been promised. The king of Jericho is put to death and an interdict (*herem*) is imposed on the war booty: it is not to be touched by anyone, everything will be destroyed except gold or silver objects and metal crockery to be contributed to Yahweh's treasure. Then Joshua puts a special curse on the city. Jericho will never rise again. In this narrative we find additional elements that parallel Moses' exploits such as the war cry that brings down Jericho's walls and which is reminiscent of the cry that rose up to God from the enslaved people in Egypt; or the king of Jericho and his tragic death which evokes the figure of the pharoah, persecutor of the Hebrews.

It is interesting to note that archaeologists' efforts to discover scientific foundations of the biblical tale, particularly of the destruction of the walls of

Jericho, moreover heavily excavated, have met with no success. On the contrary, excavations have shown that the city's bastions were destroyed during the Middle Bronze Age (around 1550 B. C.) and that this was the work of the Egyptian pharoah Thutmosis II and his troops. After this event, no fortified structure of any other urban settlement in Jericho is attested. Jericho, it would appear, at the presumed period of Joshua's attack, had been abandoned for quite some time.

Whatever the case may be, the conquest of Jericho earns Joshua an exceptional reputation in all the land and many a Canaanite sovereign fears a direct confrontation with him. One man of Joshua's people, a certain Achan, disobeys the interdict concerning the booty and takes for himself part of the spoils destined for God. This sacrilege causes the failure of the next campaign by Joshua and his men, that is, the taking of the city of Ai. In order to continue their conquest victoriously, Joshua must find the guilty one and punish him. Though Achan admits to the crime, neither God nor the people take pity on him and he is stoned to death, then burned with all his possessions; a pile of stones left upon his ashes to mark the event and to serve as a warning to any other impious men.

The sin having thus been expiated, military operations resume all the more actively. The city of Ai is conquered by a clever tactic suggested by God to Joshua and the king of Ai and all of its inhabitants, as was the case in Jericho, are massacred.

At this point, the narrative pauses for an event of holy and far-reaching impact that takes place on Mount Ebal. Obeying divine injunctions and the terms set down by Moses, Joshua builds an altar of rough stone and with great pomp offers sacrifices to the Lord; after which, he copies the Mosaic Law on stone steles and holds a solemn reading of it before the people of Israel and the foreigners living among them. By this act, Joshua wishes to mark Israel's definitive recognition and acceptance of the Law as a ritual obligation, even in the new land opening up to them and in the context of sedentary life.

Then, the movement for the conquest of Canaan resumes, in an impetuous thrust towards the south of the country, like a great tide sweeping across the land. The resistance of the local kings and coalitions that band together are in vain: the Israelite advance led by Joshua and desired by the Lord is invincible. Besides those who uselessly try to oppose the Israelites and are literally annihilated, there are also those who, such as the inhabitants of Gibeon when they hear the terrifying news circulating, devise a clever ploy (passing themselves off as inhabitants of a foreign land) and manage to establish peaceful relations with the Israelite hordes. Once their trick is discovered, however, and though their lives are spared, a treaty permanently fixes their subordinate social status (as servants, lumberjacks, waterbearers) within Hebrew society. After various trials and tribulations, all of the southern cities of Palestine including Jerusalem are captured by Joshua, whose shrewdness and wisdom are sustained by Yahweh's constant counselling and miracles.

In one episode during a decisive moment in combat, Joshua raises a hymn to the sun and moon commanding

View of the Walls of Jericho

Archaeologists have searched for traces of the biblical tale, particularly of the destruction of the walls of Jericho. But excavations have revealed that the city's bastions were destroyed by an Egyptian invader in a much earlier period. No fortified structure was ever rebuilt in Jericho which, at the presumed period of Joshua's attack, had been abandoned for a long while.

them to stop, thus allowing Israel to gain the upper hand over its enemies. This passage deserves particular mention as it later serves as the basis for the astronomical doctrine professed by the Church which, with its literal interpretation of the biblical text, defends the conception of the Earth's central and immobile position in the solar system. This will notably lead to the condemnation of the heliocentric theory worked out in the sixteenth century by Copernicus, taken up again and developed further by Galileo, a theory branded as heresy in 1564 because it contradicted the Holy Scriptures and the interpretations of the church fathers.

After conquering the south of Canaan, Joshua leads his men northward and occupies the region where he burns the important city of Hazor to the ground. At this point the conquest is nearing completion, but God reminds Joshua that many other regions are waiting to be taken. After a well-deserved rest to recover from the fatigues of the war, the victorious leader faces another new and delicate task : the dividing up of the conquered territories among all the tribes of Israel, with the exception of the two and a half tribes already settled to the east of the Jordan, and the tribe of Levi, exclusively destined to exercise sacerdotal functions without possessing any specific territory.

The final part of the Book of Joshua is entirely devoted to this distribution, which takes place in two stages, the first at Gilgal and the second at Shiloh, the text abounding with painstaking details and descriptions. However, what is of more direct interest to us here than these complex details, is the great wisdom Joshua demonstrates in times of peace as in times of war; for instance, in the handling of a very difficult task that demands of him the same firmness and serenity with which he has so successfully conducted his military campaigns. Assisted in this work by the priest Eleazar and by the heads of the families, he proceeds to distribute the land of Canaan, even providing for "refuge" cities, that is, places where, for example, an involuntary murderer might find asylum and protection from those desiring to wreak vengeance. To Joshua goes a city located on the Mountain of Ephraim which he later rebuilds and where he settles. The narrative then includes a series of speeches and recommendations by Joshua in part meant to encourage peace among the tribes, but above all to emphasize the importance of observing the faith of Yahweh.

With the fair distribution of the Promised Land achieved, all that God has foretold and meant to realize through Joshua has come to pass. The aged commander "of a thousand battles" sees the end of his life approaching and pronounces a last speech, a spiritual legacy, in line with the principles upon which his whole life has been based. Loyalty to God, scrupulous respect of the Law, purity in worship, these are the rules repeated at Shechem, site of a prestigious sanctuary to Yahweh, where the old Joshua signs a final pact with his people before going "the way of all the earth" (Josh. 23:14). At 110 years of age he dies simply and peacefully and is buried at Timnath Serah on the Mountain of Ephraim, his land.

Even if a person named Joshua, who could perhaps have been a prestigious military chief did exist, the figure described in the Bible greatly transcends history and deliberately so. The biblical Joshua is a symbol, the ideal figure, the perfect executor of divine orders who succeeds in realizing the impossible. Moreover, the conquest of Canaan is purposely presented by the editors of the Old Testament as a divine undertaking of which men are only the physical instruments. Their intention was never to give an accurate account of a moment in history through this grandiose saga written long after the events they concern. Joshua is made to be no more than a trustee of this undertaking and the skillful strategist responsible for its accomplishment in the field. He is the figure who brings an external unity to a series of very disparate and rather complex events, the ancient memory of which had certainly been kept alive, but which were later evoked to justify the conquest of a country at a definite time in history, the sixth century B. C., very far-removed from the epoch of these distant and fabulous origins. In fact, their aim was actually to legitimize the return of the Hebrew people in the period following the Babylonian exile and the reclaiming of the land of their ancestors. Thus the Canaanites are deliberately described as a population unjustly occupying a territory of which they are, in reality, the most ancient and legitimate inhabitants.

These historical clarifications naturally do not detract in any way from the "literary" Joshua who embodies and expresses high moral ideals, if only through the modest role of a man versed in the arts of war; he shows himself to be a charismatic and wise leader in times of peace as well. His combats are obviously the "battles of God," which greatly help to reduce his moral responsibility in episodes of cruelty and genocide, unfortunately quite frequent in the historical chronicles of antiquity. A passage from the Book of Ecclesiasticus best captures the salient features of our hero who paradoxically seems to gain in greatness by the very fact that he has never tried to distinguish himself from others, if only in his obedience to divine precepts:

> A valiant champion was Joshua, son of Nun, minister of Moses in the office of the prophet, made to be, according to his name a great savior of those chosen by God, to take revenge upon his enemies and give Israel its possession... Who could resist him when he fought the battles of God?
>
> (*Ecclus.* 46:1-3)

Later tradition will remember Joshua not only for his military gifts, but also for his unswerving loyalty to divine purpose; his name which is very close to "Jesus" is naturally interpreted as a sign of destiny and he is seen, in some ways, as an early incarnation of the Messiah. For, just as the Messiah frees man from his greatest enemy, sin, by offering him the kingdom of heaven, Joshua frees Israel from its enemies in Canaan by leading his people to the Promised Land. Such a comparison more than suffices to make Joshua one of the key figures of biblical history and of later Judaic tradition.

Marc Chagall, ***The Tribes of Israel***

After the conquest of Canaan, Joshua sees to the fair distribution of the territories between the Twelve Tribes of Israel and shows the same wisdom that characterized his actions in times of war.

SAMSON AND DELILAH

The Adventures of a Too-Human Hero

And, more or less, every woman is always Delilah.

ALFRED DE VIGNY, *The Rage of Samson*

The adventures of Samson, and notably his fateful encounter with Delilah, which eventually leads to his death, are narrated in chapters 13-16 of the Book of Judges. Given the deeply religious character of the story, this narrative was long believed to have been written by a prophet, namely the great Samuel. The narrative, however, which is concerned with the relationship between Yahweh and his people — a relationship punctuated by chronic infidelities of the latter — was, in fact, born out of reflections formulated by theological circles many centuries later, looking back to the past as a source from which to draw teachings. Their main interest in relating the Hebrew story was in fact to vigorously reassert monotheistic orthodoxy, banishing all that did not correspond perfectly to this ideology, and particularly those religious practices suspected of deriving from outside influences, especially Canaanite.

The Judges in question in this book — the term used to define them, *"shofet"*, being the same one used in Carthage to designate the celebrated "suffetes" — are in fact "chieftains" who, because of a unique charisma granted by Yahweh under special circumstances and for a limited time, are put at the head of their people to deliver them from oppression. This was an institution halfway between a tribal regime and a monarchy, but could not fully be considered a political responsibility in the traditional sense, in that it was neither elective nor limited by a set term of office. These Judges were looked upon as deliverers of their people and protectors of their homeland, usually interceding in times of crisis when the Israelites' acts of disloyalty toward their God had provoked some form of divine punishment, usually in the submission of the chosen people to an oppressor.

We should probably avoid making too servile use of "historical" dates in the Book of Judges, however, since although it is virtually our only source of information about the period, this work is primarily a reinterpretation of events from a very specific ideological perspective and thus, for example, shows very limited concern for any chronology regarding characters or events. The period in question is the beginning of the Israelites' settlement in Canaan, from the death of Joshua to the birth of Samuel, the last of the Judges, and the one who will give Israel its first king in the person of Saul. According to conventional chronology, this would place us at the very end of the thirteenth century to the middle of the eleventh century B. C., but the story lacks coherency and does not show any real chronological progression.

The Judges are twelve in number, six so-called "minor" ones and six "major" ones, the last of the major Judges being Samson. As we will see, the original features of this hero's character make his presence in the Book of Judges seem rather odd, to say the least. The only aspect of Samson's life which might explain his relationship to the great deliverers of Israel is perhaps the role he plays in the wars between the Israelites and the Philistines. To better set the scene of our story, perhaps we should pause here a moment to consider these historical enemies of the Hebrew people, the Philistines. Of Aegean or Anatolian origin, the Philistines belonged to the fearful "Peoples of the Sea" who infiltrated the Near East at the beginning of the twelfth century B. C., leaving a wake of destruction across the land. (Ugarit, for example, was entirely burned to the ground and abandoned.) They later attempted to invade the Egypt of Rameses III, who managed to repulse them toward Canaan. It was there, on the coastal plain of Palestine, in the area surrounding Gaza and Ashkelon, that the Philistines settled, giving their name to the entire region, "Palestine." Excellent smiths and therefore well armed, they soon began to invade the neighboring regions and eventually came into conflict with the Israelites, a struggle that would last for many centuries. Samson's exploits were not enough to quell the Philistines' threats or oppression, and the first king of Israel, Saul, fell in battle against them. His successor, David, eventually managed to defeat the Philistines, but toward the end of the tenth century, bitter conflicts between the two peoples flared up again, indeed more vehemently. Not long after, however, the Assyrians arrived on the scene, dominating all the region and forcing the payment of heavy tributes from the population, thus reducing Israelites and Philistines alike to the equal status of grudgingly faithful vassals.

This is the historical background, then, against which the story of Samson's life unfolds, adventures abounding in rich and humorous anecdotes reflecting the saga's popular folk origins. Samson is clearly a local hero famous for his celebrated exploits, who has been "fitted" into the Book of Judges, as smoothly as possible, with the help of a few editorial adjustments. Before we try to "dismantle" this mechanism invented by the Bible's editors to recover local traditions for their own ends, let us look at the story itself as it has come down to us.

The scene opens on yet another instance of the chosen people's infidelity towards Yahweh who, as punishment, has left them to languish in the hands of the Philistines for forty years. We immediately note the absence of any chronological references to help pinpoint these events in time, or any connection between these events and previous ones in the same book. Manoah, a man whose name signifies "rest," has no children, for his wife is barren. This man belongs to the tribe of Dan, the Danites, who, before emigrating to the north of Palestine, had occupied a territory northwest of Jerusalem which included Zorah, not far from Beth Shemesh. We note that this is the first mention in the Book of Judges of this region, near Philistine territory, which will be the cultural and geographical birthplace of the legend of Samson.

One day an angel appears to Manoah's wife and announces that she will bear a son. The angel warns her, however, that she must abstain from all strong drink and impure food, since the child will be dedicated to the life of a Nazirite, a man set aside for God. The Bible contains many other celebrated cases of angels announcing the births of sons: to Mary, of course, but to Sarah as well, also barren. In ancient societies this represented a serious affliction as descendants were expected to ensure proper burial of their deceased, and were entrusted with keeping their memories alive. Being a Nazirite was a special state in which, for a limited period, a person was dedicated to the Lord and took certain vows of abstinence. The verb *nazar*, from which the noun *nazir* or *nazer* (Nazirite) derives, expresses the actions of "to separate," "to consecrate," and also "to abstain." In the Book of Numbers (6:2-21) legal obligations concerning this status are enumerated and represent, in fact, sacred interdicts concerning, for example, abstaining from alcohol (wine, vinegar, liqueur, etc.), avoiding "unclean" contact with any part of a dead creature, and above all, never shaving or cutting the hair. Once these vows were taken, the Nazirite performed sacrifices and made offerings to God. He put an end to this state by shaving his hair. Other than Samson, famous Nazirites included Samuel, Amos, Judas Maccabaeus, and St. Paul. What made Samson unique was that he was pronounced a Nazirite while still in his mother's womb, and the fact that he was destined to remain so for his entire life. The angel prophesies that Samson will begin to deliver Israel from the Philistines. We will see how he will accomplish this all alone and not at the head of any army, as in the case of the other Judges.

Told by his wife of the angel's visit, Manoah prays to the Lord asking him to send his messenger again, for he would like to know what is expected of them after the birth of the child. The angel appears a second time and repeats his commands which, they are told, apply not only to the mother during pregnancy, but also to the child after he is born. Abiding by the rules of hospitality, Manoah then offers to prepare the angel something to eat, and in doing so follows the example of Abraham in the Book of Genesis and Gideon in the Book of Judges. But the angel refuses, saying that offerings may only be made to God. Manoah and his wife are unsure who the messenger really is and thus call him "man of God," and ask the angel his name. They wish to give thanks to him after the birth of their son, as they would have normally done for any seer or prophet. But the angel categorically refuses, reminding them that the names of celestial beings are an ineffable mystery, inaccessible to man. According to ancient beliefs, knowing the name of an object or a living being was the same as seizing its essence and exercising power over it. Manoah does not insist any further, and sacrifices a kid as an offering to God. As the fire consumes the animal, the angel mingles with the altar's flames and rises to the heavens, vanishing forever. The man and his wife are filled with awe and adoration at the thought that God could have provoked their deaths after manifesting himself to them in this way.

But instead, their lives are blessed by the birth of a son, whom the mother calls Samson (in Hebrew *Shimshôn*), a name associated with the word "sun" (*shemesh*). The Sun was an important divinity worshipped by a cult apparently deeply rooted in the region, and the place-name Beth Shemesh, which means "Sun Temple," could also be an indication of this. We will see later how this etymology also gave rise to a symbolic interpretation of the adventures of Samson, linking them to the concept of the sun. Chapter 13 of the Book of Judges then concludes with an important statement: while Samson is growing up he is invested by the Lord's Sprit, thus making him twice marked by God. As a Nazirite, he possesses the divine charisma which characterizes all Judges, though in his case this will not make him a military commander or political leader. On the other hand, Samson does not display any of the admirable ethical virtues to be expected of a character so clearly marked by

Guido Reni, *The Victorious Samson*

Biblical editors borrowed the figure of Samson from local folklore and fitted him, as smoothly as possible, into a "theological" plot.

A. Gelmers, ***Samson and Delilah and Samson and the Gates of Gaza***
These two episodes are excellent illustrations of the character of Samson: the first, of his terrible naivety in the face of Delilah's tactics; the second, of his formidable strength.

God. On the contrary, he is rash, impulsive, a slave to his desires and sexual drives, endowed with exceptional physical strength it is true, but certainly not a man of wisdom nor a model of conduct. The subsequent episodes, after being adroitly introduced by the prologue, are concerned with relating whether Samson respects his Nazirite vows or not, and what lies in store for him. The destiny of Israel seems to be of secondary importance in respect to Samson's adventures.

Samson goes to Timnath, a small town of uncertain location (probably Khirbet Tibneh), and falls in love with a young Philistine woman. From this passage in the text, it would seem that relations between the Israelites and Philistines there at that time were peaceful enough, although the text does stress the domination imposed by the latter over the Hebrews. Faced with his parents' opposition, who do not favor the idea of having a foreign daughter-in-law (the Philistines are not circumcised, they remind him), Samson decides to take upon himself the initiatives generally left to the parents of the future husband. During the epoch of the patriarchs, in any case, the choice of a young man's wife and the responsibility for wedding preparations were the prerogatives of his father, although the son could express a preference. From the time of Moses, however, the Law had prohibited intermarriage, that is, unions with foreign women. The success of this measure had been varied, though, depending on the times, returning to the center of attention during the epoch of Ezra and Nehemiah. The Book of Ruth, which also appears in this volume, shows very clearly that at certain epochs biblical editors presented a very positive image of these unions. The infamous Jezebel, Phoenician princess and wife of King Ahab, incarnation of evil, wickedness and apostasy, was not the only model held up to represent the foreign woman. The examples of intermarriages are numerous in the Old Testament: other than the cases of Ruth and Ahab just mentioned, we note those of Joseph, Moses, David, and Solomon. As for the editors of the Book of Judges, they do not voice any opinion concerning Samson's choice, but rather present it as part of the 'divine plan' intended to destroy the Philistines.

Returning to Timnath for the second time, Samson encounters a lion along the way and, strengthened by the Lord's Spirit, he kills it and skins it with his bare hands without mentioning the exploit to anyone afterwards. The presence of lions at the time in Palestine is historically documented, but what is striking here is the parallel between this episode and Hercules' famous slaying of the Nemean lion which he strangles in the same way, and whose skin he wears, it becoming, with the club, one of his most important attributes. However, we will return to this comparison later. Meanwhile Samson, having seen the woman of his dreams, decides to marry when, on the road to Timnath yet again (we do not know how much time has elapsed), he comes across the carcass of the lion and sees it is now filled with honey left by a swarm of bees. He scoops some out and eats it on the way home, and then without revealing where he has found it, gives some to his parents. As a Nazirite, of course, Samson was forbidden to touch any part of a dead creature and therefore by touching the honey inside the carcass, he commits his first in a long series of transgressions. The symbolism of the honey and the carcass deserves some explanation, and we will include it in our overall discussion of the significant elements of Samson's adventures.

The narrative is not at all explicit about the details of his marriage, nor are we ever told if Samson's parents finally do give their consent. In any event, they do not appear in any of the scenes which take place in Timnath, nor does Samson's bride ever leave her parents' house. Perhaps this represented

a special type of matrimonial arrangement, well documented in the Arab world, in which each of the spouses continued to live with his parents and the husband could visit his wife when he wished. On one of these visits, or perhaps even during the wedding celebration itself, a seven-day banquet is held. Fearing Samson's strength, the young Philistines arrange to have the hero escorted by thirty "body guards." The text does not say what Samson actually consumes at the feast, but one can reasonably assume that celebrations of this kind were not particularly conducive to the vows requiring abstinence from alcohol imposed upon the Nazirites. This could perhaps represent a second transgression by Samson.

Whether or not this is so, at the banquet Samson then puts a riddle to the guests inspired by his unique adventure with the lion. Whoever solves the riddle before the end of the festivities will receive a prize from Samson of thirty pieces of precious linen and thirty changes of fine clothing. If no one finds the answer, the prize will go to Samson. The riddle went like this: "Out of the eater came something to eat. Out of the strong came something sweet."

The riddle, expressed in two elegant hemistichs and based upon antomyms as well as a play on words, is in fact almost impossible to solve. Only Samson, who has seen the lion's carcass ("the eater/the strong"), with the honey inside ("something to eat/sweet") can answer it. After three days of vain searching, the Philistines threaten Samson's wife to set fire to her father's house if she does not take advantage of Samson's feelings for her to get the answer out of him. Armed with all her feminine wiles, she pursues him relentlessly, weeping, nagging, complaining, shouting abuses, until finally, a totally exasperated Samson gives in and explains the riddle to her. This is the first example of Samson's weakness towards women which will eventually lead to his ruin.

The Philistines, this time in verse as well, give the desired solution to Samson, but he retorts in two rhyming verses, quite rare in Hebrew poetry, that only by resorting to dishonesty were they able to solve the riddle. Then, wild with rage and invested with the Holy Spirit as God's armed representative in the struggle against the Philistines, he descends upon Ashkelon and slays thirty of its men, helping himself to their clothing as prizes to be given to the thirty men who have solved the riddle. Samson returns home, to the house of his parents, and his wife is given in marriage, presumably, to one of the guests at the banquet.

Some days later, Samson goes to visit the woman he still believes to be his wife, taking a kid with him as a gift. Much to his surprise and dismay he discovers, however, that because he had seemingly abandoned her, she has been given in marriage to someone else. Samson is consumed with rage at this affront and will hear nothing of his father-in-law's proposal to accept the younger sister, described as prettier, as his wife instead. He goes out and captures three hundred foxes and ties them together in twos, attaching flaming torches to their tails and sets them loose across the fields to ravage the crops of wheat, grapes, and olive groves ready for harvest.

Foxes being extremely rare in Palestine and, moreover, fiercely solitary in nature, this would seem to be more an example of the type of folklore commonly found in fables or legends. Furthermore, this remarkable episode is not unique. Ovid in his *Fasti* (*Calendar*), describes the annual celebration held on 19 April in Rome dedicated to Ceres, the agrarian goddess, during which, to purify the earth, foxes attached to torches were released in the fields. There are records of similar practices having

Medieval miniature, *Samson and Delilah*

Rash and impulsive, Samson is a prey to his instincts. He is strongly attracted to a foreign woman, Delilah, though only to become her puppet and victim.

existed in the Arab world associated with rain and fertility. Hannibal, in the midst of the Punic Wars, probably drew inspiration from this sacred tradition while devising his military strategy at Lake Trasimeno in 217 B. C.

The terrible destruction caused by Samson's punitive act incites the Philistines to retaliate and they kill Samson's ex-wife and her father. This again provokes the hero's wrath, and seized by a terrible fury, he promises to wreak vengeance. A brutal massacre of the Philistines ensues, after which Samson cautiously goes to hide in a cave. But the vicious spiral of violence is underway and the Philistines waste no time: they invade Lehi and threaten war against the tribe of Judah, inhabitants of a region near Timnath, forcing their cooperation in capturing Samson, now the declared mortal enemy of the Philistine people.

Three thousand members of the tribe of Judah descend upon the cave where Samson is hiding and, after promising to spare his life, they bind him in ropes and lead him thus to the Philistines. However, Samson is yet again invested by the Lord's Spirit and breaks out of his bonds. Catching sight of the jawbone of an ass, he seizes it and strikes "a thousand Philistines" with the curious weapon. Through a play on words using the Hebrew terms for the animal and the action of "striking" and "heaping up" he proclaims: "With the jawbone of an ass, heaps upon heaps, with the jawbone of an ass have I slain a thousand men." However, in so doing, Samson has once again broken the Nazirite rule forbidding him to touch any part of a dead creature. This episode — specifies the biblical editor — gives birth to the place-name Ramath Lehi ("the Hill of the Jawbone") just as the event which follows, when God then quenches Samson's thirst by making water spring miraculously from the ground at Lehi, gives birth to the the place-name Hakkore, a site in the same city. Chapter 15 of the Book of Judges then abruptly concludes with a statement that has no apparent connection with anything that has preceded, nor with anything that follows: "Samson judged Israel in the days of the Philistines for twenty years." Such statements customarily appear at the close of a story relating to a Judge, whereas in this case, Samson's tale is by no means over. Perhaps this peculiarity may be partially explained by the fact that chapter 16 relates Samson's capture and death, in other words, the end of his "career" as a deliverer of his people. Whatever the case may be, this once again seems to suggest that Samson's inclusion in the Book of Judges is, in fact, a rather forced "theological" manoeuvre which fails to dissimulate its real nature as a popular saga celebrating the exploits of a local hero named Samson.

Samson now finds himself in Gaza, without our being told why he has made such a long trip, where he meets a prostitute and goes to spend the night with her. Consistent with what we have already seen of this side of his character, Samson again shows his weakness for women despite the serious problems they inevitably cause him. For, informed of his presence in the city, the inhabitants of Gaza wait in ambush for Samson at the city gates, hoping to murder him at dawn as he leaves the city. Samson, however, departs at midnight and without giving his enemies a second thought, takes hold of the great city gates in his arms, ripping them up together with the two posts and the bar, and heads eastward carrying them on his back, all the way to the top of a hill near Hebron.

At this point, the woman with whom he will fall helplessly in love, the fatal Delilah, bursts into his life. The setting of their story is again the region of Samson's childhood, around Zorah and Beth Shemesh. Delilah is most likely a Philistine, though the biblical text never explicitly specifies this. In any case, the local princes put pressure on Delilah to take advantage of Samson's feelings for her to discover the secret of his extraordinary strength, and each one of them even promises her a reward of eleven hundred pieces of silver. Knowing from different sources that the Philistine territory at the time consisted of a pentapolis of five city-states, we may assume that the five heads of this confederation were offering Delilah, in the event she succeeded, no less than 5,500 pieces of silver or about six kilos, a truly considerable sum.

With disarming and, we must admit, seemingly idiotic frankness, Delilah asks Samson point-blank where his strength comes from, the best way to take him prisoner, and how to render him powerless. The dialogue between the two lovers, in fact, is not meant to be a historical account of the facts as they actually happened, nor does it even attempt to be credible, but is rather a genre portrayal of ordinary life in which irony and humor play a fundamental part. Samson plays the game, saying that seven green bowstrings still to be dried would suffice to take him prisoner and render him as weak as any ordinary man. No sooner said than done, Samson is bound up, and Delilah hurls at him, "Samson, the Philistines are upon you!" The hero easily frees himself, however not without coming into contact yet again with part of a dead creature, the bowstrings having been made from nerve fibers. Delilah is very unhappy at having been tricked, and faced with her angry reproaches, Samson then suggests she use brand-new ropes this time to achieve her objective. The outcome is the same again, however, and Delilah's anger grows. Samson's advice is then to take a loom and weave the "seven locks" of his hair into its web, fixing them tightly with a peg. After yet another failure, and with a shower of further abuse, Delilah now decides to play on Samson's feelings. She pursues him relentlessly, accusing him of not loving her, tormenting him with endless curses and tears, and begins to remind us uncomfortably of Samson's first wife trying to get the answer to the lion and honey riddle out of him. Although once again Samson will eventually surrender to feminine tenacity, and in so doing demonstrate his weakness of character, he is also, in his own way, cooperating with God's plan to eliminate the Philistines.

Samson therefore tells Delilah of his special condition as a Nazirite, a person dedicated to God, and how his hair must never be cut or shaven. "If my hair is cut, my strength will leave me and I will be as weak as any other man." Realizing that this time Samson is telling the truth, Delilah informs the Philistines who come to her with the promised payment. As soon as Samson falls asleep, his head in Delilah's lap, they cut his seven locks of hair and, as on the other occasions, she cries, "Samson, the Philistines are upon you!" Samson tries in vain to collect his strength and push them back, but God is no longer by his side. With the cutting of his hair, the Nazirite vow has been broken. Only a special ceremony performed in a sacred place could have annulled the vow and released him from this obligation. By violating it, even involuntarily, Samson has put an end to the privileged relationship which united him with Yahweh, the true source of his force and charisma.

At the mercy of the Philistines, Samson is brutally blinded and imprisoned in Gaza where, fettered with two heavy bronze chains like a slave, he is made to turn the millstone at the prison. Little by little, however, his hair begins to grow back, and with it a flicker of hope returns that his fortunes may change. The opportunity comes at the great hecatomb offered to the national god, Dagon, by the Philistines which is followed by a celebration of thanks to the divinity for having delivered Samson into their hands. Dagon was, in fact, an important Semitic god whose name was closely related to "wheat" and was, therefore, an agrarian divinity whose cult was assimilated by the Philistines when they settled in Palestine. Spirits run high knowing that at last this great enemy of the people, responsible for so much death and suffering, has been reduced to a helpless blind prisoner. In their rejoicing, the people demand to see Samson, to jeer at the great powerless giant. A young man leads the blind Samson by the hand towards the crowd, but Samson persuades his guide to let him lean against the pillars supporting an edifice, probably a grandstand, raised near Dagon's temple. Above, thousands of men and women (three thousand according to the Hebrew text, seven hundred according to the Greek Septuagint) including the Philistine chieftains, are gathered for the festivities and also to get a better look at Samson. Invoking God's help, and praying for the strength that had once made him invincible, Samson locks his arms around the two central pillars supporting the edifice, and with all his regained strength, pulls them down crying, "Let me die with the Philistines!" The grandstand comes crashing to the ground killing thousands — more Philistines than Samson had ever slain in his entire lifetime, offers the biblical text — and Samson perishes with them.

Samson's brothers and all his father's family come for his body and bury him in the family tomb alongside his father, Manoah. The story concludes with almost the very same words as chapter 15, repeating that Samson was Judge in Israel for twenty years.

As noted previously, Samson's story seems out of place in the Book of Judges and gives us the strong impression of a tale that has been forced into a theological and narrative framework foreign to it. Chronology is almost non-existent or confused, and Israel plays no part in Samson's initiatives, a hero who accomplishes all his exploits on his own, without the help of any army. Though it is true the Philistines are punished,

Guercino, ***Samson reveals to Delilah that his strength comes from his hair***

The theme of the strength that lies in a person's hair is frequent in literature and popular beliefs the world over. For example, was it not customary in France to shave the bodies of those suspected of witchcraft before leading them to the torture chamber?

P. P. Rubens, ***Samson and Delilah***

As a Nazirite, that is, a person dedicated to God, if Samson cuts his hair he will lose the divine protection that makes him invincible. Here passion proves stronger than his holy vows.

they are by no means eliminated from the history of the chosen people. In short, when the text awkwardly repeats that Samson was "Judge in Israel for twenty years," we are actually presented with tangible traces of "manipulation" and reworking of a popular tale about a powerful and courageous man, endowed with exceptional strength who, despite himself, becomes a Judge of Israel. Probably in the region which serves as a setting for these adventures, the homeland of the Danite tribe, a more or less legendary but certainly "profane" saga in oral form must have circulated in praise of a certain Samson, hero of spectacular feats performed to the detriment of the "evil" Philistines. The biblical editors used this legendary material for their own theological ends, salvaging the character of Samson whom they transformed into an acolyte of Yahweh. The process consisted in weaving the story of Samson's adventures into a religious plot, and the initial chapters accomplish this by presenting Samson as a miraculous child given to his parents by God, and bound to the Lord by a special promise to respect the vows of the Nazirite for an entire lifetime. It was then possible to apply the same development to the rest of Samson's life as the stories of the other Judges: the Holy Spirit invests him, blesses him with divine charisma, and above all with exceptional physical strength with which he accomplishes exploits equal to the greatest though, as mentioned before, very different from the collective military feats of a Jephthah or a Gideon. Samson's repeated violations of the Nazirite vows will inevitably lead to the loss of his charisma and great strength, and even to death, despite an ultimate burst of power.

This then is the story of the figure we know as Samson and of the traditions related to him. An underlying folk origin is indicated by many of the story's features as, for example, the importance of the marvelous and fantastic in his adventures which give them an "epic" quality, the presence of a riddle, and also various aspects of Samson's personality. Samson is not, in fact, a particularly edifying character. He is violent, impulsive, irrational, and at times like a brute incapable of controlling his instincts, particularly his sexual impulses. He is irresistibly drawn to women, especially foreign women, disapproved of almost consistently in the Old Testament and, as he is incapable of perceiving their wickedness, invariably ends up their puppet and victim. What captivated people's imaginations and accounted for Samson's success when his legend began to circulate, was his superhuman strength and his ability to trick the Philistines. Far from being a religious or moral figure, Samson possessed the typical qualities of the popular folk-hero whose excesses make people laugh and whose adventures are replete with tragic-comic overtones. Moreover, without ever being cited anywhere else in the Old Testament, this rather unorthodox hero has nevertheless found himself the object of both negative and positive evaluation by posterity: Martin Luther lashed out at his lack of moral integrity, his baseness, and weakness toward the opposite sex, while the great English poet Milton, in his work, *Samson Agonist*, written in 1671, presents Samson as a tragic hero painfully aware of his moral inadequacy in terms of the tasks he has been entrusted to fulfill, and who embarks on a journey of spiritual suffering in an effort to attain purification. He even manages to win Delilah over when she visits him in prison to ask forgiveness for having caused his ruin — quite a remarkable turn of events in respect to the Bible, where Delilah disappears all together once Samson is captured. In any event, Samson's saga was enthusiastically adopted by the faithful who saw in him, through his tireless struggle against the Philistines, the precursor of Saul and David. In this way, beyond the folklore and popular themes reflected in the tale of Samson's adventures, we can also recognize and appreciate a definite historical value.

Another familiar folk motif concerns the association between physical strength and a person's hair. We find references to this in all the literatures of the world, and in many beliefs up to our own times. For example, is it not true that athletes often refuse to cut their hair before a match, just as warriors before a battle? Has it not been said that many criminals have confessed their crimes after having had their heads shaved? And in France, based upon this same principle, was it not customary to shave the bodies of those suspected of witchcraft before leading them to the torture chamber? Parallels in classical mythology are many, and we know for a fact that the rites of passage sanctioning a change in status, for example from adolescence to adulthood, and consequently complete integration into the civic community, were marked by an offering of the initiate's hair, as during the famous Athenian "Apaturia."

As for riddles, according to the Book of Numbers (12:8) these represented an important vehicle of knowledge. The most famous example, other than that of the sphinx in Greek mythology, is of course that of the queen of Sheba, in the Bible, who visits Solomon to put his wisdom to test. The king of Tyre, Hiram, seems to have been another partner to the king of Israel in the use of riddles. Much has been written about Samson's riddle, some authors even having discerned an erotic motive behind it, quite well dissimulated it is true. Others more justifiably have stressed the strangeness of a riddle which only Samson could answer, having been the sole witness to the events surrounding it. However, the existence of an ancient popular tradition has recently been brought to light, supported by examples in iconography as well, according to which the carcasses of "strong" animals (horses, bulls and lions) were believed to produce special worms which, after a certain lapse of time (seven years according to some), gave birth to bees. The illustration of such a scene on a Carthaginian razor, a funerary object discovered in a tomb, suggests that this phenomenon had an eschatological dimension as well: a useful animal born out of a carcass, the triumph of life over death. Samson's riddle may not be as obscure as it seems at first sight, and in fact could be a reflection of traditional beliefs of the epoch.

Finally, based on the etymology of Samson's name ("He from the Sun" the "Solar One"), the story has sometimes been interpreted as a symbolic representation of the struggle of the Sun, defender of cosmic order, against the forces of chaos; the hero's famous locks serving as an allegory of the sun's rays. As we have seen, however, this is probably an example of a popular belief associated with the supernatural strength of the hero. As for Samson's "solar" name, we should also consider the more probable explanation that his name comes from the region where he was born, an area where the Sun cult was particularly active. In a similiar way, apart from the episode of a bare-handed struggle with a lion which Samson and Hercules both have in common, these two characters are not, in fact, very closely related. True, both of them are granted extraordinary strength through divine will, and perform acts of "purification" for the benefit of posterity. However, apart from this, there are many features which distinguish the two. Hercules' struggles are motivated by a will to dominate natural forces (for example water or animals), whereas this concern is completely foreign to Samson. Both are certainly great seducers, but Hercules' relationship with the feminine element is infinitely more complex than Samson's. Also, Hercules' relationship with the Sun, from whom he takes a goblet to descend into the underworld, offers quite different connotations than the vague etymological one which associates Samson to it.

In short, we will leave these simple comparisons aside and not be tempted by their superficiality. Let us rather conclude by considering Samson, the biblical hero who, beyond the apparent naiveness of a rather coarse character, illustrates the ambiguities of existence in which human freedom must contend with primary impulses on the one hand, and divine plans on the other. Samson is neither a saint nor a sinner, but a human being with his strengths and weaknesses, a hero who is sometimes as incredibly strong as he is pathetically weak, whom God helps when he is truly in need, and whom he uses to realize his divine plans.

Rembrandt, ***The Blinding of Samson***

The figure of Samson, so strong and yet so weak, reflects the ambiguities of existence. Neither saint nor dreadful sinner, Samson is a human being in all his greatness and degeneration, a hero whom God uses to fulfill divine plans, for example, to defeat the Philistines.

RUTH

The Model Foreigner

It was a dream in which Boaz saw an oak
growing out of his stomach that reached the blue sky.
Along it a race climbed in a long chain.
A king sang below,
Above a god was dying.

Victor Hugo, *Boaz Asleep*

Ruth is the central character of a Book whose theme deals with the possibility of integrating foreigners into the community of the chosen people. A Moabite, and therefore a foreigner, she reveals many admirable qualities and, choosing to live in the land of Judah, even becomes an ancestor of the great David. The ancient land of Moab, bordered on the north by the country of the Ammonites and on the south by that of the Edomites, is located across the Jordan river between the Wadi Mujib (the River Arnon) and the Wadi Hasa (the River Zered), and is dominated by a plateau that rises to an altitude of almost 1000 meters. It is a well-watered area and therefore extremely fertile, which explains why, as relates the Book of Ruth, the Israelites from the region of Bethlehem, hard hit by famine, seek refuge in Moab. The entire Transjordan region, in fact, is the theater of the first conflicts between the Israelites led by Moses in their quest for the Promised Land, and the Canaanites, settled in the area, who refuse to accept the new arrivals. The Moabite king at the time, a man named Balak, feeling threatened by the presence of the Israelites in the vicinity, sends for a soothsayer, the famous Balaam, and orders him to put a curse on the invaders. The Book of Numbers tells us, however, how great Balak's surprise and dismay are when the prophet, inspired by God, blesses the Israelites and curses the Moabites who, he foresees, are destined to become subjects of Israel. Co-existence with the Moabites, however, leads Israel to apostasy and disloyalty to Yahweh: the Israelites, losing themselves in debauchery with the Moabite women, venerate the local Baal, the Baal of Peor, and completely forget the Covenant that binds them to Yahweh. For this reason, in spite of his blessing, Christian and Hebrew literature will consider Balaam the symbol of the False Prophet. Also, quite importantly, we note the discovery of an Aramaic inscription in Deir Allah, Jordan, which refers to a person named Balaam as "the man who saw the gods," which represents quite a striking convergence between the biblical tale and historical fact.

During the first centuries of Israel's existence, the neighboring peoples of Transjordan are a permanent threat to the territorial integrity and survival of the chosen people and, because of this, conflicts are numerous during the epoch of the Judges. It is David who, after crushing Philistine power, conquers Transjordan and gains complete control of it. Until the ninth century B. C. the Moabite kings are vassals of the kings of Israel who collect heavy tributes consisting of, according to the second Book of Kings, "one hundred thousand lambs and one hundred thousand rams." From this period dates the famous "Inscription of Mesha," King of Moab, also known as the "Stone of Moab," a very important historical document discovered in 1868 in Dibon on Moabite territory and today preserved at the Louvre Museum in Paris; dating from the ninth century B. C., it contains the first extra-biblical reference to Yahweh as the God of Israel. The Mesha stele tells us that the Israelite king Omri oppressed the people of the land of Moab for many years and that the national god Kemosh was angered by this. We read further — and naturally the Old Testament provides substantial support of this story — that Omri's successor, Achab, puts down a rebellion led by Mesha. Some years later, it is the turn of Achab's son, Jorum, to stifle an uprising with the help of the kings of Judah and Edom. The name Elisha is mentioned in relation to these events when he miraculously supplies water to Moab's enemies. Cornered in the city of Qir Hareshet, the Moabite king seeks to be saved by a desperate act: he sacrifices his eldest son on the walls of the city and offers the child to the gods as a burnt offering. Extremely shocked by this sacrifice, the Israelites retreat across the Jordan and both of the opposing forces claim the event as their own victory. As can be seen, relations between the Israelites and the Moabites were far from peaceful, and the choice of Ruth as heroine of a biblical tale is therefore all the more significant.

The events related in this work take place in the days of the Judges, which has led some exegetes, notably as early as Eusebius of Caesarea and Saint Jerome, to qualify the Book of Ruth as no more than an appendix to the much richer Book of Judges. According to the Talmud, the work is from the pen of the prophet Samuel who lived from the eleventh to tenth century B. C. However, further study of the text has shown that things are perhaps not quite so simple. There is a strong Aramean influence evident in the language which suggests that the Book of Ruth was not at all written during the period of the events which serve as its historical background, but in the fifth or fourth centuries B. C., that is, many centuries after the events which it reconstructs. From the point of view of ideas illustrated in the story of Ruth the Moabite, we note that the editor shows great tolerance toward foreigners when he draws a very complimentary portrait of Ruth and in no way condemns mixed marriages. But such conceptions may be interpreted as a reaction to diverse historical events from different periods, such as the negative example given by the Tyrian Jezebel, the abhorred queen of the ninth century B. C., constantly denigrated for having introduced the abominable Baal worship into Israel, or the campaigns of Ezra and Nehemiah waged against mixed marriages between Jews and foreigners from the fifth to the fourth centuries B. C. In short, the dating of the Book of Ruth remains a debated question even if the hypothesis mentioned above would seem the most credible. Finally, a stylistic study of the Book of Ruth seems to indicate that the editor had recourse to an ancient poetic substrate, an old georgic cantilena that narrated the adventures of Ruth, Naomi, and Boaz, simple people of solid virtues deeply inspired by their love for others, the family, and God, and whose idyllic destinies unfold against a backdrop of fields and flowers.

The short tale that focuses on the figure of Ruth develops over four chapters, extremely rich in characters and events, related in a sober, delicate, and effective style, without digressions or moral considerations. Its presentation is linear with a prologue that serves to set the scene and sketch out the characters, and an epilogue that shows Ruth become mother of a family and David's ancestor. Between these two parts, the body of the story describes Ruth's destiny, a Moabite called upon to take her place among the people of Israel.

In the days of the Judges, severe famine ravages Israel. A man named Elimelech (most likely meaning "the [divine] king is my God"), his wife Naomi ("gracious"), and their two sons Mahlon and Chilion (whose names might refer to the situation in the story since they mean "sickness" and "annihilation"), all born in Bethlehem in the kingdom of Judah, decide to emigrate to the land of Moab reputed for its fertility since, because of its high altitude, it enjoys more favorable climatic conditions. Long ago, Abraham and Jacob were forced to emigrate to Egypt for the same reason, but far from making any negative allusions to that exile or to the country where they settled, though the Israelites' atavistic enemy, our author is satisfied to relate the facts without passing any value judgement. Elimelech dies, and after his death Naomi remains alone while her sons marry Moabite women: one of them is Orpah (a name with an uncertain meaning) and the other, Ruth, whose name could mean "friend" or "companion." Here again the compiler records this fact without commenting or taking any position on a practice that had long been contested by those who feared mixed marriages threatened the strength of the chosen people's faith and their cultural integrity. A few years later, Naomi's two sons also die and, having learned that her own country is again free from famine thanks to divine intervention, she decides to return to her homeland. Her two daughters-in-law insist upon going with her, but Naomi urges them to remain in their own Moabite families, thanking them for their devotion, and wishing the two women well in finding new husbands. She embraces Ruth and Orpah in farewell, but the two daughters-in-law burst into tears and refuse to be separated from Naomi, to whom they have obviously become extremely attached and whose genuine goodness and courage in the face of adversity they so greatly admire. The scene in its restraint is moving. But Naomi, thinking of the well-being of her daughters-in-law insists: why go with her? Why risk having to give up remarrying and having children? At Naomi's age, the birth of any more sons is unlikely, sons who, even if Orpah and Ruth had the patience to wait, might one day become husbands and fathers to their children.

Here Naomi, in a rather liberal interpretation, is referring to the Law of the Levirate (from the Latin *levir* which means "brother-in-law"). This law states that if a widow has no male children, she will be remarried to her brother-in-law and that the first son born of this union will be considered her deceased husband's child, therefore receiving his father's inheritance. This was intended to ensure a line of descendants and simultaneously to protect the family patrimony. The Book of Ruth suggests, moreover, that this obligation — which could be avoided under certain conditions — extended to family members beyond the brothers of the deceased. Naomi envisages the possibility here of her daughters-in-law remarrying

Statuette of a Moabite King

The land of Moab in Transjordan is the theater of the first conflicts between the Israelites, led by Moses in search of the Promised Land, and the Canaanites who occupy the area and refuse to accept the newcomers. The hostilities last for several centuries.

her children born of a second marriage, who would therefore be the half-brothers of the deceased Mahlon and Chilion. This would mean that the obligation of the levirate did not only concern the family nucleus strictly speaking, but rather the clan as a whole, as the rest of the story will confirm.

Orpah is finally convinced by Naomi to return to her own family, whereas Ruth vows that she will never leave her mother-in-law's side and that she will follow her like a shadow: "Wherever you go, I will go, wherever you live, I will live. Your people will be my people and your God will be my God. Wherever you die, I will die, and that is where I will be buried." From this passage it clearly appears that a restrictive relationship existed between the people and country to which one belonged, and the worship of a particular diety. Ruth, in other words, will not be allowed to worship her national god Kemosh once she goes to live on Israelite territory; she must renounce her own religion and adopt the Yahvist faith. Ruth follows Naomi to Bethelehem where the women receive them very warmly. Naomi tells them she would like to be called Marah from now on, a name that expresses the bitterness the God Almighty (*Shaddai*) has brought her after the deaths of her husband and two sons. But Naomi's sentiments go no further than this bitterness: there is no revolt, no desperate attempt, like that of Job, to comprehend what guides the hand of God. As for Ruth, by her very choice to live on Israelite soil she is integrated into the local community and is considered one of the chosen people. We note that such a simple and direct process, which prefigures the universality of Christianity, greatly contrasts with the position expressed in Deuteronomy concerning the assimilation of foreigners, particularly of Ammonites and Moabites, who because of their hostility shown towards the Israelites on their way to the Promised Land, are excluded from the community of the children of God.

The editor of the Book of Ruth then explains that Naomi and Ruth's arrival takes place at harvest time, probably at the end of May or beginning of June and, in fact, a rural atmosphere serves as the backdrop for the adventures that follow. In the synagogue, moreover, the Book of Ruth is read on Pentecost, the most important agricultural festival of the year, when thanks are given to God for the harvests. Ruth offers to go into the fields, since the two women are without any means, and gather the barley left by the harvesters, in accordance with Hebrew law that reserves this right for widows and orphans. Chance has it that she chooses a field owned by a man named Boaz ("force is in him"), an important and affluent man related to the family of Ruth's deceased husband. Boaz, after piously greeting his workers ("the Lord be with you"), inquires about the young woman; from the outset Ruth distinguishes herself by her determination, working at her task without a moment of respite. In a paternalistic tone, Boaz speaks to Ruth, telling her she may come back to the fields in the days ahead: she is welcome to gather as much grain as she likes and, drink from their wells; he reassures her that the workers will act kindly towards her. Ruth gratefully bows to him in thanks and expresses her surprise and pleasure at how amiably foreigners are treated. Boaz responds by praising the virtues she has shown to possess: in her loyalty to Naomi and in her decision to leave her homeland and entrust herself to the protection of Yahweh. In this scene we see the buddings of a romantic relationship between Boaz and Ruth that will eventually lead to marriage.

Boaz invites Ruth to sit with him at his table and even tells the harvesters to deliberately drop ears of barley in the fields so that she can gather them. At the end of the day, Ruth threshes her grain and returns to the city; she tells Naomi all the events of the day and learns from her mother-in-law that her generous protector is in fact related to the family. God's mercy has taken care of things very well. As a close relative — though the text does not specify to what degree they are related — Boaz may, according to the law, exercise protection, as a trustee, over the property of the deceased; he may buy back property which may have been sold out of necessity, and also marry the deceased relative's widow, in this case, Ruth. For this reason, and also to avoid possible ill-treatment from others elsewhere, Naomi encourages Ruth to continue to go to the fields owned by Boaz until the end of the harvest.

Naomi, who now considers herself almost as Ruth's own mother, feels the time has come for Ruth to remarry and make her integration into the Hebrew community complete. With this objective in mind, Naomi suggests, exactly as would be expected of the mother of a young daughter, a plan to achieve this aim. The object of her designs is, of course, Boaz, a rich, pious, good man, who is also a relative of Ruth's deceased husband. Naomi knows, as the well-informed woman she is, that Boaz will sleep near the threshing floor that night. The barley, once harvested, was beaten with special pitchforks and pickaxes conceived with the purpose of separating the grain from the stalks, and night was often the best time for this job with the light evening breeze that made the work easier. Taking advantage of this favorable circumstance, Ruth bathes and, perfumed, puts on a veil that is particularly becoming. Then, as also suggested by Naomi, she waits for Boaz to fall asleep and lays down at his feet. Ruth's behavior may seem calculated to us, but her actions, though guided by a specific purpose, have nothing immoral about them: they are only meant to obtain Boaz's benevolence and protection, to ensure the presence of a man in the family, represented by Naomi and Ruth, who find themselves without any moral or material support.

The text tells us that Boaz is "euphoric" that evening and that after a hard day's work and a hearty meal he immediately falls asleep. In the middle of the night he realizes a woman is sleeping at his feet and asks who she is. "I am Ruth, your servant!" she answers, and begs him to grant her his protection and redeem his right, as a close relative of her deceased husband, to marry her. Boaz agrees without hesitation and spreads part of his coat over her, a symbol which even today in the Muslim world indicates a man's intentions to marry the widow of a close relative. He then praises Ruth's virtuousness, the fact that she has not been tempted by an irresponsible marriage with any young man but has preferred to turn to a mature and dependable member of her adoptive family. Once again, Boaz asks God to bless Ruth and reward her for her devotion. The only obstacle to their union is the existence of a closer

(*opposite page*)

Willem Drost, *Ruth Demonstrates Her Fidelity to Naomi*

When Naomi prepares to leave Moab to return to Israel, her homeland from where she emigrated with her husband and two sons now deceased, her young Moabite daughter-in-law, Ruth, insists upon following her at all costs.

Portaels, ***Ruth***

This portrait, which idealizes the biblical heroine, reflects the mood of the Book that bears her name. Elsewhere in the Old Testament, however, we encounter xenophobic echoes, for example, as regards the Phoenician Jezebel.

relation than Boaz who has priority over him in the matter, and Boaz decides to sound out this relative's intentions the very next day.

The next morning, Boaz gets up early to avoid any prying eyes that might see Ruth sleeping at his feet. He does not leave her, however, without showing his attachment and generosity to her by placing six measures of grain by her side which she takes back to Naomi. The latter, once informed of what has taken place the night before, feels optimistic about the outcome of the affair. Meanwhile Boaz, at the very busy and crowded city gates, sees his relative who possesses the right to marry Ruth. In the presence of ten elders of the city who are asked to serve as witnesses — this is, in fact, a legal matter — Boaz questions the other relative in a direct and determined tone about his intentions. First of all, the land formerly owned by Naomi's husband must be bought back so that it remains, in one way or another, in the family. The man responds that he is willing to do this. However, Boaz adds, this acquisition also implies that the relative agree to take Ruth as his wife, not so much out of a legal obligation but rather a moral one, in view of the virtuous sacrifices the Moabite has made. Under these conditions, however, not wanting to jeopardize his own patrimony, the man renounces his right to marry Ruth and instead offers Boaz the opportunity of replacing him. In a symbolic gesture, he removes his sandal and gives it to Boaz to ratify their agreement.

Before the people who act as witnesses, Boaz promises to buy back the property that had belonged to Elimelech, Chilion, and Mahlon, and to marry Ruth the Moabite to "raise up the name of the deceased upon his inheritance, so that his name will not be severed from that of his brothers nor from the gate of his city." The elders and all the people approve of his words and express the hope that Ruth will follow in the footsteps of Rachel, Jacob's favorite wife and the mother of Joseph and Benjamin; and Leah, Jacob's first wife, mother of Reuben, Simeon, Levi, Judah, Issachar, Zebulon, and Dinah, the two women who established the House of Israel, and that she will also give birth to many descendants.

Soon after their marriage, Boaz and Ruth conceive a son, Obed ("servant [of God]"), to Naomi's great joy, who sees in him her consolation and support in old age. Obed in turn will have a son, Jesse, father of the great David, king of Israel. In this way, Ruth, the foreigner, becomes a predecessor of this illustrious figure and an important link in the history of the chosen people. The Book of Ruth closes with these genealogical details and leaves it up to the reader to fill in the rest of Ruth's life, spent by the side of her husband, Boaz, in Bethlehem, where she dies.

What, in fact, was the editor's real motive in narrating this pleasant experience of peaceful co-existence between the Hebrew people and a Moabite in the Book of Ruth? Was its intention solely to give added weight to David's genealogy who, in the Gospel according to Saint Matthew, also figures as Ruth's descendant? It is actually unknown whether the final genealogical verses of the Book of Ruth formed part of the original text or whether they were a later addition, but in any case they do not seem to be sufficient justification for this tale, a short work it is true, but nevertheless one rich in events and profound moral significance. Ruth demonstrates admirable loyalty to her "adoptive" family, including the deceased, to whom she appears to want to remain faithful at all costs. All the characters in the Book of Ruth impress us by their benevolence, faithfulness, generosity. Apart from Ruth, we note her mother-in-law Naomi, strong and courageous; Naomi's other daughter-in-law, Orpah, a Moabite too, but also willing to leave for Israel with Naomi; Boaz, welcoming and attentive. Idealized or not, they are examples of a gentle humanity that greatly contrast with the figures of the bloody and cruel episodes that punctuate the Book of Judges, which immediately precedes the Book of Ruth in the biblical canon. Ruth is the antithesis of the false Delilah, a Philistine and therefore also a foreigner, or the cold and cruel Giaele who murders her host. Though Deborah may be famous in the Old Testament for her ardent patriotism and charisma, she is very far from embodying the feminine ideal of the period, a period which most likely recognized in Ruth the qualities of the preferred model: devotion towards the family, attachment to her deceased husband, and the spirit of self-sacrifice and hard work.

The choice of a foreign heroine, moreover a woman who comes from a nation often hostile in its relations with Israel, must have met some specific objective which overrode any concern for historical truth. In fact, the editor of the Book of Ruth does little to try to depict the epoch with realism. The only chronological detail it contains appears in the opening of the narrative ("in the days of the Judges") and is, to say the least, rather vague. No Judge's name is mentioned, no synchronism, only a general backdrop to quickly orient the reader. The aim, therefore, is not to give a first-hand account of the period of the Judges nor of the life of a presumed ancestor of King David, but rather to relate the simple story of an encounter, in all its freshness and spontaneity, between the Israelites and a foreigner, and to show by this example that peaceful co-existence is possible. The fact that Ruth is a foreigner is therefore an essential factor to understanding the message contained in this Book. The text heavily stresses Ruth's Moabite extraction and her considerable sacrifice in accepting to leave her country, its customs, its gods, and her own family. But our heroine goes even further: she fully integrates herself into Israelite society by marrying Boaz and giving him a son and, of course, she fully embraces the religion of Israel. In this respect, a comparison with the Book of Esther will give us further insights for deeper reflection. Esther is a Jewish woman at the court of Persia who becomes the wife of the very powerful local king, Assuerus. She nevertheless maintains her cultural and religious identity; she refuses to renounce her faith and continues to worship Yahweh. At one point she even risks her life and proves her attachment to her own people by saving them from a terrible massacre. Ruth, on the other hand, voluntarily undergoes a process of complete acculturation: from the Moabite she was, she becomes an Israelite. Such a view seems to betray an idea of superiority on the part of the Hebrews who have always welcomed the converted with open arms, thus demonstrating even as early as the Old Testament the universal dimension of the Christian faith, later highlighted so well by the New Testament. Ruth is virtually conquered by Yahweh whereas Esther will not renounce this God for anything in the world. Both characters testify to God's unequalled power.

The Book of Ruth may also be considered as an answer to those who, such as the editors of the Laws of Deuteronomy or Ezra and Nehemiah, railed against mixed marriages and contacts between Israelites and foreign populations. Nonetheless, we note that never in the Book of Ruth does the editor adopt a polemical tone to take a distance from certain xenophobic attitudes of the time. Perhaps instead of an elaborate defense of his ideas, he preferred a lively and pleasant narrative of positive life experiences which, more than any eloquent speeches, demonstrate the validity of inter-ethnic contacts.

In conclusion, behind an everyday story of a foreign woman who finds a new country, we read the theological message of its editor in all its simplicity and magnitude: divine providence helps those who are good and leads them to happiness; life, of course, has its moments of suffering and pain, grief, famine, poverty, but it also offers, to those who know how to find the right path, great satisfactions. Without exaggerated pessimism, without extreme glorification, the humble Book of Ruth conveys a message of wisdom and balance, marked by the seal of divine benevolence.

Medieval miniature, *Ruth and Boaz in the Fields*

Kind and generous, placed in an idyllic rural setting, the characters of the Book of Ruth represent a gentle humanity in striking contrast with the protagonists of the countless cruel and bloody episodes related in many of the Books of the Old Testament.

SAMUEL

The "Man of God"

Loved by his Lord was Samuel,
Prophet of the Lord, he founded the royalty.
He anointed the princes to lead his people.

Ecclesiasticus, 46:13

The two Books which bear Samuel's name are, in fact, only partially devoted to the life of the great prophet who lived in the period probably around 1040 B. C. This period is marked by the transition between the epoch of the Judges, which was discussed in relation to Samson, and the monarchy, whose founding is closely associated with the holy figure of Samuel. In addition to Samuel's story, these two books also cover the lives of Saul and David, the first two kings of Israel, with the figure of Solomon subsequently treated in the first Book of Kings. The belief that these works were written by Samuel, of course, grew out of a later tradition without any historical foundation.

Samuel's father, a member of the tribe of Ephraim, has two wives: Penennah, who has given him several sons, and Hannah, apparently barren, who despite her husband's love for her is the victim of her rival's constant mockery. As he does every year, this man, Elkanah, makes a pilgrimage to the great sanctuary at Shiloh to offer a sacrifice. His wives receive, as is their due, a part of the meat from the sacrifice, but Hannah, because of her sterility, weeps and refuses to eat. Then, in a surge of optimism and confidence in the Lord, she makes a special prayer vowing that if God blesses her with a son, she will devote the child to the life of a Nazirite. The story of Samuel's birth presents obvious similarities to the birth of Samson, who was also destined to be a Nazirite, a special state of dedication to God which implies various forms of abstinence and the observance of certain rules, for example forbidding the shaving or cutting of one's hair. Here, the setting of the event is the great sanctuary at Shiloh, religious center of the cult of Yahweh Sebaot, or "Yahweh of the Armies," the God who leads Israel's troops into battle, notably against the Philistines, and who is also the omnipotent commander of the celestial armies. According to one tradition of priestly inspiration, once the Israelite penetration into Canaanite territory had been accomplished, Joshua left the Ark in Shiloh where it was later carried off by the Philistines during combat. The Ark was eventually recovered, though it was never to be returned to the sanctuary. This was also the site where Joshua distributed the newly conquered territories of Canaan to the various tribes. Shiloh, therefore, represented a particularly important center in the holy history of Israel, if only for a brief period, serving as a gathering place under the aegis of Yahweh, the symbol of the unity and faith which Samuel was called upon to perpetuate. It might be noted, however, that excavations of the modern site at Shiloh (Khirbet Selun, 19 kilometers south of Nablus) have not to-date yielded any traces of this sanctuary.

Several months after the visit to Shiloh, Hannah gives birth to Samuel ("his name is God") whom, once he is weaned, his mother takes back to the holy place, for as promised, he will be dedicated to serve God for the rest of his life. There, his mother sings a hymn to God's limitless power, attesting her faith in his omnipotence and omniscence, and then leaving the child in Shiloh, she returns home alone to Ramah, her village. Favored by God's benediction, she is blessed with five more children, three sons and two daughters. Meanwhile, at the sanctuary in Shiloh, the priest Eli's sons constantly violate the rules of the cult of Yahweh, eating the meat set aside for sacrifices and trying to seduce the women sent to the sanctuary to watch over the Ark. They scornfully disregard their father's remonstrances until finally God himself manifests himself to Eli through an oracle, announcing that the complete destruction of his family is imminent and that Eli will be replaced by a more faithful priest, worthy of serving Yahweh.

One day when Samuel is asleep in the temple where the holy Ark is kept, Yahweh calls his name. Believing it is Eli calling him, Samuel goes twice to the priest only to be sent back again. On the third time, Eli realizes that it is the Lord calling Samuel's name and he advises him to wait for the next time and then to show his willingness to receive the divine message. The Lord then announces to Samuel that he intends to carry out his terrible threats to punish Eli and his sons for their disrespect to God. The next day, Samuel tells Eli of the divine revelation and the priest declares himself ready to receive the Lord's judgement. Samuel's reputation and popularity, meanwhile, have been growing day by day and all of Israel sees him as Yahweh's spokesman.

As in the days of the Judges, particularly in Samson's time, the Philistines are Israel's greatest threat. After one particularly devastating defeat suffered by the Israelites, the elders propose removing the Ark from the sanctuary at Shiloh and taking it into battle with them to hasten their deliverance from the Philistines. Eli's two sons, Hophni and Phineas, accompany the precious object to the Israelite camp while the Philistines, warned of the arrival of the Ark, tremble in fear, but are still intent on going into battle. Launching a new offensive, they massacre the Israelite army and carry off the Ark. It is during this battle that both of Eli's sons are killed. One soldier, who manages to escape, announces the dreadful news to Eli, now 98 years old and in failing health. Eli, stunned, realizing that his sons are dead and the Ark captured, reels from his chair and, hitting the back of his head against the door, dies instantly. Here the text tells us that he had "judged Israel," meaning, that he had been its religious, moral,

Nicolas Poussin, *Plague in Ashdod*

During the days of Samuel, the Philistines capture the Holy Ark and take it to the temple of their national god, Dagon, in Ashdod. The next day, the statue is found prostrate before the Ark, and the day after that it is headless and without hands. Then, as punishment, Yahweh afflicts the city with a plague.

and political authority for forty years. Phineas' wife, whose pregnancy has almost reached its term, dies from shock after first giving birth to a son, Ichabod.

Meanwhile, the Philistines take the holy Ark to the temple of Dagon, their national god's center of worship in Ashdod. The next morning, however, the Philistines are struck dumb with amazement: the statue of Dagon is prostrate before the Ark! The next day, the same scene occurs, except this time the statue is headless and has no hands. Shortly after, Yahweh sends a plague to punish the inhabitants of Ashdod. The Ark is then removed from the temple of Dagon and sent to Gath, then to Ekron, but at each stop the people witness the same deadly effects. After seven months, the Philistine chieftains decide to return the Ark to Israel and, upon the advice of their priests and seers, they also include five pieces of gold fashioned into the form of buboes and five gold mice (the number five standing for the five city states of the Philistine confederation) in the hope that these gifts will rid them of the plague. The Ark is then placed on a brand-new chariot drawn by two prize cows. Completely on its own, the procession immediately heads towards Beth Shemesh, a clear sign that the Ark is meant to return to the Promised Land and to the chosen people.

The recovery of the Ark is celebrated with great rejoicing, the chariot completely dismantled and the cows sacrificed in a burnt offering. But Yahweh punishes the inhabitants of Beth Shemesh when they dare to open the holy Ark to look inside: of the fifty thousand inhabitants of the city, seventy will die. The Ark is then taken to Kiriath Rearm, to the house of a man named Abinadab whose son, Eleazar, is consecrated to God and designated guardian of the Ark. Twenty years will elapse before the people of Israel express their desire to return to the faith of Yahweh. This comes about when, in the hope of being saved from the Philistines, Samuel asks the population to abandon the worship of all foreign gods, the Baals and Astartes, the supreme Canaanite divinities, and to serve only the God of Israel. At Mizpah, a sanctuary located on the heights north of Jerusalem, the people gather before Samuel as he prays to God on their behalf and becomes Judge of Israel. The Philistines then attempt another attack against Israel, but Yahweh hears Samuel's pleas and those of his people. The Philistines are repulsed, humiliated, and defeated, so badly in fact, that they

Panel in faience, *The Fall of the Idol of Dagon and the Epidemic of Plagues in Ashdod*

There is an obvious connection between this composition and the famous painting by Poussin in that both illustrate the charismatic power of Samuel, the true precursor of the Israelite dynasties.

will not undertake any other attacks against Israel for the entire period that Samuel remains Judge.

Of the years immediately following this event we know very little. The biblical tale leaps from this point in Samuel's life to his old age when the figure of Saul is destined to cross his path, this being the man who will become the chief protagonist in Israel's history. Samuel, however, from behind the scenes and until his death, and even after death, nevertheless makes his presence felt and has a decisive influence on the fate of the first king of Israel. We will therefore encounter him again periodically in the story of Saul's reign, which might be considered in many ways an unfortunate period.

SAUL

The Accursed King

Only by myself, and by myself alone (miserable king),
and by myself I fear nothing.

V. ALFIERI, *Saul*

Samuel, as we have seen, represents a personality, prophet, and Judge of great stature in the history of Israel. Having become too old to lead his people, he hands over the reins of power to his sons who, however, are unable to live up to their task and to the greatness of their illustrious father. The people's desire for a monarchical power to rule over Israel therefore makes itself increasingly felt. At first Samuel is reticent, but prompted by Yahweh who sees in the people's demand for a king another form of infidelity to their God, Samuel speaks to the people and warns them of the dangers and disadvantages of a monarchy. In this discourse the king is described as a despotic tyrant to whom the people are only cannon fodder, a toiling labor force in fields and palaces, or a source of heavy tithes. Turning a deaf ear to these warnings, however, Israel resolutely reiterates its desire for a king. In reality, this story in the first Book of Samuel, which deals with the establishment of the Israelite monarchy, reveals traces of two opposing movements. The first is supported by the anti-monarchists, who contend that Yahweh is the unique sovereign and the only power capable of choosing the people's leaders, as in the case of the Judges when they are invested by the divine spirit. The other movement is made up of the pro-monarchists, for whom the various kings, and above all David, are the chosen ones and Yahweh's representatives on earth. For this reason the narrative is sometimes contradictory, on some occasions praising the monarchy and at other times criticizing it.

Fate then leads Saul to Samuel. Tall and handsome, Saul belongs to the tribe of Benjamin. One day, looking for his father's lost asses, Saul arrives near Samuel's town of Ramah. He learns that a "man of God," a prophet, lives in the vicinity and decides to visit him. When Samuel sees him approaching, he knows immediately that this is the man whose arrival God has announced, and whom the Lord has instructed Samuel to anoint as ruler over Israel, the man destined to deliver the chosen people from the Philistines. Samuel therefore invites Saul to take part in a sacrificial meal and reassures him that his father's animals are safe. That night Saul sleeps at the prophet's house and at dawn Samuel relates Yahweh's revelation to him. Even before speaking, however, he anoints Saul with the oil of consecration and then, embracing him, takes his leave after having revealed God's plans and his destiny to become Israel's ruler.

As foretold by Samuel, Saul is invested with divine charisma and begins to prophesy. Soon after, Samuel, yielding to popular demand, gathers all the tribes of Israel together and holds a draw of lots by which the first king of Israel will be chosen. As it turns out, of course, Saul is designated king, his anointing by Samuel apparently having remained a secret. As observed on other occasions — for example, in the Book of Joshua — a draw of lots is a means by which Yahweh manifests his will. The people cheer enthusiastically and Samuel then enumerates the royal prerogatives before setting them down in writing, after which he dismisses the assembly and the people return home.

The first military event in which Saul participates involves the Ammonites who lay siege to the city of Jabesh. Though the Israelites surrender and agree to conclude a pact, the Ammonites still threaten to gouge the right eyes out of all the city's inhabitants as a symbol of Israel's humiliation. Deeply shocked, Saul raises a force of three hundred thousand Israelites and thirty thousand men from Judah and inflicts a

Silver Byzantine goblet, *Samuel, Saul, and David*

The destinies of these three personages are closely interwoven. They belong to the transition period between the days of the Judges and the monarchical regime of which David is the most perfect expression.

Medieval miniature, ***The anointing of Saul by Samuel***

The Old Testament, as is often the case, gives two versions of the anointing of Saul though in both stories this act is accomplished by the great Samuel.

crushing defeat upon the cruel Ammonites. Having thus won the unanimous support of his people, Saul is again proclaimed king. Here again, we have two different versions of Saul's accession to the throne, quite skillfully reconciled to form a single story, though not without some incoherencies and contradictions.

Samuel realizes that the moment has come to step down from his functions and he addresses the people in a farewell speech that marks the transfer of his powers to Saul. As in the days of Moses and Joshua, Samuel retraces the main phases of Israel's history and of the Covenant with Yahweh. Not forgetting to point out, with the people's full agreement, the integrity he has shown in the exercising of his powers, he solemnly reminds the people to remain faithful to their God, and promises his continued mediation in favor of Israel.

Thus does Saul's reign truly begin, most probably in the years 1030-1020 B. C., the first monarch in the history of Israel. Thirty years old when his rule begins, Saul will reign for twenty years. Effectively seconded by Jonathan, his son, he wins a victory over the Philistines but then runs into difficulty against these same enemies at Michmash. For a rather obscure reason, apparently for having offered a sacrifice to Yahweh in Samuel's absence, he is severely reproached by the latter who predicts his reign's imminent and dramatic end. In the meantime, skirmishes between Saul's troops and the Philistines are increasingly frequent. On one of these occasions, Jonathan and his equerry massacre an entire unit of Philistines and this triggers a general battle that eventually results in a resounding Israelite victory. Saul forbids his men to touch food until nightfall, but his own son, unaware of the fast proclaimed by his father, eats some honey, a very serious act of disobedience which has disastrous consequences. The same holds true for the men who, after having repulsed the Philistines, freely help themselves to the abandoned livestock and eat the meat, with its fresh blood, though fully aware that according to the ritual obligations contained in the Book of Leviticus, these animals are to be sacrificed to God.

Intending to deal a final blow to the Philistines, Saul then prepares a nocturnal attack, but when a priest questions Yahweh about the outcome of the future battle, he receives no answer. To expiate the wrong they have done, Saul declares he is prepared to sacrifice his own son who, again in a draw of lots, has been singled out as responsible for God's refusal to answer. The people, however, intervene and defend Jonathan to whom, they assert, the victory over the Philistines is principally due, most certainly with God's benediction. Jonathan is therefore spared and Saul decides against pursuing the Philistines.

Over the subsequent years Saul combats successfully against all of Israel's enemies, but these victories are not enough to win back God's favor. Worse yet, Yahweh, in a vision to Samuel, expresses his regret at ever having chosen Saul as Israel's king, reproaching him indirectly for not having respected the rule that all living creatures who are enemies of Yahweh, including animals, are

to be annihilated. Questioned by Samuel, Saul tries to defend himself by claiming that the best livestock has been spared only to be offered in sacrifice to the Lord, and that in so doing he has only complied with the wishes of the majority. However his protests are to no avail. Samuel pronounces the divine sentence in answer to his disobedience: "You have rejected the word of the Lord and the Lord has rejected you as king over Israel." In spite of his good intentions and constant devotion to Israel and to his God, Saul's destiny is thus doomed in a seemingly very arbitrary or at least unfathomable way, as was true in the cases of Cain and Esau as well, this in order to emphasize once again the supremacy of divine purpose.

Saul tries in vain to prove his innocence and pleads for forgiveness. Samuel decides at the last minute not to withdraw his support, most certainly of great importance to the stability of the monarchy, and agrees to appear with Saul one last time in public. However this occasion will, in fact, be their final encounter for a short while later Samuel retires to his residence in Ramah where after some years he dies. A different version, however, which appears a few chapters afterwards mentions an episode that brings Samuel and Saul back together again.

Samuel continues, in the meantime, to be the mediator through whom Yahweh designates the next sovereign destined to lead Israel. God sends Samuel to Jesse's family in Bethlehem where he is told to anoint one of Jesse's sons whom the Lord will identify during a sacrificial ceremony. After each of Jesse's seven sons are presented to him one by one, Samuel meets the youngest son whom he finds alone tending his flocks. It is this young shepherd who will be the chosen one, for God probes deep into men's hearts to judge their worthiness and is little concerned with physical stature. David is therefore anointed in the presence of his brothers and invested with the spirit of Yahweh, though David's "official" anointing will not take place until much later.

During this time, Saul is grappling with an "evil spirit" that seems to have possessed his mind, and to sooth his fears and anxieties a musician is engaged. As it turns out, this is David, who soon becomes Saul's equerry and confidant. As for outside threats, they still persist with the Philistine army that, under the leadership of a giant named Goliath, measuring a full six cubits and one span, or almost twenty feet, challenges the Israelite troops led by Saul himself. Displaying his incredible force, Goliath dares any Israelite champion to pit his strength against his own. If the Philistine giant is defeated, Israel may reduce its enemies to slavery, and vice versa in the case of Goliath's victory. For forty days, Goliath renews his offer without one opponent willing to take up the challenge. Now, it so happens that three of David's brothers are in the Israelite army while David, the youngest, has remained at home to tend the flocks (a detail that again denotes the existence of variations within the same story since David, according to the previous chapter, should already have left Bethlehem for Saul's court). Whatever the case may be, David is sent to the "front" by his father to deliver fresh supplies to his brothers. This happens just when Goliath renews, for the last time, his unusual proposal to take on one of the Israelites in single combat. No one seems willing to step forward, not even when Saul promises that the courageous man who dares confront Goliath will be showered with riches and receive the king's daughter in marriage. Brought before Saul, David says he is prepared to take up the challenge, but Saul, incredulous, can hardly believe that this young shepherd, totally lacking in military experience, stands a chance. David, however, describes how he has fought against bears and lions to protect his flocks and says he is confident and trusts in Yahweh's help. Wearing Saul's full armor, with breast-plate and weapons, David, however, is unable to walk and therefore prefers to go to meet Goliath armed only with his shepherd's rod, a sling, and five stones, much to the amusement of the cruel giant who curses him. David then proclaims in a loud and clear voice that the source of his strength lies in God and then, taking his sling, he shoots a first stone that violently strikes Goliath on the forehead. The giant immediately collapses heavily to the ground and David, climbing upon his enemy's body, seizes Goliath's sword and pierces him through the side. Then, after decapitating the body, he carries the giant's head to Jerusalem. Awestruck, the Philistines try to escape, but Saul's armies pursue them and massacre their soldiers in great numbers. David is then taken to Saul to whom he reveals his identity; during this visit, a deep friendship is born between David and Jonathan, Saul's son, and the two swear to stand by each other until death. At the court, David is successful in everything he undertakes and is ultimately put at the head of the army, much to the satisfaction of the men and the royal ministers.

Jealousy, however, sets Saul against David. The joyous procession which escorts the victorious hero over the Philistines highlights all the more clearly David's merits and kindles the king's rage. First trying to murder his rival with his own hands, Saul then resorts to sending him on dangerous military missions. David's continued successes, however, only serve to add to his popularity, while Saul's fears mount before this charmed rival so manifestly protected by Yahweh. Saul then proposes to give his eldest daughter, Merab, in marriage to David, but the latter hesitates, feeling unworthy of such a great honor. Then, just before the wedding and without any apparent reason, Saul gives Merab in marriage to another man, and Michal, one of the king's other daughters, is promised to David instead, though he remains just as reticent. In fact, Saul's plan is to have David killed in battle and, therefore, as a wedding donation from David he demands one hundred foreskins from the Philistines, convinced that David will fall before his enemies. But much to the contrary, however, for David brings back the one hundred foreskins and wins the hand of Michal who becomes a loving and devoted wife, even further fueling the sovereign's hatred. Now determined to murder David, Saul informs his ministers and his son Jonathan of his intentions. But Jonathan, because of his great love for David, immediately warns his friend of his father's plans and then attempts to dissuade Saul against such an unjustified act. As a result, the king, at least for a while, puts off his plans and calls David back to the court where, by right, he belongs. By now, however, Saul is hopelessly prisoner of a malevolent spirit that has possessed him ever since Yahweh turned away from him. He takes up his lance and tries to kill David, but misses his target. David then truly realizes he must flee as far away as possible from the king. But Saul's envoys follow him, having been commanded to eliminate David at the first opportunity, which is what they would certainly do were it not for Michal who warns her husband of the danger and urges him to go into hiding. David takes refuge in Ramah, at Samuel's house, and tells the prophet of Saul's attempts to have him murdered. Continuing on his blind rampage, Saul despatches his emissaries

(*opposite page*)

Jean-Jacques Lagrenée, *David Insults Goliath*

Almost twenty feet tall and brandishing his incredible strength, the Philistine Goliath challenges any Israelite to meet him in single combat. For forty days he renews his offer without finding one willing opponent. Finally the young David accepts the challenge and despite his slight stature defeats the giant in one blow.

Nicolas Poussin, ***David's Triumph***

After beheading the giant, David is paraded through the streets of Jerusalem. However, jealousy sets Saul against him; the triumphant procession highlights all too clearly David's qualities and the king in a fury decides to eliminate him.

three times over with orders to kill David. But these men, invested by Yahweh's spirit, instead of accomplishing their mission suddenly begin to prophesy with Samuel. Then Saul himself goes to capture David, but suddenly transformed into a prophet himself, he remains prostrate on the ground, naked, a full day and night in Ramah.

During a secret meeting with Jonathan, David tries in vain to comprehend Saul's motives. When the two friends part, Jonathan assures David of his loyal protection. Although the previous chapter already describes David's flight, the episode is taken up again here, as if David had never left Saul's court.

Jonathan, informed of his father's decision to murder David, tells his friend, in hiding somewhere in the surrounding country, that he must flee and after a last warm embrace the two friends part. David first escapes to Nob on Mount Scopus, east of Jerusalem, where a local priest named Ahimelech, gives him some bread and a sword; then, passing through the kingdom of Gath, he pretends to be mad in order not to be recognized. He stops for a time in a cave at Adullam where he sees his family and is joined by a force of four hundred men. After entrusting the members of his family to the protection of the king of Moab, David flees to Judah. Meanwhile, Saul, advised of David's stay in Nob, orders the death of all the priests in the region, no less than eighty-five men, guilty of having helped David. Then, the king destroys every living creature in Nob, women, children, the aged; only Ahimelech's son manages to escape the massacre and goes to tell David of Saul's terrible vengeance.

David, helped by the Lord, then victoriously leads his troops against the Philistines at Keilah but threatened by Saul, is forced to escape with his men to the Ziph desert where Jonathan goes to see him. There, Jonathan confirms David's destiny to replace Saul as king, and renews his own promise of unfailing support. The Ziph inhabitants tell Saul that David has found refuge in the desert and the king, hoping to surprise and kill him, arrives, but David has already fled with his men to the Maon desert. Saul pursues him, surrounds him, but is then urgently called back to his own kingdom, under attack by the Philistines. David is thus spared from the confrontation at the last minute, but not for long. Saul's attacks resume soon after, this time in the region of the Engadi wilderness. There, chance has it that Saul finds himself at the mercy of David who, nevertheless, decides to spare him. For, Saul is still the king, the one chosen by Yahweh to rule Israel, David's revered master. Moved by this noble act, Saul repents for his unjust treatment of David and, more convinced than ever that this man is the future king of Israel, he makes David swear that he will not put his descendants to death nor eradicate Saul's name from the memory of his people. Thus a truce is established between Saul and David.

During this period Samuel dies and is greatly mourned by all the people who bury him near his home in Ramah. One day, David learns that a certain Nabal, a rich livestock breeder, mean and violent, married to a certain Abigail, a gentle pretty woman, is in Carmel shearing his sheep. David sends ten men to ask him for an offering of wool, but Nabal refuses. In the past, when Nabal's herds had crossed the desert, David and his men, helped by the shepherds, had always protected him, which was why David was now making this request. Learning of Nabal's refusal, David, with his four hundred men sets off for Carmel. Abigail, informed of their arrival by a slave, loads a donkey with bread, wine, meat, grain, and fruit and without saying a word to her husband goes out to meet David. She bows down before him, aware that this man is Israel's future ruler, and begs him to accept her offering, which David does, reassuring her that he no longer intends to seek revenge for Nabal's affront. Abigail returns home and relates the event to her husband who, greatly shocked, dies ten days later. Rejoicing over the punishment God has

inflicted on Nabal, David marries Abigail, who becomes his second wife after Ahinoam, while Michal, Saul's daughter, has been remarried to a man from Gallim.

As already related — this chapter is most likely a copy of the previous one — Saul is told where David is hiding, but David, having discovered the place where the king is sleeping, goes that very night intending to kill him. Once there, however, he decides to spare Saul's life out of respect for God's chosen ruler, confident that divine plans will see to Saul's end when the time comes. Nevertheless, as proof of his loyalty to the king, David carries off Saul's sword and his water jug, then, from a nearby height, heckles Saul and questions him on the reasons for his hostility. Here again Saul admits to his faults and promises David respectful treatment in the future. After which, each man returns home in peace.

But David has no illusions about Saul's commitment. To escape from him, David sees no other alternative but to seek refuge among the Philistines, at the court of Achish, King of Gath. The latter entrusts the city of Ziklag to David, located near the Philistine border northeast of Beersheba, and for a year and four months David and his troops serve the king of Gath as faithful vassals. In his campaigns under the Philistine king, David carefully chooses to wage combat against Israel's traditional enemies, continuing therefore to help his own people. Then the Philistines launch a massive attack against Israel. David, having been appointed the king's bodyguard, sides with Achish. Saul also mobilizes all of his troops but cannot overcome his growing fear in the face of this combat. Plagued by Yahweh's continued silence, Saul disregards the fact that soothsayers and necromancers, that is, those who question the dead to predict the future, are forbidden by official religion, and goes incognito one night to consult a famous necromancer, the witch of Endor. The woman at first is hesitant, afraid of being put to death, fully aware that necromancy as well as the worship of the dead are strictly prohibited practices. The Old Testament, in fact, considers the realm of death and the deceased as impure, marked by the absence of Yahweh. In Sheol, the biblical otherworld, the dead are abandoned to their unfortunate fate, forsaken by their God who is exclusively concerned with the living; any contact with the world of the dead, therefore, being absolutely forbidden. The repeated mention of this interdict in the Old Testament, however, leads us to believe that practices related to the worship of the dead and necromancy were in fact extremely popular among the people. It must have been very difficult to accept the idea that close kin were to be completely forgotten and abandoned after death, particularly when Canaanite culture, contrary to official Hebrew tradition, accorded so much importance to the worship of ancestors and the dead who were considered beneficial entities capable of bestowing force and good health on those who turned to them. Whatever the case may be, the witch finally rouses the spirit of Samuel, who has only recently died. Samuel appears and immediately recognizes the necromancer's client as Saul and then complains for having been disturbed. Samuel's spirit then confirms God's sentence: as Saul's punishment for his failings, Israel, in the impending battle will fall into the hands of the Philistines, and Saul and his sons will be sent from the world of the living to join Samuel.

Silver Byzantine goblets, ***Scenes from the life of David (David marries Michal; David meets Goliath; David and Jonathan; David slays a lion; David slays a bear)***

Almost all the stories in the Old Testament concerning David bear the stamp of an apologia. Loyal, sensitive, righteous, David is God's chosen one, founder of the kingdom of Israel and the ideal king, and also Yahweh's partner in a covenant destined to be renewed through the person of the Messiah, the "son of David."

Bruegel, ***The Suicide of Saul or The Battle of Mount Gilboa***

On Mount Gilboa a tragic battle ensues between Philistines and Israelites. Among the slain are Saul's sons and the king himself who, wounded by Philistine archers, throws himself upon his own sword.

Guido Reni, ***David and Abigail***

Married to Nabal, a greedy and selfish livestock breeder, Abigail bows down before David, whose wife she becomes after the death of her husband.

Filled with terror, Saul sees death inexhorably approaching. In the Philistine camp, meanwhile, the people grow more and more distrustful of David, this Hebrew who, at the height of the battle, could easily turn against the Philistines. Despite Achish's protests, David is kept from participating in the combat. Returning to Ziklag with his men, David discovers the city has been pillaged by the Amalekites. All the women, including David's two wives, and children have been taken prisoner. With the help of an Egyptian slave, David finds his enemies and massacres all except four hundred young men who manage to flee. David then sees to the fair distribution of the immense booty thus acquired and even sends a portion to the elders in Judah, with whom he has maintained good relations.

The next day, then, on Mount Gilboa a tragic battle ensues between Philistines and Israelites. The dead are too numerous to count and among them are Saul's sons, including Jonathan. Saul himself, wounded by Philistine archers, in a desperate act, as Ajax during the Trojan War, throws himself upon his own sword and kills himself. Without slackening their pace, the Philistines seize all the neighboring territories abandoned by the fleeing Israelites. The next day, the Philistines behead Saul's body and strip it of its armor. The two trophies are exhibited to the Philistines and Saul's weapons are then donated to the temple of Astarte while his body and those of his sons are exhibited on the walls of Beth Shan, the present Beisan. A commando unit made up of inhabitants from Jabesh, a city that had once been saved by Saul, goes at night to Beisan to remove the bodies of the dead king and his sons. They burn them according to accepted ritual in Jabesh where the remains are then properly buried under a tamarisk. Thus Saul disappears from the scene, a just king, devoted to his people, chosen by God and then rejected and even "accursed," whose life was destined to unfold in the shadow of the great David.

DAVID

The Model King

Just as the fat is set apart in sacrifice,
So was David among the sons of Israel.

Ecclesiasticus, 47:2

Indeed, as we have seen, just as the destinies of Samuel and Saul are inextricably interwoven, so David's presence in the biblical narrative overlaps with the reign of Saul, as if David is, in fact, just waiting to be called by God to finally assume the position destined to him. It is true that David holds a very special place in the history of Israel and that he will forever remain the model of the great king. The second Book of Samuel opens with the story of his reign and is entirely devoted to this great moment in the adventure of the chosen people.

It is in Ziklag that David is informed of the death of Saul and his sons. Contrary to the events in the last chapters of the first Book of Samuel, we are told here that the king, afflicted by severe dizzy spells, is killed by a young Amalekite passing near the battlefield. The young man runs to David to announce the news, taking with him as proof of his story Saul's diadem and chain. David and his people mourn the sovereign and have the man put to death, the one who dared raise his hand against Yahweh's chosen one. David then composes an elegy to Saul and Jonathan preserved in written form in an anthology entitled, *The Book of the Righteous*, today unfortunately lost to us. "The heroes have fallen! Their arms of war have perished!" laments David, particularly mourning the loss of his cherished friend Jonathan. Urged by Yahweh, David then goes to Hebron with his two wives and his troops and is officially anointed king of Judah. Meanwhile, the commander-in-chief of the army, Abner, has already designated Saul's son, Ishbosheth, as king of Israel and this gives rise to an open conflict between Judah and Israel, a struggle which will continue for several years and from which David will emerge victorious.

During this period, several children are born to David, six in fact, by his two wives in Hebron. A woman is then the cause of Abner's defection when Ishbosheth accuses him of having seduced the deceased king's concubine. This prompts the powerful general of the Israelite troops to change sides and join David, bringing with him as proof of his good intentions Michal, Saul's daughter, once David's wife but later remarried to another man. Abner also convinces the elders and the people of Israel of the legitimacy of David's claim, Yahweh's chosen one. Abner is just about to rally them all to this cause when, after a peaceful visit to Hebron, he is assassinated by one of David's men, a certain Joab. His brother had been killed by Abner in combat. Learning of Abner's death, David puts a curse on the house of Joab and Abner is buried in Hebron with all the honors due to him. To demonstrate his innocence, David undertakes a fast.

Soon after, it is Ishbosheth who is assassinated by two gang leaders from his entourage. The men behead his body and take the awful trophy to David, who, as he had done in the case of Saul's presumed murderer, has the two men put to death while Ishbosheth is buried in the tomb where Abner's body already rests, in Hebron.

Thus, Judah and Israel, with the unanimous consent of all the tribes, are brought under David's rule, who concludes a pact with the elders and is anointed king of Israel. He is thirty years old at the time, the biblical text tells us, and will reign for forty years. One of the first acts of his unified rule is to take the city of Jerusalem, inhabited by the ancient Jebusites, and its fortress, Zion, which becomes the "City of David," his permanent residence, ideally located between the two kingdoms under his jurisidiction. David's power becomes more and more evident, even abroad, when the king of Tyre, Hiram, sends David cedar, carpenters, and masons to help construct the palace at Jerusalem, now the religious and political capital of the land. This gesture, in fact, will mark the beginning of a very fruitful exchange between Israel and Tyre, which will develop and intensify under the reign of Solomon, as we will see.

In Jerusalem, David takes other wives and concubines who bear him several children, notably Solomon. The peaceful interlude, however, proves to be short-lived. The Philistines renew their atavistic attacks against Israel all the more violently, even threatening Jerusalem itself. However, Yahweh suggests a strategy to David and, with divine support, David dominates his enemies and drives them back to their own territory. It is then that the Ark, after a three-month stop in Gath, is solemnly brought into Jerusalem to the sound of trumpets and cymbals, preceded by David, girded with the holy ephod, a belt of fine linen, as he joyously leads the procession. The Ark is placed in the center of a tent specially intended for the purpose. Shortly after, David makes plans for the construction of a temple to house the Ark, but through the voice of the prophet Nathan, Yahweh, recalling with some nostalgia his past as a nomadic God, tells David that not he, but rather David's son should accomplish this task. God's prophecy goes even further: "It is not you who will give me a house," Yahweh says in essence, "but I who will guarantee the stability and permanence of your house," that is, the line founded by David. Then of David's seed God tells him, "I will be a father for him and he will be my son," a statement that clearly evokes the figure of Christ, David's descendant. In short, contained in this passage we have the first prophetic message of the coming of the Messiah.

Nevertheless, warfare is David's common lot. He challenges the Philistines, then the Moabites, who become his vassals; a prince of the region of Anti-Lebanon, then the Arameans, and many others, accomplishing a meteoric expansion of the kingdom of Israel and dedicating to God all the precious metals taken as booty from his enemies. David extends his generosity to Jonathan's son, in memory of his childhood friend, a certain Mephibosheth, who is crippled and cannot walk. David restores all of Saul's possessions to him and invites Mephibosheth to dine at his table every day.

It is now the Ammonites who stage a revolt. After they insult David's ambassadors sent to their country following the death of their king, Nahash, a faithful and friendly vassal to Israel, hostilities break out and the Arameans, having joined the Ammonites, are also defeated in the joint battle by David's troops. The next year, David's army launches a new campaign against the Arameans in which a certain Uriah, a Hittite mercenary, takes part alongside the Israelite ranks. His wife, a strikingly beautiful woman, is seduced by David in Jerusalem and a child is conceived from this union. David, wishing to marry her, orders the commander-in-chief of the army to send Uriah, her

Medieval miniature, *David and the Musicians*

David, according to tradition, is the author of seventy-four Psalms and many poems. His love for music is emphasized in the Old Testament.

View of Jerusalem

The citadel of Jerusalem, Zion, becomes the "City of David," his permanent residence, but Solomon also greatly contributes to the embellishment of the capital notably by the construction of a magnificent Temple dedicated to Yahweh.

husband, to the front lines and, as David had hoped, this costs Uriah his life. David is thus free to take Uriah's wife as his own. This act, nevertheless, provokes God's strong disapproval. David is told, through the prophet Nathan, that because he has broken the moral code and his personal pact with Yahweh, David will be victim to the same fate he has inflicted on Uriah. However, when David solemnly repents and recognizes how wrong his action was, Yahweh "limits" himself to condemning to death the son born of David's union with Uriah's widow, Bathsheba. Not even seven days go by after the birth of the unfortunate child that the prophecy proves true, but David and Bathsheba conceive a second son, Solomon, whom the Lord favors and who is, according to God's wishes, affectionately called "loved by Yahweh" (Jedidiah). Meanwhile, David's troops have defeated the Ammonites and conquered the capital Rabbah, the present-day Amman, the worship center of the national god, Milcom.

The chapters which follow give a detailed account of the court intrigues that plague the monarchy and in which David's son Absalom plays a main part. First, David's eldest son, Amnon, attracted by his half-sister, the ravishing Tamar, manages, by a clever ploy, to lure her into his room and rapes her. After this, developing an extreme repulsion to her which proves even stronger than his previous passion and desire, he drives her away. She seeks refuge at Absalom's house where her brother advises her to say nothing of her misfortunes, and though this does not keep David from eventually finding out, the king does not intervene, given his great affection for Amnon, his eldest son. Two years later, Absalom, to avenge the affront to his sister Tamar, invites all the king's sons to a banquet and has Amnon assassinated by his servants, after which Absalom flees to Aramean territory leaving David alone to mourn his dead son.

After spending three years in exile, and thanks to a clever initiative by Joab, the commander-in-chief of the army, who presents David with a similar case to judge and thus gets David to admit that the return of Absalom is only fair, Absalom is then called back to Jerusalem. He is ordered, however, to remain in his residence and not to present himself before the king. For two years, Absalom, whose striking good looks the biblical text points out, patiently abides by his father's wishes and finally obtains David's forgiveness. However, immediately after this, by popularity-seeking tactics and loud criticism of his father's judge, Absalom gains remarkable popularity among a certain minority of the population. Under the pretext that he has a sacred vow to fulfill, he goes to Hebron where he proclaims himself king, rallying the support of a great many Israelites. David then decides to flee from his son's threat and goes into

Silver Byzantine goblet,
David Playing a Lyre

Though initially engaged in the service of the king as a musician, David soon becomes Saul's equerry and confidant.

Donatello, ***David (in bronze, right)***

Completed in about 1440, this statue was the first full nude since antiquity. It represents the young shepherd David, in the bloom of youth, with a slightly effeminate body.

Donatello, ***David (in marble, left)***

This statue by Donatello was completed a quarter of a century prior to the David in bronze, it was also destined for the Bargello in Florence.

exile in the desert with his ministers and his people. Leaving the Ark in Jersualem, he wonders if he will ever see it again. He meets many people on his journey: some assure him of their support, others betray him, and he even encounters a member of Saul's family who curses him, but David accepts this and sees in it a sign from God.

Meanwhile, Absalom has occupied Jerusalem and taken over the palace, including the harem quarters where David's concubines live. He then devises a plan to have his father killed and the people brought back to Jerusalem. At the head of his troops, Absalom crosses the Jordan and meets David at Mahanaim. A fierce battle ensues — the biblical text refers to twenty thousand dead — from which David's loyal followers emerge victorious. Absalom, despite David's orders to his men concerning his treatment, is immediately killed and buried upon the battlefield. David is deeply saddened by his death and the victory is overshadowed by the sorrow of his mourning. However Joab, head of the troops and the man who has killed Absalom, comes to shake him out of his grief. Finally David, reproached for giving too much importance to the death of a traitor and not enough to the courage of his people who have risked their lives for their king, goes before the people to celebrate the victory.

The people of Israel and Judah clamor for David's return to Jerusalem, appealing to him to reclaim the throne. During his return, he meets the same people he had passed before, but this time all of them unanimously agree that he is the uncontested king of both Israel and Judah. However, tension still persists within this two-headed hybrid kingdom. A brief uprising led by a certain Sheba from the kingdom of Israel, where he has rallied support, is quickly put down by David's troops, while the kingdom of Judah during this time remains loyal to David.

The biblical text records various episodes for posterity related to David's reign. For example, the brief story of a three-year famine which is brought to an end when the king allows the Gibeonites, a tribe of Amorite origin, to execute seven of Saul's descendants. Saul had wanted to wipe out this people, settled in the territory of Benjamin and bound to Israel by a treaty of vassalage, though Gibeon was the site of an important Yahvist sanctuary. Then, also noted here are: another battle with the Philistines; the text of a hymn almost identical to Psalm 18 attributed to David who is, moreover, according to tradition the author of seventy-four Psalms and many poems; the transcription of David's last words which, as those attributed to Jacob in Genesis and to Moses in Deuteronomy, represent a spiritual "testament;" a list of the most valiant warriors who served David. Then, the details of a census organized under David's initiative and his subsequent punishment by Yahweh who sends a deadly plague over Israel that lasts three days, is followed by the building of an altar to Yahweh to bring it to an end. The second Book of Samuel thus closes with these short and disparate notes, while the end of David's reign and Solomon's accession to the throne open the first Book of Kings.

David, in fact, is now an old man and his son Adonijah, Absalom's brother, as good looking as his elder brother so tragically killed, schemes against David and even eventually proclaims himself king. Some of David's entourage side with Adonijah, but others suggest to Bathsheba, Solomon's mother, that she should claim the rights of succession for her son. David then decides to openly choose his successor and anoints Solomon king. The ceremony is followed by great rejoicing and in Adonijah's camp the men flee, leaving the rebel alone to await his fate. David, however, once again demonstrating his unfailing devotion to his children, calls his son back to Jerusalem and forgives him.

Feeling that death is approaching, David sends for Solomon and counsels him, "Be strong and show yourself a man. Observe the Law and respect Yahweh's will, your God." For, David reminds him, only by obeying the divine Commandments will Yahweh keep the House of David on the throne of Israel. David dies and is buried in Jerusalem after ruling his people for forty years, a truly exceptional reign. Indeed, almost all the stories in the Old Testament concerning David bear the stamp of an unqualified apologia. Loyal, sensitive, righteous, he refuses to take part in the cruelties nevertheless common for his time. David, a name of uncertain etymology, is God's chosen one, Yahweh's partner in a covenant destined to be renewed through the embodiment of the "son of David," the Messiah. Founder of the kingdom of Israel, fervent worshipper of Yahweh, he is the ideal king, the model of the just and pious sovereign.

SOLOMON

The Wise Builder of the Temple

Solomon reigned over days of peace.
God gave him rest
so that he could prepare
a sanctuary for eternity.

Ecclesiasticus, 47:13

When he is still quite young, Solomon succeeds his father David to the throne, and Bathsheba, as queen mother, rules by his side. One of Solomon's first acts as king of Israel is to eliminate his adversaries: his elder brother Adonijah, Joab, the army commander-in-chief who had supported him against Solomon, and Saimei, a member of Saul's family who had once cursed David, though he eventually made up with him, when the great leader was on his way into exile. By this "purge," Solomon consolidates his power putting an end to the internal friction which had plagued the last years of his father's reign.

Solomon, to whom the title of "sage" is attributed, shows himself to be, as his father David, a righteous and pious man and Yahweh hastens to appear to him offering to grant the sovereign anything he needs. But Solomon, given his young age, simply asks God for the wisdom to make him a just ruler and the ability to discern good from evil in the governing of his country. The request greatly pleases Yahweh and he bestows the gifts of wisdom and intelligence upon the young ruler: "Never before was there a king like you, nor will there ever be," and also promises fortune and glory and, finally, tells Solomon that if he remains loyal to the Covenant, he will enjoy a very long life.

Solomon, who to obtain the support of the pharoah of Egypt marries the sovereign's daughter, does in fact become a renowned judge, and the famous "Judgement of Solomon" testifies to this. Two prostitutes who have just given birth go before him; of the two sons they have borne, one has died during the night and each of the two women declares the dead infant was the son of the other woman, each woman therefore claiming to be the mother of the only surviving child. To solve the case, Solomon asks for a sword and proposes to divide the child in two so that each woman may take a half; his objective, in fact, being to reveal the real mother who, moved by her maternal love, will even accept to give up her child to the other woman as long as he is not killed. This is in fact exactly what happens and Solomon is thus able to recognize the real mother's rights over the infant.

Divinely inspired wisdom is a very important feature of Solomon's personality. His spirit is, says the Bible, "as vast as the sands of the sea," and his wisdom "surpasses that of all the sages of the East." Three thousand proverbs and one thousand and five poems are attributed to him. Biblical tradition, in addition, also adds the Song of Songs, the Book of Ecclesiastes and the Wisdom of Solomon, without mentioning a few Psalms. His reputation as a judge is such that people from all nations, including kings, come to Jerusalem to hear him. Solomon is also respected for the vastness of his territorial possessions: "from the

Medieval miniature, *The Coronation of Solomon*

The last years of David's reign are weakened by plots hatched by his own sons against him. Weary and pressed by his entourage as well as Bathsheba, Solomon's mother, David finally openly designates a successor and anoints Solomon.

River (Euphrates) to the land of the Philistines and to the borders of Egypt." All pay tributes and are loyal to him in a climate of peace and well-being extremely rare for the age.

This is therefore the general atmosphere in which Solomon undertakes the building of the great Temple of Jerusalem intended to house the Ark of the Covenant. To accomplish his task, he calls upon the logistical support of the king of Tyre, Hiram, who had also been on excellent terms with David and had helped him to build his palace. Hiram supplies Solomon with cedar wood from Lebanon which he sends by sea and in exchange, Solomon agrees to ship him annual reserves of wheat and oil. Thirty thousand men are put to work cutting the wood, seventy thousand are responsible for its transportation, and eighty thousand for cutting stones in the mountains. This grandiose building project, fruit of a mutually beneficial alliance between the Israelites and Tyre, is implemented during the fourth year of the reign of Solomon. The biblical text gives a detailed description of the Temple's dimensions, its exterior and interior appearance, the decoration, the furnishings of a royal shrine that would go down in history for its unparalleled beauty and sumptuousness. In substance it was a rectangular building consisting of three rooms leading one into the other, a vestibule, a large worship room, and the "most holy place," Holy of Holies. This inner sanctum located at the heart of the Temple, secret and hidden, was slightly elevated and consisted of a cell entirely covered in gold. There, the sacred Ark was housed, protected by a veil and cherubs that spread their wings over the precious object. Two famous bronze pillars "Jachin" and "Boaz," by a Tyrian bronze-smith, also named Hiram, were erected in the vestibule. From this same craftsman also came bowls, vases, cauldrons, and other various smaller pieces, all of an exceptional artistic quality. The Phoenicians, it is true, excelled in the working of metals, a fact which Homer also affirms in the *Iliad*.

Seven years after its commencement, during the eleventh year of Solomon's reign, the work is finally completed. All the elders of the people of Israel, all the heads of the various tribes, all the local potentates are invited to Jerusalem for the transferring of the Ark from Zion to the Temple. This gesture pleases Yahweh and, in the form of a cloud, his presence fills the sanctuary. Solomon then addresses the people and, praising the glory of Yahweh, calls for each individual's absolute loyalty to the Covenant. Solomon then asks Yahweh for his support against Israel's enemies, to grant them rain and fertility, to spare his people from cataclysms and epidemics, to render them hospitable to foreigners and, finally, to protect them from deportations. Solomon's prayer is followed by a grandiose sacrifice and seven days of celebration in all the land.

Next, work begins on the construction of Solomon's royal palace, an undertaking which will last thirteen years and, because of its abundant use of cedar wood, will be known as the "forest of Lebanon." During this period Yahweh appears to Solomon again to congratulate him on his building projects and reminds the king and his people to remain faithful to God. For if not, Yahweh warns, he will quickly abandon them and their Temple will be nothing but a joke for everyone to mock.

Twenty years after the erection of the Temple and the palace, to thank Hiram of Tyre for his collaboration, Solomon offers twenty villages in Galilee to him. Despite Solomon's objections, Hiram supposedly gives him twenty gold talents as payment. This strange episode, its logic being unclear even to scholars, seems to reveal Solomon's diplomatic and commercial skillfulness to impose upon the king of Tyre a rather unprofitable commerical transaction and transfer of sovereignity. Probably at about the same time, Solomon begins various other building projects in different cities of his kingdom with the use of forced labor gangs taken from the remaining ancient local populations. Solomon then turns to foreign trade, which also attracts him, and, to realize his plans, once again calls upon the collaboration of the king of Tyre, whose city is reputed for its sailors and commercial activity in the Mediterranean. Solomon has a fleet built on the banks of the Red Sea and, with the navigational expertise of the Phoenician sailors, sends these ships to Ophir, most likely another name for East Africa, somewhere near Somalia and Sudan, from where they return with abundant quantities of gold, precious stones, and fine wood. In addition, every three years a special fleet is sent to Tarshish to carry back gold, silver, ivory, and exotic animals,

Guido Reni, *The Judgement of Solomon*

Solomon's wisdom becomes famous. Some three thousand proverbs and one thousand and five poems are attributed to him, as well as the Song of Songs, the Book of Ecclesiastes and the Wisdom of Solomon.

notably monkeys. The exact location of the country of Tarshish is still much disputed: Asia Minor, in the area around the city of Tarsus? Or alternatively, Southern Spain, in the ancient Tartessos region whose rich mining resources were famous during antiquity?

The reputation of Solomon's wisdom and wealth gives rise to the famous visit of the queen of Sheba who travels from the southwest region of the Arabian peninsula (the present day Yeman) all the way to Jerusalem to put the king to test. Escorted by a procession of camels bearing gold and precious stones, this *Thousand and One Nights* heroine sees all her riddles answered in a snap by the king of Israel. Astounded by the majesty and splendor of Solomon's surroundings, the queen of Sheba sees in them the signs of a superior God and showers Solomon with royal gifts. The king does likewise, and the queen sets off on her journey back to Arabia. This episode takes a surprising turn in Abyssinia when ancient local traditions trace the

Nicolas Poussin, *The Judgement of Solomon*

Two prostitutes go before Solomon to claim a child. Solomon asks for a sword and proposes to divide the child in two, so that each woman may take half. Moved by her maternal love, the real mother accepts to relinquish the child to save its life, and Solomon is thus able to unmask the imposter.

Lorenzo Ghiberti, ***The Encounter between Solomon and the Queen of Sheba***

The queen of Sheba goes to Jerusalem with camels bearing gold and precious stones to test the wisdom of the king. This episode takes a surprising turn when ancient Abyssinian traditions trace the local dynasty back to the union between Solomon and the queen, an event never mentioned in the Old Testament.

ruling dynasty back to a union between Solomon and the queen of Sheba, a union of which the Old Testament is completely unaware.

Solomon is now at the peak of his dynastic "career." Renowned the world over for his great wisdom, he regularly receives visitors from the four corners of the earth and is literally flooded with prestigous gifts — gold, silver, fine garments, arms, spices, horses and mules. In Jerusalem, money and precious stones abound and cedar has become commonplace. But Solomon is already on the brink of his decline and, as is often the case in the Old Testament, it is women who will be the cause of the faults he commits. For, Solomon takes foreign women among his wives: Moabites, Ammonites, Edomites, Phoenicians, Hittites, who all practice religions other than the faith of Yahweh, the biblical text referring to a total of seven hundred women of royal descent and three hundred concubines in Solomon's household. Taking advantage of the aged Solomon's feebleness, his wives easily win him over to foreign gods, the Phoenician Astarte, the Moabite Kemosh, and the Ammonite Milcom. Betraying his father's lifelong loyalty to Yahweh, Solomon has worship places erected to these divinities and provokes the wrath of his national god. Out of respect for David and his love for Jerusalem, Yahweh postpones the execution of his sentence, but he warns Solomon of his decision — a part of Solomon's royal power will be taken from him, or more precisely, from his son. In this message Yahweh announces the great "schism" which will split the territory and give rise to two independent kingdoms, Judah and Israel. Yahweh intends in this manner to humiliate David's descendants, although he adds that this will only be a temporary situation.

The withdrawal of Yahweh's support nevertheless makes itself felt immediately. Externally, foreign enemies rise up against Solomon and, on the domestic scene, Jeroboam, one of his servants, leads a revolt against him, a prophet having told Jeroboam that Yahweh intended to grant him the leadership of ten of the twelve Tribes of Israel because of Solomon's apostasy. Solomon's attempts to have the rebel killed prove unsuccessful and Jeroboam takes refuge in Egypt until Solomon's death. After forty years of rule, in 931 B. C., Solomon dies and is buried in the City of David, at Jerusalem. His son Rehoboam succeeds him and goes to Shechem to be made king before the people, again reunited. Jeroboam, however, faced with the young king's intransigence, stirs the people to secession and only the tribe of Judah remains loyal to Solomon's son. Thus the schism foretold by Yahweh is realized in 931 B. C. and gives birth to two separate kingdoms, Israel and Judah. With this event, an exceptionally properous period, a golden age in the history of Israel draws to a close, an epoch marked by the prophetic figures of Samuel, David, and Solomon, who led Israel to unequalled heights of expansion, prosperity, and prestige.

ELIJAH AND ELISHA

Sworn Enemies of Baal

Then did Elijah rise,
a prophet like fire, his word like a burning torch.

Ecclesiasticus, 48:1

Elijah and Elisha, the former a famous seer and prophet, the latter his disciple and perpetrator, are two figures best studied side by side in view of the numerous similarities and, at the same time, important differences which characterize them. They both share, in any case, the same zeal in their service to God and in their lives totally devoted to the struggle against the Canaanite cult of Baal.

These two figures, whose true historical background is unknown to us, were the object of a cycle of tales which progressively formed around their lives, probably first circulating in oral form in prophet circles before being committed to writing and accepted by biblical canon. These episodes, which could be considered much like the French *gestes*, sets of medieval epic poetry, were pervaded by a legendary atmosphere in which episodes in two versions were often proposed, first with Elijah and then with Elisha as the hero. The Old Testament has preserved these tales in the first and second Book of Kings, though numerous references to the figures (particularly Elijah) are found elsewhere in the Bible, including in the New Testament. In the tales of their adventures, we encounter many narrative folk motifs which should be considered in terms of the religious beliefs and the cultural climate of the times, open to syncretism. Indeed, the stories of Elijah and Elisha, particularly the main narrative motifs, in order to be truly understood must be read against the background of Canaanite conceptions of Baal worship and the conflict that opposed Hebrew monotheism and the polytheistic religion of the people of Canaan.

Chronologically and geographically speaking, details in the narrative allow us to set Elijah and Elisha's story sometime in the ninth century B. C., at the northern border of the kingdom of Israel. This was the area of Palestine closest to Phoenicia and therefore the most exposed to cultural and religious influences originating from that country, not only due to ethnic contacts, but also official relations between one court and another. Elijah and Elisha must fiercely oppose Israel's sovereigns in order to defend Yahvist orthodoxy and loyalty to the worship of one God, so greatly threatened by the devotion to Canaanite divinities shown not only by the royalty but also by the people. Our two heroes, therefore, represent in Hebrew tradition the voice of intransigence that opposes the introduction of new cults of worship and, because of this role, they are presented as trustees of divine charisma and endowed with supernatural powers.

After the epoch of David and Solomon, and even during their reigns, Hebrew culture progressively absorbed Cannanite influences, not only in cultural and artistic fields, but also religiously. The custom of taking foreign wives — a practice that attained its zenith in the union between King Ahab and Jezebel, a Phoenician princess — reinforced the trend towards syncretism. This was particularly due to the zeal shown by the new queen who, so resolutely attached to her own ancestral divinities, was determined to oust the religion of Yahweh in favor of her own form of worship. It should be pointed out, however, that the Bible presents a much too negative image of Jezebel to be historically true: the biblical editors made her into a totally evil symbol of all the vices and most reprehensible idolatries imaginable. She was considered the emblem of that "other" religion which it was so imperative to combat and eradicate from the hearts of the Israelite people who, on many occasions and in various epochs, had shown a very strong attraction to Canaanite divinities and cults, so very different from the austere faith of Yahweh.

This religious conflict was rooted in two different world views, irreconcilable and even sometimes conflicting. For, Yahvist monotheism was, with its severe moral code and exclusive ritual, as rigid as the polytheistic Canaanite religion was tolerant (at least in terms of the multiplicity of cults). The former was based upon the exclusive relationship between God and the chosen people and the latter, upon a relationship between the divinities and their territories (the city). The Yahvist faith was a nationalist cult, chauvinistic, closely related to the ethnic and cultural identity of its followers, whereas the Canaanite religion was more "open" and the plurality of gods made cultural exclusivity aimed at defining a specific national identity impossible. Whatever the case may be, in the adventures of Elijah and Elisha the biblical setting is again, as it has been many times before, the fruit of reflection of a much later period and therefore cannot be considered entirely reliable from a historical point of view. Though it is undeniable that Hebrew monotheism ends up getting the upper hand over Canaanite polytheism, it is also implictly understood from the story that, during the time of Elijah and Elisha, the souls not only of Israel's sovereigns but of its people as well were turned more favorably towards the cults of the Baals and Asherahs than towards the faith of Yahweh, defended only by an elite though determined minority.

This therefore brings us to Elijah and Elisha and their adventures. Despite many points in common,

Fragonard, *Jeroboam Sacrifices to the Idols*
Jeroboam rebels against King Solomon who tries in vain to murder the rebel; when Rehoboam succeeds his father Solomon, Jeroboam incites the inhabitants of Israel to secession. However, as almost all the kings before him, Jeroboam also worships Baal, an attitude that soon provokes a strong reaction from Elijah and Elisha.

these two men also present, as mentioned initially, certain differences mainly in terms of character and personality. Their destinies will eventually differ significantly as well. An important distinguishing feature between them is the fact that Elijah seems quite disinclined to seek the company of others, whereas Elisha apparently is just the opposite. Elijah, in fact, is a solitary person destined to be a hermit and an ascetic. Elisha, however, is well integrated into the urban communities (the cities of Jericho, Samaria, and Dothan) where he ministers, often collaborating with the "sons of the prophets" (that is, a group of people devoted, body and soul, to the Yahvist faith) and, completely unlike Elijah, he does not find it disdainful to take an active part in politics.

Elijah

Elijah is a renowned prophet of extraordinary powers and guardian of a special charisma that he has received directly from God. His name, moreover, reflects a life of absolute and exclusive devotion to Yahweh since it signifies "Yahweh is [my] God." Unlike the other prophets whose genealogies the Bible usually provides, the text offers very little information about Elijah's background which leads us to believe he is more a traditional figure than a historical personage. He is described, in any case, as an austere and solitary man accustomed to wearing only an animal skin held by a belt, the normal attire of ascetics and hermits at the time. He prefers, also as they do, rural life to the cities, which he regards with suspicion as places where only confusion, sin, and moral degradation prevail.

A native of Tishbe in Gilead, Elijah lives and prophesies in the southern kingdom of Israel, whose capital is Samaria, under the reigns of Ahab (875-854) and his son Ahaziah (854-853). As mentioned before, this is the Palestinian area closest to Phoenicia and therefore the most vulnerable to influences coming from that highly refined culture. Ahab is, in the Old Testament, the example of the "accursed" king, presented in a very negative light and roundly condemned for his idolatry (he notably erects a temple to Baal in the capital city) and for having married Jezebel, the daughter of the Phoenician king Etbaal, accused of having introduced her own cults into Israel. It should be noted, however, that biblical chronology is not completely consistent here since other allusions associate Elijah with the king of Judah, Joram (852-845). The difficulty of reconciling these chronological details and the fact that the biblical editors have not perfectly integrated Elijah into historical reality therefore forces us to evaluate this figure in a legendary context rather than a historical one. The story opens in Gilead as Elijah the Tishbite, a man of rare spiritual stature, prophesies to King Ahab and warns him of a terrible drought about to descend upon the land, a cataclysm which only God himself will finally bring to an end. The reasons for divine anger, as we already know, are related to the idolatrous behavior of the king and his court. To escape Ahab's furious reaction and his certain reprisals, Elijah follows God's advice and flees east of the Jordan, near the brook Cherith, where he lives in complete solitude. In this desolate wilderness he is able to survive thanks to ravens that bring him bread and meat. However, because of the continuing drought, the brook finally dries up and Elijah, listening once more to God's counsel, leaves for Zarephath, in Phoenicia, where he is told a kind widow will take him in.

At the gates of the city, Elijah in fact meets the woman and asks her for some bread and water. But the prophet's request surprises the widow. Not even a crumb of bread is left to offer him, a fistful of flour and a little oil, she admits despairingly, is all she has. She was just getting ready to cook it after which, for lack of food, she and her son could only look forward to death. Elijah then performs his first miracle. He commands the woman to make him some bread from the flour, and to use the remainder for herself and her son, telling her not to worry, for God would see to it that neither the flour in the jar, nor the oil in the pitcher would be consumed for as long as the drought would last. Elijah's predictions prove true and they have enough to eat until the end of the famine. In this episode we already get a glimpse of a rather transparent anti-Canaanite argument based upon a confrontation between the powers of Yahweh and those of Baal. Although the latter is traditionally known as a god closely related to rain, who bestows fertility through its abundance, Yahweh is shown here with powers independent of meterological conditions, and capable of providing food at will without the need of precipitations.

A short while later, the widow's son falls seriously ill and even appears to stop breathing. His mother, believing he is dead, is overcome with grief and blames Elijah, saying that his presence has caused the terrible misfortune. Imperturbable, the prophet takes the child upstairs and lays him on a bed, then invokes the Lord to have mercy on the person who has shown him such generous hospitality. The prophet then covers the child's body with his own, three times, calling upon God to return the child's soul back to the lifeless body. Yahweh answers his prayer and the boy comes back to life. As Elijah takes the "resuscitated" child downstairs and returns him to his mother, the widow sees in Elijah, the miracle-worker, a "man of God."

A while later, the Lord tells Elijah that it will finally rain very soon and asks the prophet to go to King Ahab. Elijah thus departs for Samaria, a city which, as all the rest of the country, is crippled by famine. The king, who is still looking for Elijah in the hope of punishing him, one day orders the royal major-domo Obadiah to accompany him across the kingdom to find cattle fodder or they will be forced to kill the animals for lack of food. We are told that this man Obadiah is, in fact, a follower of Yahweh and has saved "a hundred" (this number representing "many") of the Lord's prophets from the persecution of the Phoenician queen Jezebel, by hiding them in a cave and bringing them food in strict secrecy. It is Obadiah then who, while Ahab is travelling on another road, runs into Elijah and immediately recognizes him. Obadiah bows down before the prophet and Elijah asks him to inform his king that he wishes to see him. But Obadiah greatly fears Ahab's reaction, who is still trying to capture Elijah, particularly if the prophet eventually changes his mind and decides not to appear before the king afterall. However, reassured by Elijah, Obadiah goes to announce the prophet's arrival.

The encounter between Ahab and Elijah is dramatic. To the king who accuses Elijah of having caused Israel's ruin, the prophet answers that the guilty one is he, the king, and also his family. Elijah reminds him that it is they who have betrayed God to become followers of the Phoenician Baal. A challenge is then inevitable. Elijah commands the king to summon all the prophets of Baal (one hundred and fifty without including the prophets of Asherah, who number four hundred and fifty according to a late biblical note) so that Elijah may challenge them in the name of his God, before all the people of Israel. After severely reproaching the crowd for having neglected their traditional faith in Yahweh by willingly following Baalite customs, the prophet anounces the terms of the challenge: the prophets of Baal will place the pieces of a young slain bull upon a pile of wood without, however, setting fire to it, and Elijah will do the same. They will then each invoke the intervention of their own god to set fire to the wood, only the divinity who responds positively will be decreed the true god. The prophets of Baal set to work preparing their burnt offering and then invoke their god Baal, but in vain. Their prayers are answered only by an eerie silence. Elijah then scoffs at them: perhaps their god is hard of hearing, asleep, or maybe on a trip? This is a rather obvious allusion to religious Canaanite notions according to which the divinity went into dormant periods when it would have to be "awakened" by means of special ceremonies and sacrifices. Such conceptions reflected an anthropomorphic view of the divinity who, it was thought, needed to be supplied food, drink, and clothing. At any rate, the prophets of Baal continue to invoke their god and finally even resort to making incisions on their bodies, which causes much blood to be shed, but still all in vain!

Then it is Elijah's turn to act. He takes twelve stones (a symbolic number representing the tribes of Israel), erects an altar to his God, and digs a trench around it big enough to contain two bushels of seeds. Then he prepares a pile of wood and lays the pieces of the young bull upon it. Calling to the crowd, Elijah asks them to flood the altar with four barrels of water (according to the "magic of opposites" fire is attracted by water) and has them repeat this action three times, until the water begins to flow into the trench. Then, Elijah invokes the God of Israel to appear to the people so that all may know he is the only true God. Fire, like a bolt of lightening, is unleashed from the sky and the wood and altar burst into flame, the water vanishing instantly. Before this miracle, the people, now a riotous mob spurred on by Elijah, proclaim Yahweh the one and only God and rise up against the prophets of Baal, murdering every one of them.

This event virtually puts an end to the famine. Elijah goes to Ahab telling him to eat and drink to his heart's content for abundant rains are imminent. The prophet sends his acolyte six times to scan the horizon, but it is only on the seventh time that he sees a small cloud far off in the distance. Shortly after this, torrential rains finally end the interminable drought.

The events on Mount Carmel certainly do not help ease Ahab's resentment towards Elijah nor his thirst for vengeance. In fact, the king, and especially his wife Jezebel, after hearing that the prophets of Baal have all been killed, decide to subject Elijah to the same fate as the pagan priests. The prophet receives a very threatening letter from the wrathful queen and, fearing for his life, he seeks refuge in Beersheba, in the kingdom of Judah, and then continues fleeing until he finally reaches the desert. Exhausted and only desiring death to put an end to his suffering, Elijah falls asleep under a juniper tree in the hope that the Lord will mercifully end his days. However, instead, an angel appears twice to him in his sleep telling the prophet to eat and drink for the road is still long. This is God's way

Guercino, *Elijah is Fed by Ravens*

Elijah goes to live in solitude east of the Jordan. In this desolate wilderness ravens, as instruments of divine Providence, bring him bread and meat.

of telling Elijah that he must stay alive and continue acting in the name of the Lord. Revitalized, not only physically but also morally, after forty days and forty nights Elijah reaches the Mountain of God, Horeb, the place where Yahweh had once appeared to Moses and made the Covenant with the chosen people.

In this, the holiest of places in Hebrew tradition, a theophany, another appearance of God, takes place. Inspired by his ardent belief in the Lord and more determined than ever to see that the Israelites respect the only true faith, Elijah sees God: first, a raging wind rises, then an earthquake breaks loose and finally flames of fire shoot up, but the biblical text emphasizes that in none of these phenomena is the Lord materially present (precisely to underline the transcendence of the one God opposed to the immanence of Baal). After these divine occurrences, a light breeze begins to blow and Elijah, filled with his love for God, leaves the shelter of his cave and suddenly hears a "still small voice." God tells Elijah that he must anoint, that is, consecrate three men: the king of Damas, Hazael; the future king of Israel, Jehu; and finally Elisha, who will become Elijah's disciple and perpetrator. Through these men, God's vengeance will be wrought against all those who have fought against Yahweh or renounced him. If a man escapes one, he will die at the hands of another of the three. For, in all of Israel only seven thousand people remain whose "knees have not bent down to Baal," and only they will be spared by the Lord.

After leaving Horeb, Elijah meets Elisha and, as we will see in more detail further on, calls the young man and takes him into his service in a consecration ceremony filled with symbolic meaning. The subsequent chapters of the first Book of Kings are devoted to a description of the political and military background of the period, important to understanding the adventures of the two characters, but which is not necessary to present here in detail. We will limit ourselves to recalling that the story unfolds in the days of the wars between the Arameans and Ahab, king of Israel, who manages to victoriously rout the enemy thanks to the help of a prophet. But Ben-Hadad, the Aramean king of Damascus, does not accept this defeat and, the next year, makes another attempt. Once again, thanks to the support of the "man of God," the Israelites get the upper hand. Ahab generously pardons his enemy and returns all the cities taken from him and proposes to sign a commercial treaty. The clan of prophets, however, condemns Ahab's attitude, considered as a sign of weakness, since God himself had doomed the Aramean enemy to death. Consequently, another prophet announces to Ahab that he and his people will soon pay for the Aramean lives so unjustly spared.

After this military digression which serves to create an even more negative image of the king of Israel's conduct and character, the biblical text continues to further describe the reprehensible behavior of Ahab and his wife, Jezebel. The king wishes to buy the vineyard of a man named Naboth — a piece of land right next to the royal palace — to use as a garden for his residence, but Naboth refuses to sell, the land being an inheritance from his ancestors. Hearing about this, Jezebel decides to intervene personally and promises her husband that he will soon become owner of the vineyard. The treacherous queen lays a trap for the poor Naboth whom she slanders before the elders and the city officials with false accusations, even calling him a traitor to God and to the king. Framed by false testimonies, the unfortunate Naboth is stoned to death and the king is free to take possession of the much desired property. But Yahweh intervenes. He appears once again to Elijah and sends him to the court of Ahab. Inspired by God, the prophet accuses the king of murder and usurpation and predicts that Ahab will meet his death on the same spot where the innocent Naboth has been slain. All of Ahab's family and descendants will be annihilated, adds Elijah, and Jezebel will be devoured by dogs in Naboth's field. Hearing Elijah's terrible prophecies and omens, the king is overcome with a feeling of repentance. He dresses in mourning and begins a fast to atone for his faults. God therefore tells him that the extermination of his family will not take place during his own lifetime, but during that of his son's.

In another digression of a military nature in the text, Jehoshaphat, the king of Judah, convinces Ahab to organize an expedition against the Arameans to recapture Ramoth and Gilead, fallen to the enemies. Before going into battle, the court prophets are consulted (of course these are "impure" prophets who are not directly inspired by God given their dependence on the king). They predict victory, but Jehoshaphat, who is not at all convinced by their response, wishes to consult other seers. Though Ahab is reluctant, they send for another prophet by the name of Micaiah, not very well thought of by the king since he is a follower of Yahweh. This prophet, filled with true divine inspiration, first announces a positive prophecy in an ironic tone, then in all seriousness foretells an impending defeat and explains that because his own God has willed it, the other prophets have not told the truth. Ahab has Micaiah flogged and thrown into prison. During the battle, Ahab is mortally wounded by an arrow and, carried out of the fray, he dies at dawn. Upon the news of his death, the soldiers are overcome by panic and the king's lifeless body is taken back to Samaria where it is buried.

With Ahab's death, one of Israel's most negative sovereigns in biblical tradition disappears. Jezebel survives him, but she will also have to face divine wrath. In the meantime, war between Israel and Moab breaks out when the Moabites rebel against Israelite dominion. Ahaziah, Ahab's son, has ascended to the throne of Israel and, as a worshipper of Baal just as his mother and father had been, he strongly opposes Elijah. And, true to the prophet's prediction, this will provoke Yahweh's terrible vengeance.

It is not long before the tragic destiny foretold to king Ahab comes to pass. One day, Ahaziah falls from a balcony and is injured. He then orders that a foreign god be consulted, the "lord of Ekron," the Philistine Baalzebub (his name, which means "Baal of the flies," is a biblical distortion of his original name, Baalzeboul, or "Baal, the prince") in order to find out about the prospects of his recovery.

Tintoretto, *Elijah is Fed by an Angel*

Hunted down by Ahab and Jezebel, exhausted and in despair, the prophet falls asleep under a juniper tree hoping the Lord will grant him eternal peace. But an angel appears to Elijah urging him to eat and drink: God tells him he must continue acting in the name of the Lord.

But Elijah is there, standing in the new sovereign's way. Obeying Yahweh's explicit instructions, the prophet reproaches the king's envoys for turning to a foreign god when there is a God of Israel. Ahaziah will pay for his infidelity, proof of his idolatry, by never recovering. The king, greatly angered, despatches a group of soldiers to the mountain where Elijah lives in solitude with the order to capture him. When he hears the soldiers ordering him to surrender, Elijah invokes the Lord's help and a devastating fire descends upon the men, killing all of them. The same thing happens to a second contingent, who are annihilated just as the first. The royal captain of the third contingent, filled with terror, begs the prophet to show mercy, not wanting to meet the same fate as those before him. Elijah therefore spares his life and fearlessly descends the mountain with the soldier. Going before the king, the prophet makes an ominous prediction: Ahaziah will never rise from his bed again and will soon die. After his brief reign, continues Elijah, having no heirs, his brother Joram will succeed him as king.

Elijah's earthly existence, at this point, has almost come to an end and finally God decides to take Elijah away with him. One day the prophet, accompanied by Elisha, feels irresistibly called by God and tells his disciple that he must now let him go. But Elisha wants to remain with his master at all costs. The two of them arrive in Bethel and the "sons of the prophets" also tell Elisha that God will take his master away that very day. But Elisha, who already knows this, nevertheless insists on following Elijah to Jericho, and then right up to the banks of the Jordan, refusing to listen to those who say the prophet must go alone to meet the fate God intends for him. On the banks of the Jordan, before the eyes of fifty witnesses who watch from a distance, Elijah takes his mantle and strikes the waters of the river and the waters divide, allowing the prophet and Elisha to cross. Then Elijah asks what he can do for his disciple before he leaves him forever, and Elisha answers that he would like to receive a "double portion" of his master's spirit. If Elisha witnesses the moment his master is taken up to the sky by God, Elijah replies, then he will know that his wish has been granted. A chariot of fire drawn by horses of fire suddenly appears in the sky. Elijah climbs upon it and, in a whirlwind, rises to the heavens. When he has completely disappeared from view, Elisha, after having invoked the Lord during the entire prodigious scene, tears his clothes in a gesture of mourning and picks up Elijah's mantle. Returning to the river again, just as his master had done, Elisha strikes the waters with the garment. The river divides, allowing him to cross to the other side. At the sight of this new miracle, the "sons of the prophets," who have followed the entire scene from afar, bow down to Elisha. All now know that the spirit of Elijah has invested his disciple. Elisha is reluctant when they want to search for Elijah, but he finally agrees to accompany them. The search, of course, proves in vain. Elisha knows very well his master has left them forever and that it is now up to him to continue his master's work on earth.

In Judeo-Christian tradition, the figure of Elijah is of considerable importance. He is one of the most passionate defenders of the faith of Yahweh, a solitary and invincible warrior whose relationship with God is so privileged that he even seems to escape the lot of all common mortals by a celestial "abduction." This singular episode is charged with feelings of hope and waiting for the beatification of Man; and Ecclesiasticus, after having reiterated the inimitable greatness of the prophet ("How great were you, Elijah, by your miracles! Who could boast they were your equal?" (Ecclus. 48:4) then adds significantly:

> Happy those who have seen you
> And who in love went to sleep!
> For also we will surely live!
>
> *Ecclus.* 48: 11-12

Elijah's ascent into heaven, therefore, carries profound eschatological and messianic implications which have always appeared at the heart of theological reflection. Moreover, in the days of the New Testament, belief in (and the waiting for) Elijah's return one day, was quite widespread in the popular mind. The ancient champion of the faith of Yahweh honorably takes his place beside Moses in the famous episode of the Transfiguration of Christ (Mark 9:4) and, according to the teachings of Jesus himself, the new Elijah, the supreme prophet John the Baptist, is a reincarnation of the ancient defender of the faith, whose memory is still venerated to our day by Christians, Jews, and Moslems alike because of the universal values it holds.

Elisha

We have seen the figure of Elisha appear in Elijah's story as the great prophet's disciple and perpetrator, even though, as already mentioned, quite a few characteristics distinguish Elisha from his master. For, Elisha is a military advisor and politician, an expert in the field of foreign affairs (particularly as regards King Jehu and his dynasty) which is a dimension totally unknown to Elijah. In addition, rather than an authentic holy man and moral teacher, Elisha is presented as a great thaumaturge and his story is replete with "miracles" and "wonders" (some of which are very similar to those performed by Elijah). He ministered, if we go by the biblical narrative, during the reigns of no less than four sovereigns, Joram (853-842), Jehu (842-815), Jehoahas (814-798 and Joash (798-783), but it is impossible to organize the events of his life in any coherent chronological order. The episodes that make up the Elisha "cycle" are quite disparate and the biblical text juxtaposes them without any concern for constructing a precise sequence.

We have already seen how Elijah, after communing with the Lord on Mount Horeb, meets Elisha (whose name means "God has helped") while he is busy plowing the fields with his oxen. Inspired by the Lord, the old prophet, without a moment's hesitation, throws his mantle over Elisha in a gesture that calls the young man to enter into his service. Elisha leaves everything to join Elijah, saying farewell to his family for the last time. To demonstrate his willingness, Elisha not only kills his two oxen, but he uses their yoke as firewood to roast their meat. In this act, Elisha cuts all ties with his former life, to which he will never be able to return, and from that moment on commits himself body and soul to a life dedicated to serving Elijah and God.

After the episode describing Elisha's call, we return to him at the moment when Elijah is taken to heaven by God, the details of which have already been related, and where the role played by the disciple has been highlighted. Elisha receives the spirit and powers of his departed master, which he immediately demonstrates by the episode of the mantle, when the miracle performed by Elijah is repeated by Elisha who again divides the waters of the Jordan. After Elijah has risen to the sky, Elisha continues his master's work and performs many miraculous interventions that clearly recall those of his master. One day he happens to be in Jericho and hears the inhabitants lament that the water is contaminated and that all the women have become barren or have had miscarriages. Elisha puts some salt in an unused bowl and goes to the spring. He pours the salt into the water and, in the name of God, pronounces magic words that have the power to cleanse the waters which, after this, become pure and limpid.

While on his way to Bethel, a group of young boys make fun of him because of his "baldness," referring, most likely, not simply to a physical defect, but rather to the special tonsure adopted by prophets. Since Elisha is a man of God, and it is as such that the boys ridicule him, their insults are a sacrilege. In the name of God he puts a curse on the boys and two ferocious bears immediately charge out of the forest, attack several of them, and tear them to pieces.

Meanwhile, the king of Israel, Joram, has joined forces with both Jehoshaphat, the king of Judah, and also the king of Edom, in view of regaining dominion over the Moabites ruled by King Mesha. The Moabites have proclaimed their independence and refuse to be subject to the tribute. On their march towards Moab, the coalition army is faced with a severe drought which becomes so critical that they decide to consult a prophet of God. The prophet, of course, turns out to be Elisha. Though he opposes Joram because of his idolatrous practices, out of respect for Jehoshaphat he agrees to prophesy and, to the sound of his lyre, Elisha tells them that an abundance of water is imminent and that the allied troops will get the better of the Moabites. The next morning, just as foretold, a hurricane and storm flood the land and the water settles in pools on the battlefield. The Moabites, tricked by the reflections, believe they see pools of blood and

Medieval miniature, *Elijah Is Taken into the Heavens*

For Judeo-Christian tradition, Elijah is the passionate defender of the faith of Yahweh: he escapes the lot of common mortals by a celestial "abduction" and will appear beside Moses in the famous episode of the Transfiguration of Christ related in the Gospels.

decide that the allied troops, in dissension, have turned on each other during the night. The Moabites charge their enemies' camp but are easily defeated, their cities are destroyed and their territory sacked by the joint forces. Only the fortified capital defended by King Mesha escapes the butchery and resists the assault. The king, in a desperate act, offers his own son in a burnt offering upon the walls of the city, appealing to the Moabites' national god, Kemosh, and this extreme act so profoundly shocks the Israelites and their allies that they retreat. This rather mysterious event should be considered, from a historical point of view, as an Israelite defeat as confirmed, moreover, by the remains of a very important historical document, a stone stele engraved by King Mesha himself. Upon the stele, today preserved at the Louvre Museum in Paris, the king records these events and boasts of his victory over his adversaries.

But let us now return to Elisha and his miraculous works. The next episode's heroine is a widow of one of the prophets' disciples. She is driven to despair by a creditor who is about to take her two sons and reduce them to slavery. Elisha, to whom the widow has turned for help, asks her for her only remaining possession, a phial of oil. It miraculously becomes enough to fill several pitchers. The widow is thus able to pay her debts without seeing her sons forced into slavery.

Just as Elijah had once resuscitated a widow's son in Zarephath, Elisha also accomplishes a similar miracle. A well-off woman from Shunem, who is childless and lives with her elderly husband, convinced that Elisha is a holy man, offers him a room in her house so that he will have food and lodging when he passes through the city. One day when Elisha and his servant Gehazi are staying with her, the prophet, wishing to show her his gratitude, prophesies that she will bear a son. Although the theme of miraculous birth is not unusual in the Bible, the woman is incredulous. Nevertheless, despite her disbelief, the prophecy comes true. Some years later, however, the young boy is victim to an unexpected illness and dies. His grieving mother goes to Elisha and reproaches him. She has tragically lost a son whom she had never even thought to bear, and Elisha has deceived her. Elisha intervenes immediately and sends his servant ahead of him to place the prophet's staff over the child's face to try to revive him. But the servant is unable to pull the child out of his torpor. Then Elisha himself goes to the corpse lain on the bed; he spreads his body over the child's body and, little by little, the child begins to warm up and comes back to life. The mother bows down before Elisha, so overcome with gratitude that she offers the prophet her house as a gift. We find a continuation of this episode further on in 2 Kings 8:1-16, included erroneously in Elisha's adventures, which takes place during the Aramean wars. The woman, following Elisha's advice, takes her son and leaves her famine-stricken city to seek refuge for seven years in the land of the Philistines. When she returns, the king allows her to reclaim all her property and belongings. We note that the story seems to suggest that Elisha is no longer alive at the time, since no mention is made of him upon the woman's return to Israel.

Elisha then returns to Gilgal and finds the country afflicted by a serious food shortage. The prophet's disciples prepare a simple meal of wild gourds cooked in a cauldron, but soon discover these are poisonous and therefore inedible. Elisha then throws some meal into the cauldron and the gourds immediately lose their bitterness and their poison. A man comes to Elisha with twenty loaves of bread and some cereal. Elisha orders the disciples to distribute the food to all present, but there are more than a hundred people waiting to be fed and it seems far too little for such a crowd. The prophet nevertheless insists, saying that there will even be food left over. And so it is, they see there is still more bread and cereal after everyone has eaten. It is of course unnecessary to point out the parallel between this episode and the miracle of the loaves and fishes performed by Jesus and related in the Gospel according to Saint Mark.

The commander-in-chief of the king of Aram's army, a certain Naaman, enjoys great respect but is afflicted with leprosy. Having heard from a young Israelite slave of Elisha's extraordinary powers, he asks his king for permission to go to see the prophet. The Aramean king agrees, and even sends precious gifts to the king of Israel to announce Naaman's visit, explaining his hope of being cured. Joram, who misunderstands the king's message and thinks that it is he who is expected to cure Naaman and that this is all some ploy, becomes very angry. But Elisha learns of the incident and intervenes, asking the king to send the unfortunate Naaman to him, the true prophet. As he is just about to reach Elisha's house, the prophet sends Naaman a message to go to the Jordan and bathe in its waters seven times. Feeling offended by such treatment and considering the cure much too banal, Naaman is ready to give the whole trip up when, heeding his servants' advice, he decides to obey Elisha's instructions and goes to the river. He is immediately cured and cleansed and is free to return home. However, before doing so, wishing to reward the holy man, he goes to see Elisha and tells him of his sincere desire to convert to the faith of Yahweh. When Elisha refuses, Naaman then asks if he may take some soil back with him from the land of Israel to make a small holy oasis in Aram, where he may worship Yahweh. He also puts a moral dilemma to Elisha: as a high official in the king's court, he must continue to participate in rites honoring the Aramean god Rimmon, though in his heart he will be completely devoted to Yahweh. Elisha gives him his complete absolution and Naaman takes his leave.

As an appendix to this story, we find a short scene in which the protagonist is Elisha's servant, Gehazi, and where Elisha's visionary powers are fully demonstrated. While Naaman is on his way back to his own country, Gehazi tries to take advantage of the situation to obtain for himself some of the gifts the Aramean has offered, in vain, to Elisha. He catches up with Naaman and tells him that his master has changed his mind, for two young disciples have just joined them, and Elisha would like to accept Naaman's money and garments for the new arrivals. Naaman is delighted and gives the gifts to Gehazi who takes them home and then returns to Elisha as if nothing has happened. But Elisha, despite his servant's lies, already knows all the details, having been witness, in spirit, to the entire scene. He therefore tells his servant to keep everything he has stolen for, in any case, a different punishment awaits him. The leprosy from which Naaman suffered has infected Gehazi and all of his family and, in fact, as Gehazi is leaving Elisha's house, he sees the signs of the disease already appearing.

Another wonder of a different kind is performed by Elisha when, one day near the Jordan, accompanied by other members of his community, he is busy cutting beams for a house. The blade from one of the men's axes falls into the river, and the worker is greatly upset since he had borrowed the tool from a friend. Elisha then throws a piece of wood into the water, right where the blade has fallen, and the object miraculously rises to the surface.

Many of Elisha's adventures unfold against the backdrop of the wars between Israel and the Arameans. Here, the prophet does not limit himself to performing wonders, but also plays the role of military advisor to the king (in this case, Joash) with great success. After having caused several Aramean ambush attempts to fail thanks to his prophetic powers, Elisha goes to Dothan, but is pursued by the king of Aram's men who hope to capture him there. The enemy troops surround the city, but the prophet strikes them all blind and then sends them to Samaria. There, they are all taken prisoner and the king of Israel, Joash, listening to Elisha's counsel, instead of putting them to death, sends the soldiers back to their homeland, thus putting an end to the series of sporadic Aramean raids on his territory.

But the Aramean king Ben-Hadad, engaging all his troops, lays siege to Samaria and the city is rapidly brought to misery and starvation. The conditions of the inhabitants of the city become so desperate that mothers even resort to killing and eating their own children. Faced with these scenes of horror, King Joash is so enraged he even wants to eliminate Elisha, who naturally defends the position of resisting at all costs. Becoming more reasonable, however, the king then goes to the prophet to find out what fate the Lord has in store for the inhabitants of Samaria. Elisha then predicts an extraordinary abundance of food for the next day, to the complete disbelief of the royal dignitaries. Meanwhile, four lepers at the city gates, in despair because they will never be able to enter Samaria, decide to go to the Aramean camp in the hope the enemy will show pity on them. But they find the encampment completely deserted, the Arameans having fled in great haste. God, in fact, has misled the troops into believing that the Hittites and Syrians, allies of the king of Israel, are bearing down on them. The four lepers eat all they can in the abandoned camp and help themselves to quantities of gold, silver, and clothing. Then, they decide to let the city officials know of their enemies' flight. King Joash, at first skeptical, sends some of his men to explore the Aramean encampment, but it is soon obvious that the lepers have told the truth. The entire population of Samaria, rejoicing, throw themselves upon the site and sack and pillage it. One of the royal dignitaries who had doubted Elisha's prophecy is captured and put to death by the crowd, never having known the joy of this blessed day, which had been foretold by the prophet down to the last detail.

A new work of healing, this time, concerns the Aramean king Ben-Hadad. Having heard of Elisha's arrival in his country, the ailing king sends his right-hand man, a certain Hazael, to ask the holy man what future awaits him. Elisha answers that Ben-Hadad will definitely recover, but then, suddenly overcome by sadness, the prophet adds that the king's death is imminent. Seeing Elisha's tears, Hazael asks him why he is weeping and Elisha reveals that it will be Hazael himself who will be the cause of much suffering and destruction for the people of Israel, since it is he who is destined to become king of Aram. Upon his return to Damascus, Hazael repeats Elisha's prophecy to Ben-Hadad, and the very next day he murders the king by suffocating him and ascends to the throne as usurper.

At this point, 2 Kings tells us of the ascension of Jehoshaphat's son, Joram, to the throne of Judah, a king whom the biblical editors present in an extremely negative light because of his moral and religious conduct. During his reign, a rebellion in Edom breaks out and the people there proclaim their independence. Joram is succeeded by Ahaziah, also judged an "evil" king since, as his father, he is related to the house of Ahab and has also followed in the accursed king's footsteps.

These details serve to introduce the story of Jehu's coup, an initiative in which Elisha plays a fundamental role, openly taking a stand against Joram and siding with the usurper, a very zealous servant of Yahweh. The prophet therefore sends one of his disciples to Ramoth in Gilead to secretly anoint Jehu, consecrating him king of Israel. Until then, Jehu had been but a military chief, though granted, one of the most prestigious. The first and most important task of the future king, stresses Elisha, is to destroy the house of Ahab where Jezebel is still living, who will meet her death by being attacked by a pack of dogs. Jehu's officers, having learned of the consecration of their commander, immediately support this choice and also proclaim him king as well, thus recognizing the legitimacy of the prophetic investiture. Jehu then undertakes to mount a conspiracy against Joram and sets off for the royal palace. The king, having just returned from a battle with Hazael, is wounded and therefore bed-ridden and Ahaziah, king of Judah, is visiting him. Worried by the fact that the scouts he has sent ahead to meet Jehu have still not returned, and fearing military complications, Joram, accompanied by Ahaziah, decides to go to meet Jehu. The encounter between the two men proves dramatic. In answer to Joram's offers of friendship, Jehu reproaches him for Jezebel's licentiousness and idolatries. The king is just about to flee when Jehu mercilessly shoots him in the back with an arrow that pierces his heart. Jehu then orders his men to throw his corpse in Naboth's field, where Naboth was slain, the innocent victim of Jezebel and Ahab's greed. Ahaziah, the king of Judah, is not spared either from Jehu's vengeance and is also killed, his body carried back to Jeruslem and buried in the family tomb.

Console de Louvain, *Jezebel Devoured by Dogs*

Jezebel, in biblical tradition, is the archetypal evil foreigner who imposes pagan cults and persecutes Yahweh's followers. We are not surprised, therefore, when she meets a dreadful and dishonorable death.

The time has come for Jezebel to pay for her crimes. Informed of the recent events and not having any other alternative, she decides to face her destiny with dignity. In elegant dress and make up, she confronts her adversary, Jehu, with her head high and does not spare him her irony. The usurper nevertheless makes her fall from the window of the royal palace and her body is trampled by horses. When the time comes to bury her, only her skull, feet, and hands are found, the rest having been devoured by dogs. Thus Elisha's sinister prophecy concerning the Phoenician queen comes true. But vengeance against Ahab's family does not stop there. The deceased sovereign also has numerous relatives and descendants in Samaria, and Jehu therefore sends a letter to the officials of that city to find out what their intentions are. Paralyzed by fear, they declare themselves ready to serve Jehu. Jehu then asks them to meet him the next day in Jezreel, bringing with them as proof of their loyalty, Ahab's "head" heirs (the biblical text playing here on the double meaning of "head"). The officials from Samaria obey Jehu's instructions to the letter and bring him the sinister trophies: the heads of Ahab's relatives, that they heap in a pile at the gates of the city for all to see. The usurper then eliminates all the remaining members of Ahab's family and all of those who had served him.

On his way to the capital, Jehu meets Ahaziah's brothers who are on their way from Judah to visit the sovereigns of Israel, obviously unaware that Joram and Jezebel have been killed. They also perish at the hands of Jehu who is intent on sparing no one. Then, after having been joined by Jonadab, head of the Rechabites, a Yahvist sect, Jehu enters Samaria where he completes the annihilation of the last remaining members of Ahab's family.

There, Jehu gathers all the people together and pretending to be a fervent worshipper of Baal, he announces his intention to offer a great sacrifice to the Canaanite god and tells the people they must participate under penalty of death. His aim is, of course, to get all the Baal followers together so that he can get rid of them all at once. The population pours into the city from all the land to attend the event and gathers in the temple of Baal. Then Jehu, after performing the sacrifice, orders his men, in waiting, to throw themselves upon the crowd and to kill all the pagan followers. None of the Baal worshippers escape the massacre and the temple is desecrated, then destroyed, the Canaanite cult thus definitively eradicated. Jehu, who rules for twenty-eight years, is rewarded by God for his acts: four of his descendants will reign on the throne of Israel, but the usurper himself proves himself just as guilty of idolatry as many of his predecessors had been. The Lord thus allows the territory of Israel to be partially taken over by the Arameans who capture the region east of the Jordan and overrun Gilead.

We have related Jehu's story in detail not only because of the important role Elisha plays in them, but also for a better understanding of the political and religious climate of the period, a context the editors of the Book of Kings use as a background for Elisha's activity in perpetuating the faith of Yahweh. After these events, the biblical text relates various phases in the kingdom of Judah's history during the years that follow, of which we may limit ourselves here to a brief summary.

Athaliah, Ahaziah's mother, after the death of her son, takes over and tries to eliminate all pretenders to the throne among the members of the royal family. But Jehosheba, Joram's daughter and Ahaziah's sister, manages to rescue Ahaziah's son, a certain Joash, and hides him for several years in a temple of Yahweh. Then comes the revolt of the high priest of Jerusalem, Jehoida, who, during the seventh year of Athaliah's reign with the help of guards and mercenaries, takes Joash out of hiding and officially proclaims him king in the Lord's temple. Athaliah is then executed and the people joyously acclaim the new sovereign while the last repressive outbursts against the Baalist cult shake the country. A new covenant is concluded between God, the king, and his people, thanks to the mediation of the high priest.

Tradition has remembered Joash as a just king, which does not at all mean that Canaanite divinities will disappear because of him. Thanks notably to a system of oblations, the Temple of Yahweh, that had greatly suffered from time and neglect, is repaired. On the foreign front, the Aramean threat represented by Hazael is halted by the king who pays a heavy tribute to him by despoiling the Temple and the royal palace.

After the kingdom of Judah, the biblical editors turn to the kingdom of Israel, governed by Jehu's dynasty. It is now Jehu's son Jehoahaz on the throne, another "negative" king from the Yahvist point of view, who is then succeeded by his son, Joash, just as sinful and idolatrous. It is under his reign that Elisha dies. The prophet is seriously ill and the Aramean threat makes itself increasingly felt.

King Joash therefore goes to visit Elisha and weeps when he sees the holy man on his deathbed. The prophet tells him that instead of weeping, he should take a bow and arrow and shoot an arrow towards the East, after which, he predicts the king's victory against the Arameans at Aphek. Then, he asks Joash to strike the ground with his arrows, which the king does three times, and then stops. Elisha then reproaches him violently. If the king had continued to strike the ground, he would have won a total and definitive victory, whereas now, he could only expect a partial and temporary success.

After this final prediction, Elisha dies and is buried, though not without, even after his death, giving another example of the power of his charisma. Some men trying to escape from the scene of a sacking, hastily get rid of a body by leaving it in Elisha's tomb and then running away. But the lifeless body, by simply touching Elisha's bones is resuscitated and stands up.

Thus ends the prodigious life story of a man endowed by God with extraordinary supernatural and magic powers. The evaluation contained of him in Ecclesiasticus is certainly the most evocative:

> During his life no prince could conquer him,
> He was dominated by no man.
> Nothing was too great a task for him,
> Even from his tomb his body prophesied.
> During his life he worked wonders,
> Even after death his works were marvelous.
>
> *Ecclus.* 48: 12-14

The Elijah and Elisha "cycle" includes many heterogenous events, a mixture of history, legend and fable. Many of these episodes appear to be rooted in authentic popular traditions. In the background of all the miracles, prophecies, and other wonders performed by our two heroes, we nevertheless discern the harsh historical reality of the confrontation between Yahvist monotheism and the cults in favor of Canaanite divinities. In Elisha's adventures in particular, we catch a glimpse of the biblical editors' work, who tend to "strip" the Canaanite Baal of his own prerogatives in order to transfer them to Yahweh: the power over fire, which is central to the formidable scene on Mount Carmel; the control over rain, sent by Yahweh to end the famine; the production of oil and wheat, goods normally granted by Baal, that the prophets multiply in the name of Yahweh; and finally, the capacity to heal and even resuscitate the dead. This was a power usually attributed to the Canaanite god in accordance with a very ancient local mythological tradition. Elijah's ascension to heaven suggests that Yahweh's powers also extend into sidereal space, a dimension that traditionally belongs to Baal, who Ugarit texts significantly refer to as "Auriga of the clouds." What is more, in the same way that Baal dominates the chaotic entities of Yam ("the sea") or Nahar ("the river") in ancient Canaanite myths, the biblical text wants to show us that God, through his men, has no difficulty dominating the waters of the Jordan. The intention is therefore polemical and is aimed at "re-evaluating" Baal's role and powers. What better evidence of this than the symbolic episode on Mount Carmel during which Baal is described as a simple human being who eats and sleeps, and pays no attention to his faithful, is even apathetic when confronted with the omnipotence of the victorious God, the God of Israel.

When we look closely, this is the driving force behind the existences of Elijah and Elisha, who have gone down in history as the proudest and most determined adversaries of Canaanite religious traditions, destined to be vanquished by the faith of Yahweh, the one God. If Baal eventually lost this battle, as the Old Testament would like us to believe, it is also because, serving God, were men made of the stuff of our two miracle worker-prophets.

JUDITH

The Pious Beheader

Judith! Judith!
This name, which has always signified a flower to us,
a secret to the end, so velvet, so tender,
Hear the hammering, barking make of it for eternity
an appeal for harshness, sterility...

JEAN GIRAUDOUX, *Judith*

Throughout the Old Testament the identity of the chosen people is expressed through their veneration, more or less loyal, of a unique God whom they call Yahweh. For, contrary to the neighboring Phoenicians, Arameans, Egyptians, Bablylonians, and other peoples who worship a multitude of gods and goddesses, the Hebrews do not practice polytheism, or at least, no longer do when the Old Testament is compiled and edited. There is good reason to believe, however, that at one time the Israelites also gave themselves to a cult of several gods and goddesses. We even find distant echoes of this in the Bible itself though the editors tried to erase all allusions to a period when Yahweh had any competitors or "colleagues." One of the most notable consequences of this "purge" was to eliminate any female figure in the Old Testament who could have been close to Yahweh in the way that Baal was flanked by Astarte in Phoenicia or Isis was Osiris's companion in Egypt. However, this attitude does not necessarily mean a systematic diminishing of the feminine element in the Hebrew Bible where many women play an important role and are even glorified. This is particularly true in the case of Judith who is the main character of a Book which, for a long time, was considered as part of the Apocrypha and then finally accepted in the biblical canon by the Catholic Church only.

The Book of Judith opens with the figure of Nebuchadnezzar, the great king of the Babylonians, in the sixth century B. C., a personage who also frequently appears in the Book of Daniel. He is busy preparing an important campaign against a certain Arphaxad, the king of the Medes, the biblical text indicates, resorting to an imaginary name that is never mentioned anywhere in any historical document. The Babylonian king therefore sends his messengers to various peoples to ask them to join forces with him, but the Cilicians, Syrians, Palestinians, Moabites, Ammonites and Egyptians refuse his call to unite, and Nebuchadnezzar, furious, promises to take vengeance for this affront. However, in the meantime, he combats the Medes and wins an impressive victory. Upon returning to Nineveh, his capital, he indulges in banquets and festivities for a hundred and twenty days before undertaking a new expedition against the peoples who had dared refuse his proposal.

Nebuchadnezzar summons his ministers and officials to the palace to hold a council in great secret in order to work out their strategy. This is when Holofernes enters the scene, the supreme general of the Babylonian army, a figure who holds the second highest position in the state hierarchy, just below the sovereign. The magnitude of Nebuchadnezzar's plans is equal to the degree of his resentment towards the previously mentioned peoples, whom he refers to as "westerners": "Take strong men with you, about 120,000 infantrymen, and a multitude of horses and their cavalrymen, about 12,000." When Holofernes reaches the enemy's territory, he is to command the inhabitants to "prepare land and water," a common expression which indicates unconditional surrender. Nebuchadnezzar guarantees his enemies such terrible sackings and massacres that their valleys and rivers will overflow with the dead. After having reminded Holofernes to follow his orders to the letter, without the slightest deviation, the king sends them on their mission. The formidable Babylonian army begins its march on the western lands, with a mass of men accompanied by animals of every kind — camels, asses, mules, sheep, cattle and goats — "like a swarm of locusts," comments the biblical text, using an example typical of the region where the story takes place.

Holofernes' army, after three days on the march, wreaks terror throughout the land, leaving only death, fire, and destruction in its wake. Cilicia, a region located at Syria's northern border, is the first victim, then it is the Damascus plain to be attacked, where its fields are burned, herds destroyed, cities plundered, and all the young men put to death. The Phoenicians and Philistines settled on the coast, terrorized at the thought of the fate awaiting them, send a message of peace to Nebuchadnezzar's general. He therefore peacefully takes over the coastal areas where he is welcomed with garlands, music, and dancing. This, however, still does not hinder him from destroying all the temples and holy places in the land, under the pretext that Nebuchadnezzar intends to be the one and only "god" of the people. This incident naturally serves to characterize Nebuchadnezzar as such an impious man that he will stop at no sacrilege, a pagan without even the slightest respect for other pagans, the personification of Evil. Reaching the borders of Judah, Holofernes calls a halt for about a month to sort out all the booty accumulated along the way.

The inhabitants of Judah are terrorized by the proximity of Holofernes and his army and fear the worst for their holy city, Jerusalem, particularly for the Temple of Yahweh that has just been restored since their return from the Exile. In reality, these latter events come after Nebuchadnezzar's reign. We will come back to this tendency of the author of the Book of Judith to weave historical details from other periods into his story. Measures are therefore taken to protect the territory, in particular the area where Holofernes is expected to penetrate into Judah. But Israel's salvation depends above all upon God and it is to him the people direct their pleas for help against the invader. The inhabitants adopt garments of sackcloth, a coarse fabric normally worn only during periods of mourning, and cover their heads with ash. They begin a period of fasting and offer sacrifices to Yahweh in a constant prayer for their deliverance from Holofernes.

The general, informed that the Israelites are making military preparations, sends for the chiefs of the neighboring peoples, only recently brought under his control, and asks them for details on how the Israelites are organizing their resistance. He asks them where the Israelites' strength and vigor lie, who their leader as king and commander of their army are, and adds, "why have they disdained to come before me, contrary to all the other peoples who inhabit the

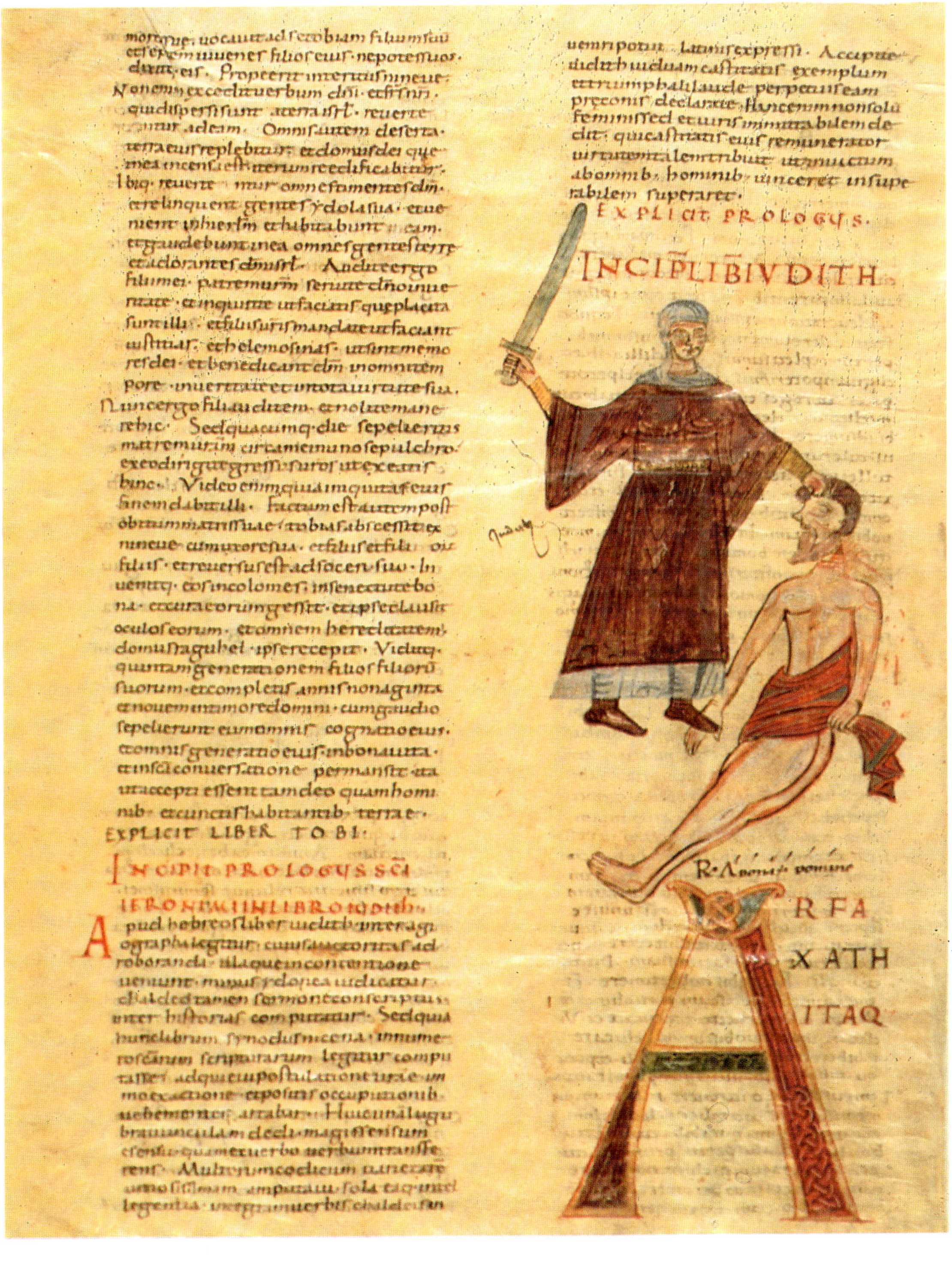

Medieval miniature, *Judith Decapitates Holofernes*

Judith's shrewdness and charm will be a flail against the impious Holofernes, Nebuchadnezzar's general. Judith acts with extraordinary determination and beheads her sleeping enemy in two strokes of the knife.

Guercino, ***Judith Holding Holofernes' Head in Her Hands***

Judith, by her name, is the ideal of Jewish womanhood, as well as symbol of a nation and a people. Far from being a historical account, the Book of Judith shows the universal and eternal struggle of the chosen people against the pagan, par excellence, embodied for this purpose by Nebuchadnezzar.

(*opposite page*)

Massimo Stanzione, ***Judith and Holofernes' Head***

God's will may be accomplished even by the most humble. In the face of Nebuchadnezzar's power, the weakest among the weak, a widow, her only strength being her faith in God, will change the course of history.

West?" Achior, chief general of the Ammonites, then answers the general and recounts the history of the chosen people: originally from Chaldea, this people worshipped only one God who commanded them to settle in the land of Canaan. After a very difficult existence in Egypt, where famine had forced them to seek refuge, these people for a time abandoned their faith in their God and, because of this infidelity, were stricken with many misfortunes including exile. Now having recently returned, they were reconciled with their God. Achior then goes even further: if God is on their side, it is useless to take up arms against them, for Yahweh's protection is unfailing. These words are met with indignation by the Babylonian troops and allies and Achior the Ammonite is arrested and delivered to the Israelites, near Bethulia, Judith's city. Holofernes intends to have him meet the same deadly fate as the Israelite enemies, to be annihilated by the Babylonian army. Achior is therefore tied to a tree in the mountains near Bethulia and left there to meet his certain death. The inhabitants of the city, however, rescue him and bring him before the city officials, the elders, and all the population. Questioned about his presence in Bethulia, Achior delights the Israelites in repeating his words to Holofernes about them, and this earns him an invitation to stay with Ozias, one of the notables of the city.

The next day Holofernes, resolved not to let Yahweh's followers intimidate him, launches his campaign against Bethulia and the entire surrounding region. At the sight of the Babylonian army, the Israelites are filled with consternation: "Now they will graze over the surface of the entire earth and not even the mountains, ravines, nor hills will bear their weight." Listening to the advice of his allies, and to spare the lives of his soldiers, Holofernes decides against a direct attack on the people of Bethulia, who know the mountainous terrain perfectly and therefore benefit from a definite advantage. Instead he chooses to take control of the various springs that feed Bethulia and to force its inhabitants, for lack of water, to surrender without fighting. Surrounded from all sides, subjected to a total blockade, dying of thirst and hunger, the desperate people resist thirty-four days against Holopherne's siege. Women, babies, young people perish in numbers and the inhabitants urge their local chiefs to surrender. "Do not lose hope, brothers, we must resist five more days and the Lord our God will show his mercy on us, he will never abandon us. If these five days pass without God coming to our rescue, I will do as you ask," are Ozias's words to the demoralized crowd.

At that moment, when the situation is at its most critical, Judith appears on the scene, a widow, young, beautiful, rich, pious, courageous. Ozias's speech has not at all pleased her and she sends for the elders of the city. "So who do you think you are — you who have gone before the people today in God's place?" It is up to God alone, continues Judith, to decide whom he will help, when and how, and it is for men to bend to his decisions

Caravaggio, ***Judith and Holofernes***

Judith's beauty and power of seduction are never finalized, as they generally are in the Old Testament, by procreation but rather become an instrument of death at Holofernes' expense.

whatever the circumstances. When Ozias begs Judith, as a wise and pious woman, to pray to the Lord for rain on their behalf, to save Bethulia, Judith hints at her plan: "Listen, for I am to do something that will be told to our people's children, to all the generations after their generation. Be at the Gate tonight when my servant and I leave the city. The Lord will save Israel through my hand before the day comes to surrender our city to the enemy. Do not try to question me, for you will be told nothing until I have accomplished my act."

Judith then prays to God and asks him to arm her against Holofernes. She invokes the God of the humble, he who rescues the unfortunate and is a refuge for the weak, the protector of those who have lost hope, the savior of those in despair; the Lord of the sky and the earth, the creator of the seas, the king of all creatures. Judith's cleverness and charm will serve as a flail against the impious who threaten God's sanctuary. Judith then prepares for the fatal encounter with Holophernes. She adorns herself as if she were a young bride before her wedding. She removes the sackcloth she has worn since the beginning of the siege and bathes, perfumes her body, places a diadem in her hair. Then puts on the festive clothes she has not worn since her husband's death, adding her jewelry. She prepares a pouch of wine, a flask of oil, some flour, figs, and bread to take with her and, accompanied by her loyal servant, escapes beyond the city walls. Once outside the city, an enemy sentry stops her and Judith tells him she has left Bethulia before its surrender, which is now imminent, to show Holphernes safely through the surrounding mountains. Escorted by some of the men, Judith, a "miracle of beauty," is led to the tent where Holofernes reclines on a divan under a purple canopy brilliant with gold embroidery and precious stones.

To the general, dazzled by her beauty, Judith, who presents herself as his servant and his slave, confirms Achior's declaration. If the Israelites are protected by their God, they will be untouchable. However, she confides, exhausted by the siege and worn out by the shortage of food and water, the inhabitants of Bethulia, just as the people of Jerusalem, are now thinking of eating the foods set aside for God: the meat which the Lord has forbidden for consumption, the first pickings of the harvest, the wine destined for Yahweh's priests in Jerusalem and God's altar. This is why Yahweh, angered by such behavior, will let Judith know when they commit these acts of sacrilege, and Holofernes, when she informs him, will be free to take Bethulia and the entire land of Judah without the slightest effort. "You will lead them like a flock without a shepherd and not one dog will growl at you," promises Judith.

Holofernes is seduced by Judith's words and promises her, if her plan succeeds, that she will sit on the throne at Nebuchadnezzar's palace and will be celebrated the world over. During the three days and three nights of her stay in the Babylonian camp, Judith carefully avoids all contamination. She eats only the food she has brought with her, and prays constantly to God. Finally, on the fourth night, Holofernes invites Judith to dine alone with him, intending to seduce her. For the occasion, she dresses in all her feminine finery. Nebuchadnezzar's general, more blinded than ever by her charms, drinks too much and, ordering his slaves to leave him alone with Judith, falls into a drunken sleep. Then, invoking God's support as she performs her act for the salvation of Israel, Judith seizes Holofernes' hair and beheads him, letting his body roll to the ground. Leaving the tent, she entrusts the terrible trophy to her servant who hides it in her pouch of supplies. Both of them, as is their habit and, therefore, without arousing any suspicion, leave the encampment to go to pray, but this time they return to Bethulia instead, without anyone paying the slightest attention to them.

Judith's mission is accomplished. Her cold-blooded courage and physical force — the text points out that she decapitates Holofernes with only two strokes of the knife — earn her the admiration of all. The people, the elders, and the officials of the city, all gathered together, discover the horrible trophy and rejoice, praising God's great mercy in granting them salvation through Judith's mediation.

Holofernes' head is exhibited on the ramparts of Bethulia and Achior the Ammonite finds his mortal enemy is dead, victim of Judith's courage. Overcome by the power of the God of Israel, he decides to convert to the Israelite religion and is circumcised.

The next morning, following Judith's counsel, all the inhabitants of Bethulia in arms descend into the valley to confront their enemies who, in great amazement, run to their officers. They go to Holofernes' tent where they expect to find him asleep in Judith's arms after a night of love. But instead, they discover the horrible assassination and cry out in pain and rage at having been defeated by a woman. Then panic spreads through the besiegers' camp, making them easy prey. From every direction, including Jerusalem, the Israelites charge against their enemy, and win an effortless victory.

Judith receives homages from the high priest Jehoiachim, and the Elders of Jerusalem. "You are the glory of Jerusalem! You are the pride and joy of Israel and of our race!" All the women fete her as a great heroine, crown her with olive leaves, and dance in her honor. All the valuables in Holofernes' tent are then presented to Judith; silver, furniture, vases, which she immediately offers to the Temple of Jerusalem. She then sings a hymn to God which, in many respects, recalls the Psalms. The people's victory celebrations last for three months, after which, Judith returns to Bethulia and, though her fame has reached the ends of the earth, she takes up her former life again. Many men are touched by her charms, but none will conquer her heart. She lives until the venerable age of 105 years in her deceased husband's house, after freeing her servant. Knowing death is approaching, with wisdom and serenity she divides her estate among her deceased husband's relatives and after she dies, is buried by his side.

The figure of Judith is fascinating perhaps because she combines beauty, seductiveness, feminine charm, with cold-bloodedness and determination, qualities that are more readily attributed to men in ancient and modern literature. She is obviously much more than just a young widow living in Bethulia during Nebuchadnezzar's reign. She embodies the very soul of Israel with its fierce desire for independence and the consciousness of an identity that must be protected at all costs.

Judith is presented from the outset as Merari's daughter. The author (or authors) of the biblical Book that bears her name, as soon as she appears in the text give her a long genealogy which, besides her father, totals fifteen ancestors of which the most distant significantly bears the name Israel. Is Judith herself not, by virtue of her name, the Jewish feminine ideal, the symbol of a nation and a people? Many other features of the biblical tale encourage us to believe that, despite appearances, the Book of Judith far from being a story with a historical purpose, contains instead an evocation of the universal and eternal struggle of the chosen people. Judith is, in a way, the

Botticelli, ***The Return of Judith to Bethulia***

After having decapitated Holofernes, Judith leaves his tent and entrusts the terrible trophy to her servant who hides it in a pouch. Both then leave the camp and return to Bethulia.

Botticelli, *The Discovery of Holofernes' Body*
For the Florentine Republic of the fifteenth century, Judith, immortalized by many artists, was the symbol of freedom and the just rebellion against the excessive power of the Medicis. Art, therefore, knowingly bestowed upon Judith a universal dimension already suggested by the biblical text.

emblem of this, against the Pagan par excellence, embodied for the circumstance by Nebuchadnezzar.

The Book of Judith opens, in fact, with a curious chronological note: "... the twelfth year of Nebuchadnezzar's reign, king of the Assyrians in the great city of Nineveh, during the time of Arphaxad, king of Media in Ecbatana." However, Nebuchadnezzar was never king of Assyria, but rather of Babylonia, and the great metropolis of Nineveh was destroyed in 612 by his father, Nebopolassar. As for Arphaxad, this name is totally unknown to historians of the Persian empire! We immediately get the impression that the author of the Book of Judith has voluntarily blurred the picture to stress the fictional character of the work that uses the vicissitudes of the Hebrew people for strictly theological purposes, that is, to illustrate God's divine plan of which Judith is no more than a chance executor. The modern visitor to Israel will search in vain for the traces of Judith's city, Bethulia, which must have been a literary invention. Its etymology is certainly not to be ignored. Bethulia, in fact, means "House of God" and consequently is an allegory of Israel, the Promised Land. Here we see taking shape, little by little, behind the names of people and places, behind the pretended historical setting, symbols of universal scope.

Chapter 8 of the Book of Judith, in which the heroine is introduced for the first time with her lengthy genealogy, relates she is the widow of a certain Manasseh, who had died three years before during the barley harvest, victim of a violent sunstroke. After he is buried in the tomb of his ancestors, Judith lives alone, for no child has been born of their union. Judith's piety and respect for ritual usages are constantly pointed out in the text. She dresses in widow's mourning, fasts almost every day and is faithful and God fearing. But Judith is also beautiful, seductive and rich, her husband having left her all his fortune in gold, silver, land, slaves. She is, all in all, an independent woman and respected by the entire community of Bethulia.

If we wanted to describe Judith's personality, we would have to resort to a myriad of attributes one more laudatory than the other: wise, a good counsel, ascetic, courageous, pure, honest, sensitive, pious, God's confidante, beautiful and rich, in short, a perfect woman who is admired and envied by all. However, in the context of social conceptions reflected in the Old Testament, we cannot help finding such a presentation astonishing for a widow like Judith. Widowhood, in fact, was considered a temporary condition, only meant to last a short period before remarriage. Deuteronomy is very clear on this subject: "When brothers live together and one of them dies without any sons, the wife of the deceased may not belong to a man outside the family. Her brother-in-law will go to her, will take her as his wife, and will perform his duty to her as brother-in-law. The first born whom she bears must perpetuate the name of the deceased brother. Thus his name will not be erased from Israel." It was therefore inconceivable that a woman, after leaving her father's protective wing when she got married, could lead, after the death of her husband, an independent existence, without tutelage, without a guarantor.

Judith, though, has been a widow for three years and has no children, but nevertheless she does not seem to have any intention of remarrying. She even enjoys remarkable autonomy: she lives alone, manages her deceased husband's estate, which was left to her as an inheritance, and plays a fundamental role in the destiny of her city and of Israel. When Bethulia is threatened by Nebuchadnezzar's ambitions, she takes the initiative of sending for the city elders whom she receives in her own house and feels free to criticize the speech Ozias has made before the people. We are therefore, with Judith, far from the image of the timorous widow living in seclusion between her four walls and only concerned with domestic duties. The cleverness and determination of Judith's actions prompt the author of the biblical text to even comment that she acts "like a man" which must have been, for the time and the cultural milieu so strongly marked by masculine supremacy, an extremely valuable compliment.

In the Book of Judith almost all the men, whether the heroine's enemies or fellow-citizens, appear but pale shadows compared to her. They are petty, limited, cowardly, naive, and incapable of dealing with a situation which Judith alone manages, very quickly, to bring quite under control. It is certainly for a good reason that the editor of the Book of Judith devotes the first seven chapters, on the one hand, to a description, meticulous and richly detailed, of the feverish preparations of the military campaign on both sides, and on the other hand, of the resistance that opposes the masculine figures who seem like ants uselessly bustling about in an overwhelming universe. Then in chapter 8 Judith appears and takes the situation in hand, proposing a solution as rapid as it is effective. However, far from being a glorification of women or a "feminist" text, the Book of Judith wants to demonstrate the fact that God's will may be accomplished *even* by the humblest. In the face of a political and military giant, represented by Nebuchadnezzar, we see the weakest of the weak, a woman, worse yet, a widow, her faith in God her only strength, capable of changing the course of history. God's act is made all the more remarkable since it is accomplished through Judith.

This being said, the unusual status mentioned previously which the biblical text bestows upon Judith, leads us to believe that the text was also influenced by the epoch, perhaps the second century B. C., when the condition of women, of the widow in particular, was being somewhat re-evaluated. Nothing revolutionary, certainly (we are far from the Suffragettes!), but some progress compared to previous periods. Judith, her mission having been accomplished and the celebrations in her honor over, goes home, as any anonymous widow, far from the hubbub of public meeting places and palace intrigues. If there is progress, it is definitely limited to exceptional circumstances.

It may also be added that what makes Judith's profile unique is the fact that she is childless. The biblical text's esteem for her could thus indicate that women are no longer exclusively bound to functions of fecundity and maternity. They are capable of rendering other services to the community than those of procreation, even though this remains their principal role. Judith's beauty, her power of seduction, are never finalized as they normally are in the Bible, by procreation, by life, but rather become an instrument of death at Holofernes' expense. In contrast to the impotence of men's armies and their strategies, Judith's beauty is a formidably efficient arm. The editor of the Book of Judith does not blame her in the least for using her charms to kill, since this act ensures the salvation of Israel. Seduction, lying, assassination are justified here by the fact that they serve a just cause: the faith of Yahweh and the defense of the chosen people. It is therefore of little importance to know whether the union between Judith and Holofernes is ever consummated — something many biblical commentators have asked themselves in vain — what is more important is that our "femme fatale," though sacrificing herself for Israel, still remains pure and uncontaminated, protected as she is, by her honesty to Yahweh.

Judith is not the only biblical heroine to play a decisive role in the destiny of Israel. Deborah, evoked in the Book of Judges, is also remembered for having helped the Israelites during the days when they were attempting to settle in the Promised Land. Having come up against the incursions of the Canaanites, the Israelites were having difficulty resisting the advance. It is Deborah, just when Israel's spirit seems to be failing, who gives renewed vigor to the troops calling them to rise up and free the land which God has promised them. The hymn celebrating these exploits is generally considered the most ancient poem in the Bible. Concise, sober, rhythmic, it is truly a literary masterpiece. It also introduces, in addition to Deborah, an Israelite named Giale who, worthily emulating Judith, smashes Sisera's skull when the Canaanite commander, while escaping, asks her for water. Just like Judith, Deborah is inspired by God himself who dictates a type of behavior extremely unusual for a woman, but beneficial for Israel.

Judith has greatly inspired artists from Botticelli to Michclangclo to Klimt. Donatello has also given us a splendid Judith, pathetic and expressive, recently restored and returned, more breathtaking than ever, for the Florentines to admire. For the people of the Florentine Republic of the fifteenth century, this statue was the symbol of freedom and just rebellion against the excessive power of the Medicis. Art, therefore, knowingly bestowed upon the figure of Judith the universal dimension the biblical text had already so vigorously emphasized.

Gustav Klimt, ***Judith I***
This modern representation of Judith shocked Klimt's contemporaries by the provocative sensuality and langorous expression of the heroine's face. Here she embodies the femme fatale and recalls Salome. The decor used in the background was taken from an Assyrian relief.

ESTHER

A Jewish Woman at the Court of Persia

Leave tears, Esther, to these young children.
In you rests all the hope of your unfortunate brothers.
They must be rescued. But time is dear:
The hours are fleeting and soon will come the day
When the name of the Hebrews must perish never to return.

RACINE, *Esther*

With Esther we are once again confronted with a biblical heroine whose uniqueness lies in the fact that she does not live in Israel, but in Persia, and more precisely at the court of the great king whose wife she is destined to become. Esther's amazing story will serve as another illustration of the exceptional force of the Covenant that binds Yahweh and his chosen people.

As was the case with the Book of Judith, the Book of Esther, which has come down to us in a Hebrew as well as Greek version, the latter slightly lengthier and of a later date, is a recent addition to the biblical canon. Luther did not like this work at all and during the period of transition to the Christian era, the famous sect of the Essenes of Qumran, which gave us the famous Dead Sea Scrolls, did not recopy it. We know, however, that the Jews of the first centuries of the Christian era upheld this work as even holier than the Prophets.

The Book of Esther, whose narrative and literary qualities have long been recognized, presents other similarities with the Book of Judith, for that matter with the Book of Tobit as well: firstly, the great liberty the authors of these books take with historical and geographical details. Certainly, though, we will see descriptions of the royal court of Persia in the Book of Esther which stand a good chance of corresponding to the historical reality that other written sources and archaeological excavations have reconstructed for us. In spite of the quality of certain data and the absence of the supernatural in this work, we do note some obvious improbabilities clearly indicating, once again, that it would be wrong to consider the Book of Esther as a historical work. History, in fact, is only a backdrop, a pretext for staging the all-powerful action of Yahweh whose name, curiously enough, never appears in the Book of Esther. He is, however, very much present, this God who dictates to Esther her exemplary conduct, based on courage and intelligence, which will deliver the Jewish people from a terrible threat. Just like Judith, Esther is a liberator, a woman who despite her disadvantaged condition — she is a foreigner in Persia and an orphan at that — is solely responsible, thanks to her moral force, for the survival of thousands of Jews, victims of prevailing intolerance. The central theme of this work, therefore, is the great reversal of a situation in favor of the oppressed, faced by the threat of the powerful, but who, through Esther, are helped by God. This is, moreover, a theme we find echoed in sapiential literature, notably in the Book of Proverbs. Finally, before considering the narrative and the outlines of our heroine's personality in detail, it should be noted that the story of the Book of Esther is explicitly associated with a Hebrew liturgical festival, Purim, that annually commemorates the rescue from massacre, thanks to Esther, of the Jews of Persia.

When the tale begins, the great Ahasuerus reigns in Persia, in whom we recognize Xerxes I (486-465 B. C.), the king who led the second Median war against the Greeks and who was defeated in the famous battles of Salamis (480) and Platea (479). It was precisely because the Persians were the Greeks' historical enemy that the Hellenic historians and geographers frequently took an interest in this land, in its mores and customs, sovereigns, history. This gives us an opportunity to compare certain specific points in the Book of Esther, whose aim is anything but "ethnographic," with the writings of the Greek authors such as Herodotus, Xenophon, Ctesia or Strabo who claimed to relate what they had seen or heard on the spot. We will point out these instances of cross-checking as we go along. This being said, we must guard against looking for an echo of the adventures of Esther in Persian history as revealed to us by historical sources. The story is definitely fictional and uses history solely for its own theological purposes.

As the Book of Esther opens, we find ourselves in the "year II" of the reign of Ahasuerus of Persia, in the city of Susa, ancient capital of Elam, one of the Persian royal residences such as Ecbatana and Persepolis. There, a Jew by the name of Mordecai, who is employed at the royal court, has a dream: two dragons are on the verge of fighting one another, they are soon joined by entire nations that threaten the Jewish people. The people implore God for help and their common cry gives birth to a river. Finally, the chosen people are victorious and devour their enemies.

The existence of the Jews in Persia is historical fact. The Books of Ezra and Nehemiah confirm this situation after the Babylonian Exile of the Jews, but what is less credible, on the one hand, is the attributing of Mordecai's deportation to the great king of Babylonia, Nebuchadnezzar, which would have meant that

Mordecai had lived for more than 150 years, and on the other hand, the intolerance which the Hebrew presence provokes among the Persians. Moreover, this detail, which serves as the basis for all the vicissitudes related in the Book of Esther, contradicts historical accounts of the situation which, on the contrary, distinguish the Achaemenides sovereigns as being particularly respectful of cultural diversity, a feature that characterized the vast Persian empire.

Mordecai, soon after this dream, successfully foils a conspiracy hatched by two palace eunuchs responsible for the protection of the king and he receives, in gratitude, a promotion to the royal chancellery, at the "King's Door," that is, the building located at the entrance to the royal palace where the guests wait to be received. This promotion provokes Haman's jealousy, the all-powerful vizier, the sovereign's closest and most influential advisor. It is within this framework of intrigues and rivalries that the event which will mark a turning point in Esther's life takes place, and who makes her first appearance at this point. The king, whose immense kingdom the biblical text heavily stresses, describing its hundred and twenty-seven provinces spanning from India to Ethiopia, decides to give a banquet to all the princes, ministers, army commanders, province governors, and other dignitaries, in a great show of his wealth and power. The festivities last no less than 180 days followed by seven days of rejoicing for the common people, who are received in the courtyard of the royal garden.

The biblical text dwells at length on the splendor of the celebrations in a *Thousand and One Nights* decor: royal wine served in vessels of gold; marble pillars and purple hangings with silver rings; beds of gold and silver upon a pavement of marble, red, blue, black and white, and the brilliance of precious objects everywhere. What remains of the ruins of ancient Susa give us an idea of the fabulous wealth of Persia's past. The city of Shushan, the ruins of which are quite damaged, was discovered in 1851 and excavated mainly at the end of the nineteenth century. Its impressive royal palace, a vast quadrilateral of more than five acres, is set upon a fortified hill and consisted of numerous rooms and vast walled gardens connected to the palace by gently sloping ramps. The famous frieze of the archers of Susa, today preserved in Paris at the Louvre Museum and brought to light when the ruins on the four hills of ancient Susa were discovered, allow us to relive just a fraction of the splendor of the Achaemenides' art. This magnificence is also the subject of an inscription from the epoch of Darius I, Xerxes' father, alias Ahasuerus, which describes the splendor of the palace constructed with precious wood procured from Lebanon and India, gold from Sardis, silver and copper from Egypt, ivory from Ethopia, and so on.

At the same time as Xerxes' festivities, the queen, named Vashti, in Persian meaning "the excellent," offers a banquet to the wives of the dignitaries of the Empire. Perhaps out of exaggerated pride or under the influence of too much drink, the king demands that the queen deck herself out in all her finery and parade before the guests. Indignant, she refuses and this provokes her immediate repudiation by the king who fears all the women in the kingdom may rebel against their husbands' wishes. The king makes his repudiation known in all the provinces and in all the languages of the kingdom. The Persian empire, in fact, was a veritable Tower of Babel where a great number of languages existed side by side: Persian, Babylonian, Elamite, Aramaic, Sanskrit, Lydian, Carian, Egyptian, Arabic, etc., and diverse systems of writing: alphabetic, cuneiform, hieroglyphic.

At this point in the story we note an interesting parallel to the tale by Herodotus concerning the king of Sardis, Candaules, which shows certain similarities with Vashti's misfortunes. Candaules, in fact, was so convinced that his wife, whose name is not given, was the most beautiful woman in the world, that he wants to reveal her charms to Gyges, his bodyguard and favorite. Hesitant at first, faced with this embarassing situation, Gyges however finally accepts and hides in the royal couple's bedroom in order to have the queen's hidden splendors revealed to him. But the queen notices the strategem and decides to take revenge for the affront. She orders Gyges to kill Candaules in his

Relief from Persepolis with a representation of the royal court

The setting of the Book of Esther is the Persian royal court where the young Jewish orphan manages to attain a place of honor as the wife of the "king of kings."

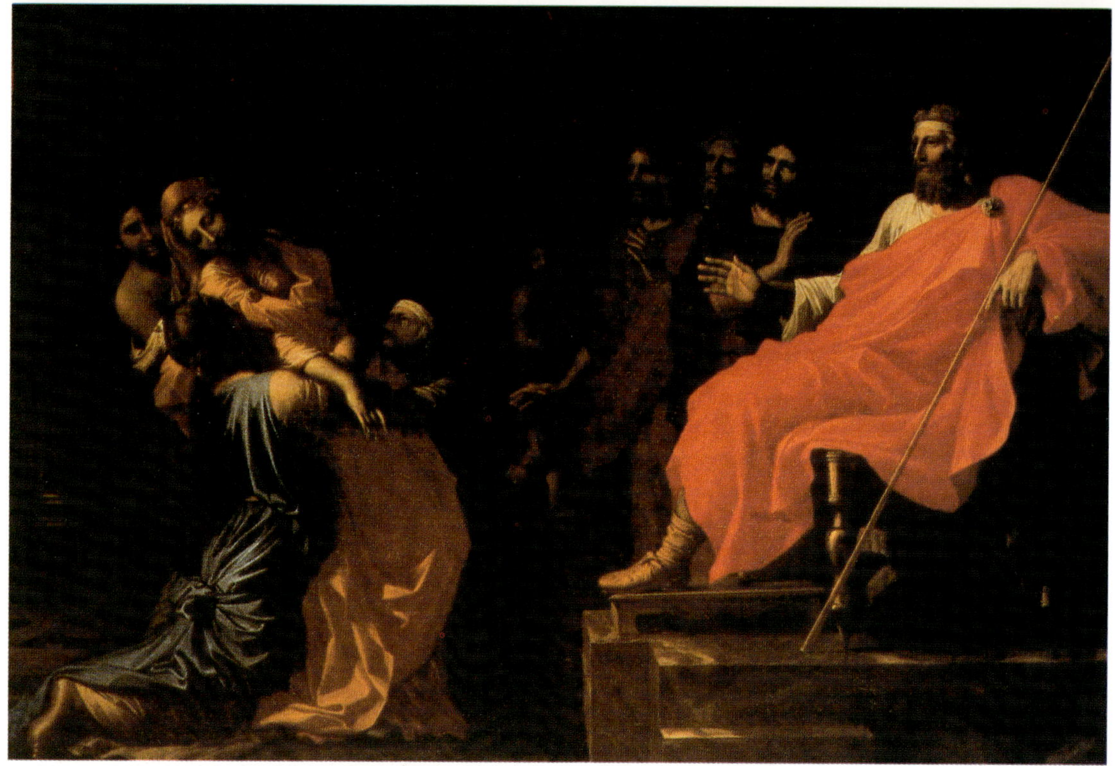

Nicolas Poussin, *Esther Goes before Ahasuerus*
According to Persian custom, anyone who presents himself before the king without being summoned by him risks punishment by death. Wearing her most brilliant garments and jewels Esther, nevertheless, goes to see the king, her husband, to plead her people's cause.

sleep and to marry her, which is what the bodyguard does, thus becoming the new ruler of Lydia and ancestor of the famous Croesus.

But now King Ahasuerus must find a new wife. All of the most beautiful virgins in the kingdom are therefore brought to Susa and are subjected to interminable preparation, then put through a long examination, including various "tests," the king remaining the one and only judge in the matter. At that moment Esther, also called Hadassah, a young Jewish orphan brought up by her cousin Mordecai, enters the lists. If Hadassah is a name connected with the myrtle, a plant also used in nuptial celebrations in the classical world, the name Esther could be derived from the name of an Assyro-Babylonian goddess of love, but also perhaps of war, Ishtar, or then again, a Persian word meaning "star." Whatever the case may be, hiding her true ancestry and her relation to Mordecai, Esther, after twelve months of preparation before all to see, is finally presented before Ahasuerus who, in the seventh year of his reign, selects her and makes her queen of Persia.

Meanwhile, the eunuchs prepare another conspiracy, foiled again by Mordecai, when he has Esther warn the king. Haman the vizier, in the meantime, continues his slow but sure political ascension within the palace ranks and finally reaches the highest functions in the administration, earning him a show of constant deference by everyone around him. Only Mordecai behaves differently, even refusing to bow down to him, as custom obliges, and provokes Haman's hatred who, to get his revenge, is determined to annihilate the Jewish people. He convinces the king of the validity of this course of action, using as a pretext his claim that the Jewish people live shut off from the rest of the world with their own laws, and that they are hostile to Persia and therefore a threat to the internal stability of the kingdom. Haman also holds out the prospect of the riches which would pour into the royal treasury as a result.

In the twelfth year of Ahasuerus' reign, therefore, a royal edict to all the provinces of the Empire proclaims the imminent extermination of all Jews living on Persian territory, young and old, men, women, children, and the sacking of all their property. Haman draws lots to determine the date and place of this extermination: the thirteenth day of the twelfth month. This strange practice of drawing lots, well attested in antiquity notably for the nomination of certain magistrates whose selection was thus left up to destiny, gives rise to the Hebrew celebration Purim, to which we will return, since the term "pur" in Accadian, the language of Babylonia, means "lot."

In Susa, consternation is immense within the Jewish community. All the Jews perform ritual gestures ordinarily meant for funeral ceremonies. They wear garments torn in shreds and sacking for tunics, cover their heads with ash, their cries of desperation rising to the sky. They also turn to prayer and to their God, Yahweh. Mordecai begs Esther to intercede in favor of her people before the king, though Persian custom dictates that anyone who presents himself to the sovereign without being summoned by him, risks punishment by death. For three days and three nights, in solidarity with the Jews of Susa, Esther prepares for this encounter, which she knows will be as dangerous for her personally as it will be decisive for all the Jewish people whom she represents and whose destiny she embodies. After dressing in her most brilliant garments and jewels and hiding her anxiety behind a calm and radiant expression, Esther presents herself before the king, fearing the worst. The tension is so great in fact that she faints, and this elicits the king's tender sympathy for his wife, whom he pardons, though she has acted in serious breach of custom. Instead of revealing her intentions to him all at once, Esther chooses a more indirect approach. Proceeding in a skillfully diplomatic and wise manner, she invites the king to a banquet at her residence in the company of the all powerful and so greatly feared, Haman. This first meeting goes very well and the king, delighted by Esther's charms, is ready to offer her anything she desires, even half of his empire. But Esther, as a clever strategist, stalls him and postpones her intercession on behalf of the Jewish people until the next day. In the meantime Haman, more self-confident than ever, and believing himself in the queen's favor, has a gallows erected where he intends to have Mordecai hanged the very next day.

Upon returning to the palace, the king, suffering from insomnia re-reads a few pages from the

Chronicles of his reign. As we know from a few surviving copies, the Near Eastern sovereigns were in the habit of having journals kept where, from year to year, the main events of their reigns were recorded. Ahasuerus then realizes that Mordecai, as a zealous servant of the throne, has saved his life upon several occasions, and he decides to duly honor him. He first sends for Haman to question him about the best way to honor a worthy man. Believing the king is thinking of him, Haman suggests dressing him in the royal robe and crown and having him parade through the streets of Susa to the cries of "here is the man whom the king wants to honor." Herodotus and Xenophon confirm the fact that the granting of ceremonial regalia, the Median or Persian royal dress, was an exceptional distinction. But how great are Haman's surprise and rage when he learns from the king himself that the recipient of these honors is no other than his mortal enemy, the man he is just getting ready to hang, Mordecai the Jew.

During the second banquet given by Esther for the king and Haman, the truth is finally revealed to Ahasuerus. Esther tells him of her Jewish ancestry and holds Haman responsible for the unjust massacre to take place in a few days. Haman pleads for the king's mercy, but he is hanged without pity upon the very the gallows he had intended for Mordecai. The king, as originally planned, then has Mordecai honored and, from a penitent dressed in sackcloth and pleading God to save the Jews from massacre, he sees himself become an honored dignitary with the insignia of royalty. He receives, notably, as a sign of the king's gratitude, Haman's house and the royal ring of the hanged man as well. This is most likely a ring bearing the royal seal, used for the sealing of official documents, similar to the one the Pharoah gives to Joseph (Gen. 12:42) and is therefore an exceptional sign of trust. Esther, naturally, sees that the king revokes the decree proclaimed previously under Haman's instigation. In a dramatic reversal of the situation that could only have been inspired by Yahweh, Ahasuerus not only annuls the previous decision concerning the massacre of the Jews, but declares that on the days designated by the first decree, these people will have the right to exterminate all who intend to do them harm. So here the oppressed become, in a way, the oppressors, at least if they decide to avenge the harm others want to inflict upon them. This will to vengeance, sometimes very violent as is the case here, seems foreign and contrary to Christian morals, but nevertheless appears frequently in the Books of the Old Testament, for example, in Psalms or in the Book of Nehemiah. The avenging and nationalist character of the Book of Esther is, most likely, a reflection of a firmly rooted mentality in certain Jewish milieus victims of persecution and hungry for vengeance.

Esther, in any case, appears as a savior and benefactress of her people for whom she receives the king's protection. In Herodotus we read of an event that takes place at the court of the Persian king Darius which recalls somewhat the story in the Book of Esther. This concerns a man who is arrested with all of his relatives and threatened to be put to death. His wife, after great pleading, manages to be received by the king who grants his pardon for one of the relatives of her choice. Much to Darius's great surprise, she does not choose to spare her husband or one of their sons, but rather her brother, arguing that she could always remarry and have more children, but since her mother was dead, she would never be given another brother. Impressed by her wisdom, Darius spares the brother of the woman as well as her eldest son. Here again, the text stresses the supplicant's charm and her power over the king. Whatever the case may be, the Jews of Persia, who are referred to as the "children of God" in the second decree, rejoice and celebrate the good news. Many other subjects in the kingdom convert to the Hebrew religion, so powerful have the Jews become and how greatly feared is

Medieval miniature, ***Scenes from the Life of Esther***

Esther is the only Jewish woman living in a foreign land celebrated by the Old Testament. Like Judith, she became an important symbol of the Jewish patriotic spirit and the triumph of faith and justice over blind persecution.

Tintoretto, ***Esther and Ahasuerus***

Proceeding in a skillful and wise manner, she invites the king to a banquet with the greatly feared Haman, sworn enemy of the Jews. Then, as a clever strategist, Esther stalls the king and postpones her intercession on behalf of the Jewish people until the next day.

(opposite page, above)

Rembrandt, ***The Triumph of Mordecai***

The Book of Esther shows how Yahweh can provoke the complete reversal of situations in favor of his faithful. The case of Mordecai, the king's servant promoted to the position of vizier, is a most notable example.

their vengeance. Eventually, on the fixed day, they gather together in arms and kill their enemies, helped even by the local authorities who fear the powerful Mordecai, now having become extremely influential at the court. In Susa, five hundred dead are recorded, not counting Haman's sons who are also hanged. Esther has the king agree to extend the measure of impunity another day and three hundred more enemies of the Jews fall in Susa, whereas in the provinces the dead amount to the astronomical, and not very credible, number of seventy-five thousand (the Greek Septuagint reduces the number to fifteen thousand, the handwritten traditions being more prone to alterations when it came to numbers). No sacking accompany these punitive acts which are, however, followed by banquets and the exchange of gifts to celebrate the end of the oppression of which the Jews have felt victim.

The end of the Book of Esther, which apparently serves to establish the liturgical festival of Purim and provide the key to the interpretation of Mordecai's initial dream, tells us that the latter, having become the second highest dignitary in the kingdom, arranges for all these events, of which he has been a privileged witness, to be recorded. He also sends a letter to all the Jews the world over urging them to establish an annual celebration to commemorate these great moments in the history of the chosen people. As a result, on the fourteenth and fifteenth of March each year the Book of Esther is read in all the synagogues of the world to recall the way in which Yahweh, once again, saved his people from annihilation thanks to the courage and determination of a woman. From Jewish sources, in particular the Talmud of Jerusalem, we know that a special ritual, in ancient times at least, accompanied this Purim celebration, a festival whose name, as already mentioned, comes from an event in the Book of Esther, that is, the drawing of lots (*pur*) for the date on which the Jews of Persia were to be massacred. On the thirteenth, therefore, the eve of the great day, the Jews fasted and gave alms to the poor, after going to the synagogue to hear the reading of Genesis. On the fourteenth, banquets and rejoicing marked the moment of salvation and in the evening, to the light of torches, the Book of Esther was read in the synagogue while the people mimed the massacre of Haman and his sons, crying out curses and hitting the benches with their hands. On the fifteenth, finally, a type of carnival with costumes was celebrated. These features have led to the belief that the celebration in question was, in fact, originally a pagan festival related to the return of Spring which, by its linking to the personage and adventures of Esther, acquired a new significance and dimension, that of the deliverance of the Jews by Yahweh. This is, however, only a hypothesis and is very difficult to confirm.

Confronted with the figure of Haman, who embodies blind hate, irrational and therefore "diabolical," towards the Jewish people (and who prefigures, as more than one Jewish author has noted, Hitler's genocidal madness in the twentieth century), is Esther, the uncontested heroine of this story — she is cited some fifty-five times, which is more than any woman in the Bible — the only Jewish woman living in a foreign land celebrated by the Old Testament. This is probably why, because of the vicissitudes that she endured, she became, much as Judith, an important symbol of the Jewish patriotic spirit and the triumph of faith and justice over blind persecution. "Star" by her name, she guides her people and, thanks to her sensible reasoning, leads them safely and soundly to salvation. She is, of course, the instrument of God's will and desire. She courageously accepts her destiny, marked first of all by her ascension to the position of queen, then her role, so very risky, as mediator between her own people and her husband, king of Persia. Without enjoying an artistic popularity as widespread as Judith's, she has nevertheless inspired a Racine drama, several paintings of which, notably, a Tintoretto, and an oratorio by Handel.

Stained glass, *Esther and Ahasuerus*
Esther's adventures are an exemplary illustration of the exceptional power of the Covenant that binds Yahweh to his people, related throughout the entire Old Testament.

Durer, ***Job Refreshed by His Wife***

Everything in Job's life exudes happiness and perfect fulfillment until the day when, with Yahweh's agreement, Satan decides to test Job's faith, after which not his wife nor his friends can do anything to relieve his suffering.

JOB

The Righteous Sufferer

Patience is the most heroic of virtues, precisely because there is no indication of heroism.

GIACOMO LEOPARDI, *Zibaldone*

Indeed the figure of Job and the questions raised by the biblical Book bearing his name represent a high point in Man's reflection on the human condition. At the heart of the discussion between Job, his friends, and God are concepts as fundamental as good and evil, sin, suffering, sickness, death, the meaning of life, and divine justice, in short, the questions which have always tormented Man and will continue to do so for as long as humanity exists. With Job, therefore, we will attempt to examine in depth an essential step in Man's advance towards his understanding and acceptance of a condition often characterized by contradiction and ambiguity. After having related the essential points of a book which is unanimously considered a masterpiece of universal literature, we will also try to demonstrate how Job's reflections fit into a particular current of Near Eastern sapiential literature which is unfamiliar, no doubt, to the general public though it is certainly worthy of the greatest interest.

The structure of the Book of Job is quite complex and has naturally given rise to lengthy discussions among specialists. The Book opens with a brief prologue which introduces the figure of Job and his conceptions concerning the way God deals with good and evil. Then comes a lengthy dialogue in verse between Job and his three friends who each defend, repeatedly, their points of view on the question. This forms the main part of the Book of Job which closes with an epilogue in prose and an intervention by Yahweh himself who refers to the questions raised in the prologue. Yahweh comments on the opinions expressed up to then and finally sides with Job. Given the complexity of its structure and the depth of the subject matter under consideration, it is not an easy task to date the drafting of this text. We are prompted to share the opinion of biblical scholars who place it somewhere between the second half of the sixth century to the fourth century B. C., it being understood that Elihu's speeches in chapters 32 to 37 are obviously quite a later addition. Nevertheless we are led to believe, notably based on parallels in Near Eastern literatures, that the Book of Job, in its form as well as in its central ideas, drew upon much more ancient traditional sources.

Job's genealogy (*ijjob* in Hebrew, a name of uncertain meaning) is unknown to us. We are only told that he is a foreigner, since he lives in the land of Uz, a region located in southern Palestine near the Arabian peninsula most likely in Edomite territory. Job is therefore not Hebrew, but this does not keep him from being attributed remarkable moral qualities. He is "blameless and upright, fears Elohim and turns away from evil." Everything about him exudes happiness and perfect fulfillment: seven sons and three daughters, seven thousand sheep, three thousand camels, five hundred pairs of oxen and five hundred donkeys, not to mention a throng of well-fed slaves. In short, the text continues, "he was the greatest of the sons of the East." The numbers in the text serve a symbolic purpose since in Semitic culture three and seven were believed to represent perfection. To the picture thus outlined must also be added Job's scrupulous concern for keeping himself and his family free from sin, all conjuring up an image of the ideal family, blessed by God and rewarded for its efforts by an extremely privileged condition. Not only in this story but also in the Book of Ruth, whose heroine is a Moabite, do we find streaks in the Old Testament of universal aspirations that must have been pitted against the narrow nationalist conceptions held by certain fringes of society, notably theologians' circles, to whom we owe the final form of the early texts. It is in fact only in the New Testament, with the figure of Christ and his apostles, that the universal dimension of the biblical message will be truly developed.

A challenge put out by Satan to God will plunge Job's existence into misfortune and suffering. To God, who praises his servant Job's uprightness and piety, Satan answers that Job's goodness is solely motivated by the material rewards his righteous attitude has continually earned him. It is therefore a form of gratitude and not blind disinterested obedience to his God. "Put Job to the test" says Satan, "and you will see that he will curse you." Yahweh then gives Satan his permission to test Job and entrusts everything that Job possesses to Satan except his own person.

As a result, a series of misfortunes rain down on Job, his family, and everything they possess. In four minutes, he receives news of four disasters. First, all his oxen, donkeys, and slaves are massacred by the Sabeans; then lightening destroys all his flocks of sheep and the shepherds. After that, the Chaldeans steal all his camels and kill the guards. Finally, a tornado destroys a house where his children are gathered, killing all of them. When news of these tragedies is brought to him, Job rises solemnly to his feet and, in the usual outward signs of mourning, he tears his outer garments and shaves his head, then throws himself to the ground. Despite his despair, however,

Georges de la Tour, *Job and His Wife*

Job's wife rarely appears in the story and plays a negative role. She suggests to her husband to renounce his natural goodness and curse God in order to escape his suffering through death. But Job persists in his heroic struggle.

he does not blame Yahweh and accepts his terrible fate with greatness and submission: "Yahweh gave and he has taken away, blessed be the name of the Lord."

When Satan again presents himself before God, the latter immediately expresses his pleasure at Job's continued righteousness and regrets ever having agreed to make him suffer so unjustly. But Satan insists: "If you smite him in his flesh," he affirms, "he will eventually curse you." Yahweh therefore consents to a further test, though reminding Satan not to put Job's life in danger.

Then Satan afflicts Job with a loathsome and painful disease that covers his body from head to toe. Job's skin dries up and is covered with scabs and sores, his body's limbs decompose and feel like dead weights, he grows so emaciated that his bones protrude from under his blackening skin. Then, consumed by a constant burning inside, he is racked with attacks of nausea and anxiety. His eyelids turn dark and his face inflamed from sobbing. He is pursued by an implacable relentless enemy whose poisoned arrows torture him without respite. It would be useless to search for a name for Job's illness, it is the sum of all the physical and mental afflictions a human being can possibly endure. Job has been stripped of everything he possesses and afflicted with diseases that surpass the imagination, reducing him to a groveling, wretched state. At the same time he remains, unfortunately perhaps for him, perfectly lucid, capable of understanding what is happening to him and, in his anguish, of asking what has made him the victim of such violent and merciless torture.

His wife, who now appears for the first time and plays an obviously negative role, suggests that Job renounce his natural goodness and put an end to his suffering by uttering blasphemy against God, which would thus cause his certain death. But Job persists in his heroic struggle and thinks, "If we accept all that is good from Elohim, why must we not accept the bad as well?" Then, informed of Job's terrible misfortunes, three friends, Eliphaz, Bildad, and Zophar, go to visit Job in the hope of consoling him. They remain with him for seven days and seven nights but their efforts are awkward and in vain. The main section of the Book of Job, in verse of remarkable beauty, relates the debate that ensues between Job and his friends.

Job opens the discussion. He curses the day he was ever born since, he says, it was the origin of all his suffering. In a fit of anger, he wonders why he had not been put to death on that very day since he was destined anyway to such a fatal existence. With the moving intensity and poetic mastery we can admire throughout the entire Book of Job, the author describes a man's absolute refusal of life and his great longing for death, for a state of non-existence where he can finally find rest and peace. Job also wonders what meaning such a hopeless and absurd life can possibly hold, and asks why God purposely puts up barriers around Man, pitting him in a constant struggle against some invisible irrational enemy. For the first time, therefore, Job accuses God of being responsible for his daily suffering, so incomprehensible and tyrannical, and asks him *why*, exclaiming in anguish, "I have no peace, no rest and my troubles never end."

Job's soliloquy gives way to Eliphaz's speech who reminds Job of how, in better days, it was Job himself who had always helped the weak and unfortunate. Eliphaz, in this way wants to encourage his friend not to lose faith or hope now that he finds himself, and not only others, the victim of misfortune. Eliphaz then develops the famous theory of retributive justice which is at the heart of all the debates in the Book of Job. Man is free to act according to positive or negative moral criteria, but he should be aware that God acts in consequence. He rewards the good and punishes the bad, and those who sow the seeds of evil and injustice will perish by God's spirit. Therefore, if Job is convinced of his good intentions and righteousness, he should not question God's attitude towards him.

To give more weight to his argument, Eliphaz presents his theory as a divine revelation and relates a dream he has had. A shroud comes to him and whispers a message in his ear. Man is a creature of God, it says, his slave and his servant, a weak and ephemeral being who can lay no claim to perfection. Therefore, who is there better than God to know men's weaknesses, and who more justly than God to punish them? One must not rebel but rather accept the good and the bad in life in total trust. God is omniscent and omnipotent, benevolent and just. Eliphaz even comes to the conclusion that pain and sorrow should be praised and proclaims the bliss of the righteous who suffer. For, he asserts, affliction is a lesson from God that offers men the possibility to grow through trust and submission. Only by totally and unconditionally surrendering himself to God, will Job successfully deliver himself from his desperate plight since God will then want to reward him. "You will know that your tabernacle is in peace, and when you visit your dwelling you will not be disappointed. You will know also that your seed will be great, and your offspring like the grass of the earth. You will go to your grave in a full age, like a shock of corn comes in its season!" In harmony with the world, nature, men, and his God, the righteous man will be restored to his place in society and emerge from his ordeal with increased stature.

But Job is not at all convinced of the validity of Eliphaz's theory and develops his own viewpoint based on his terrible experience. First, recalling the reasons for his sorrow, Job reiterates his wish to die which would bring consolation and deliverance from a life that is but a series of misfortunes, a slow death anyway, without reason. Then, speaking to his friends, he criticizes their behavior. For, just as a river, he says, swollen by the waters when the snow and ice melt, but dry when the heat comes, so Job's friends left him when his household was hit by disaster, leaving him abandoned and in despair; and yet, Job had not asked them for anything but a show of solidarity. Moreover, Eliphaz's theory does not at all explain why Job has been so harshly treated. What faults has he committed to be judged so severely by his friends who are obviously convinced that he is guilty?

Then, turning to God, Job wonders what the meaning of life is: servitude, waiting, interminable anguish without hope. Job describes his difficult condition with striking realism: "My flesh is covered with worms and sores, my skin is raw and festering."

Job's state is that of the living dead, his body appears already in the stages of decomposition. The fact that he had once known happier times cannot console him and he lives with the conviction that "salvation is impossible" and worse, that if God tries to find him, to certainly pardon him, he will search in vain for, "whoever descends into Sheol will never be brought back." Job likens his experience to death, a descent into Hell with no return. Convinced that his end is near, he is intent on denouncing, because of the urgency of his desperate condition, the injustice of which he has been a victim. More incisively than ever Job reproaches God for torturing him without respite, as if he were like a sea monster that must be constantly kept on its guard, imprisoned in a jail of pain. He wishes for death to release him from this endless suffering. Who is Man, asks Job finally, to be of such great interest to God, intent on testing him continually and spying on him night and day? What a strange and perverse relationship is this which binds Man to his God! What has Job done to become the object of such divine fury, and why may he not obtain God's pardon and be granted peace?

As we can see, Job's questions touch upon the very essence of the relationship between humanity and God based upon the concept of sin and forgiveness. Job denounces a mechanism he sees as too rigid and inhuman with its "divine retribution" which seems

Medieval miniature, *Job and His Friends*

Learning of Job's terrible misfortunes, three friends, Eliphaz, Bildad, and Zophar, try to console him. They debate with Job for seven days and seven nights without convincing him of the validity of their points of view.

P. P. Rubens, *Job*

Job's three friends, shown here as very pious, are in fact extremely harsh with the afflicted Job and their attitude even prompts God himself to reproach them at the end of the story.

monstrous to those who, not even consciously, might have strayed from the right path and suddenly find themselves the victims of extreme and excessive punishment without the slightest prospect of deliverance, if not only through death.

At this point Bildad intervenes for the first time and strongly reproaches Job for his angry speech, "like a hurricane." He reaffirms with vehemence the doctrine of retribution previously presented by Eliphaz and contested by Job. Divine justice is perfect. Therefore, if Job's children perished it was because they had sinned against God. As for Job, if it is true that he is blameless and upright, God will deliver him from his suffering and everything he possessed before, and even more, will be restored to him. Bildad urges Job to recognize the experience of past generations and the validity of the traditional point of view adhered to by his friends, instead of proposing a new vision, questionable and dangerous, of the relationship between men and God. Through various metaphors Bildad demonstrates to Job that not life, happiness, nor fulfillment are possible without God, the humus in which all forms of life are rooted. Bildad concludes his defense of divine justice on a note of hope, evoking the possibility that Job may still save himself and know joy and laughter once again in his life.

Job speaks again conceding, first of all, that of course he is foolish to say that he is right and God is wrong, to question he who can move mountains and shake the earth, who is the ruler of the sky, sun, and stars, in short, the creator and master of all things. God acts according to his own will and no man may ask him to account for his actions. As his friends have suggested, Job therefore surrenders himself to God's omnipotence though he continues to insist that he is innocent. For, in the face of such an adversary, whether a man is right or wrong, he can only bow down before God and beg for clemency. Far from seeing this situation as an expression of God's benevolence and justice, Job sees in it an expression of the law of the jungle, brutal and blind, that denies the weak the slightest right. Initially taking up the viewpoint of his listeners, that is, the necessity of accepting God's judgement, Job skillfully uses this element to better support his own protest against a God whose right is based on coercion and arbitrary power. Job insists upon his innocence and criticizes the relentless persecution of a God who, turning a deaf ear to reason, is determined at all costs to punish him, apparently treating pious and impious with the same blind cruelty. Job's God is a being who knows no pity and even takes pleasure in seeing the innocent plagued by misfortune. Contrary to what his friends assert, when they hold him responsible for his own misery, Job believes that men's fate depends exclusively upon God.

Again turning to God, Job asks in great bitterness to let him know the reasons for his condemnation. What is it that pushes God to use violence and injustice against men. Am I not, wonders Job, one of your creatures? "In skin and flesh you clothed me and with bones and sinew you wove me; then with life you graced me and your constant love has kept me alive!" What are God's reasons for wanting to destroy what he has created? Why punish him with such harshness? Guilty or innocent, why this ignomious misery? Why does God hunt him like prey and attack him like an enemy? Job closes his speech with a new plea for death and deliverance. For, compared to his agony, death even in a terrifying world of darkness and chaos, would mean peace and rest to him.

Zophar answers Job severely. He accuses Job of acting as if he believed he were omniscent by asserting his righteousness although only God can express such judgment. God's designs are beyond men's comprehension and Job is foolish to demand an explanation. Zophar tells Job to repent and turn his back on wickedness. Only then will God deliver him from his suffering and restore peace to him.

Zophar reaffirms, therefore, the doctrine of retribution and attributes Job's misfortunes to some grave sin of which only God is aware.

A lengthy reply from Job concludes the first part of the debate with his friends. Job ironically observes his three companions who take themselves to be the embodiment of universal wisdom and who, at the same time, demonstrate such disdain for a friend, unfortunate victim of fate, whom they prefer to destroy rather than offering him help. Job's anger grows as he hears them preach from on high, in the comfort of their well-being, and at the thought that God rewards these people and their likes, whereas he, the righteous man, is made to suffer without a moment's respite. After disputing the validity of traditional wisdom, Job reaffirms God's immense powers only, however, to then emphasize their irreversible, arbitrary, and even destructive quality. Job pronounces a very hard indictment against God. At the root of all deviance there is God who plays with men, creating and destroying them at will and sending them into darkness, to wander alone and homeless.

Job directs more barbed remarks at his friends. They are in no way superior to him, are completely incapable of helping him in this ordeal, and would show more wisdom by being silent. Considering to be as intelligent as his friends and just as capable of understanding the world around him, Job refuses any other interlocutor but God himself. Instead of humiliating himself by admitting to a sin he has not committed, rather than plead for a pardon that has no reason to be, Job wants to speak with God, discuss with him, as if they were in court where each party is allowed to defend his own point of view.

Job's friends have appointed themselves the defenders of God and his acts, however, points out Job, are they really worthy of this function and would it not be better to first examine their own consciences? Silence, therefore, Job tells them, for he will settle this directly with God, whatever consequences await him. For Job knows very well that in so doing, in wanting to dialogue directly with God, he risks death. But he also believes that his innocence and piety will protect him. Job therefore asks God to question him just like a judge facing a defendant and, prepared for whatever his sentence will be, Job begs God not to resort to his terrible power. Faced with the silence of his interlocutor, Job presents the questions himself and makes the case against his arbitrary and violent God: what are Job's crimes and sins? Why has he become God's enemy? What are the reasons for this relentless persecution of a man who is already utterly destroyed?

Job then pronounces an elegy for Man and his destiny, basing his thoughts on his own tragic plight. With the restless existence of a fleeting shadow, Man is consumed from the inside like a dying tree. God hunts and judges Man, never letting him out of his sight and, though he has already signed his death sentence for a specific day, renders life impossible. Then, when life leaves him, Man dies never to relive again, contrary to nature with its perpetual rebirth. What meaning is there to human destiny? Job even considers the idea, strange as it may seem, of seeking refuge for a time in Hell from where God, once placated, will have him return and resume the course of his happy existence. If only God would agree to pardon Job, he could correct any possible failings and forget the past misfortunes. But nothing of the sort appears on the horizon, and God destroys even Man's hope. Death puts an end to human existence without Man ever understanding the meaning of it and without even knowing what will remain of him afterwards, on earth, in the memory of those who were close to him.

Job has got everything off his chest now and in the dock of this imaginary court sit God and the self-appointed divine defenders, Eliphaz, Bildad, and Zophar, who one by one again expound on their viewpoints, each time provoking Job's vehement reaction. The discussion becomes extremely heated and the attacks more and more cutting. Eliphaz, first of all, calls Job a false sage whose reasoning is based on ignorance. Worse, Job sounds like the unrighteous when they speak, his words prove he is inspired by wickedness: "You are condemned by your mouth, not by me; and your own lips testify against you!" Eliphaz is ironic about Job's wisdom that dares reject the traditional doctrine which the three visitors have applied to their lives. Who is Job, then, to think himself superior to others? Returning to the ideas developed in his first speech, Eliphaz insists upon the imperfection of Man. As naturally as he drinks water, Man sins, simply because this is part of his nature. Referring once again to accepted tradition and his own mystical experience, Eliphaz graphically describes the fate that awaits the impious who, contrary to what Job claims, are always the victims of divine punishment. Their daily lot is anguish, death, hunger, and unhappiness, the sanctions desired by God.

Job denounces the inane remarks of his interlocutors and complains about their aggressivity towards him. Then he comes back to God again describing his cruel actions with their terrible consequences. Job's indictment is fierce against his executioners who act on behalf of a sadistic warring God. They are intent on destroying a ruined man though he is blameless. Job desperately appeals to God to declare him innocent before he dies. He is certain that death is near and begs God to hasten this end. Death, Sheol, the final

Sculpture, *Job*

Like a saint, Job is the object of a cult in this church and is shown here with his countless afflictions.

Guido Reni, ***The Triumph of Job***

After a long spiritual voyage, the double of what he has lost is restored to Job who also regains the esteem and affection of his kin. Again rich and fulfilled, Job lives a hundred and forty years, enjoying a longevity worthy of any of the great Patriarchs.

destination of all creatures, where even cherished ones are reduced to worms in the earth, seems his only prospect at the end of a tunnel of darkness.

Bildad, feeling the target of Job's accusations, immediately reproaches Job for his offensive tone. He draws a terrifying picture of the fate that awaits the wicked, all the while implying that this is Job's destiny. As if it is not enough that the person will be afflicted with all the world's misery, the sinner is also, according to Bildad, destined to meet a horrible death and afterwards pass into total oblivion; without children or descendants, the sinner will arouse only feelings of dread and repulsion in all the world.

Job naturally cannot agree with such a vision, and once again complains about his friends' cruelty. His misfortunes have been caused by an act of divine injustice from which he cannot manage to escape. Job tirelessly describes the wrongs he has endured and the violence of his punishment. He expresss his total solitude, everyone has left him, brothers, friends, relatives, acquaintances, neighbors, servants, and even his wife. Utterly alone, racked by pain, Job cries out for a sign of pity from God and men. He says he is convinced that one day someone will stand up for him and come to his defense and then, his innocence established, he will finally be able to see God, regain his trust and his protection, no longer be considered his enemy but once again be his friend. Contrary to his friends' belief that by repenting and surrendering himself to God's judgement Job can obtain God's pardon and a return to a normal existence, Job, convinced that he is blameless and sure there is nothing for which he can be reproached, waits for the intervention of some outside force, God or another defender, to finally vindicate him.

Zophar insists again upon the belief that the wicked are always punished, a belief all of tradition supports and which Job proposes to question with his foolish belief in the possible reversal of his situation. Even if sinners seem to be enjoying a good life, God is only waiting for the moment when he can better punish them. Consequently, Zophar tacitly argues, Job should not expect any deliverance whatsover if he continues sinning, only total annihilation awaits him.

With Job's seventh speech we enter into a new phase of the debate where he adopts a different tactic. Job analyzes the concept of divine retribution constantly supported by his friends and, by means of his questioning, reveals its inconsistency and incoherency. First asking his friends for their undivided attention, Job tells them to consider his plight in order to appreciate what he is going to say. Contrary to his friends' theory, Job sees the wicked and impious all around him enjoying prosperous existences, free and unpunished, living and dying happily. So then, what purpose does piety, loyalty, uprightness serve? Why does God afflict certain sinners and not others? Why, inversely, do some of God's faithful servants emerge unscathed while others fall victim to his terrible fury? In short, the principle of retribution is not valid: reality disproves it. Men are not equal during life nor are they at the moment of death, however, once buried, all lie equally still.

Adopting Job's style, Eliphaz attempts to respond to his objections by more questions meant to trap Job and force him into admitting his guilt. Eliphaz stresses that Man is responsible for provoking the destiny that awaits him for though God is, of course, sovereign he is not arbitrary. He punishes the wicked and rewards the righteous. Job is described by his friends as an impious man who has led a sinful existence. "You never offered the thirsty man water, you refused bread to the starving... you sent away widows empty-handed and mistreated orphans." Job's punishment is therefore perfectly logical and fair, for no one can escape God's judgement. Concluding his invective against Job, Eliphaz entreats him to make peace with God, to humble himself as a sinner before him, in a sign of his acceptance of God's verdict. Job will then surely see everything restored to him, happiness, fortune, divine favor, success in all endeavors. Deaf to his friends' arguments, Job confirms his rebellion against the God who afflicts him. But how can Job find God in order to talk to him, to question him, to obtain the recognition of his innocence and certain triumph? Job continues to trust in God and contrary to Eliphaz's speech, Job declares that his conduct has been upright. But is God reasonable? He does not act at all according to the logic of human retribution, Job insists, but according to a divine pre-established and obscure plan that confuses his faithful.

The four chapters that follow, chapters 24 to 27, have given rise to much discussion among specialists as they include considerations that are difficult to attribute to one or the other of the interlocutors, or are exceptionally brief comments placed under the name of one or the other person. In short, we do not completely understand their nature or the place of this material in the structure of the Book of Job. Diverse themes are considered: the misery of the oppressed, the acts of criminals in the night, the vigilance of God over men; the greatness and power of God confronted with the misery of the human condition; the punishment of the wicked whose existences are marked by weakness, instability, violence, desolation, oppression, anguish. In a brief speech Job then solemnly swears that he is innocent, thus performing a religious act of potentially far-reaching consequences, for a perjurer in Job's time risked severe sanctions, including death. Job proposes to demonstrate the power and wisdom of God, which is the subject of chapter 28. Certain exegetes consider this to be a later addition, an "artistic pause," before the resuming of the debates, whereas others accept the passage as serving to give the discussion a new direction, a transition to finding a solution to the problem, which necessitates some reconciliation between the two positions until then so diametrically opposed.

This discourse in praise of divine power begins by referring to the activity of mining for metals, a dangerous but useful task, that requires a special technique and considerable effort to reach the heart of the earth where the metals lie. "And Wisdom, where does it come from and where is Intelligence found?" continues the author who compares the search for wisdom to the perilous journey of the miners and their unremitting toil in the bowels of the earth. Nothing is as valuable as wisdom, not even gold or silver, coral or crystal. However, it is impossible to find it, to extract it, for it is hidden from men's eyes and belongs to God alone. Man is left, therefore, to only fear and revere wisdom.

After having pronounced this important speech in which he recognizes the intrinsic wisdom of God and the necessity for Man to submit to it, Job brings the debate to a close in a lengthy monologue and reiterates the themes developed previously. He presents his views with renewed force and conviction in the hope that this might provoke the confrontation with God he so ardently desires. Job begins by recalling when he was happy, respected and honored by all, when people sought him out and followed his counsel. A man of prestige and power, Job was also regarded as a benefactor of the poor and the oppressed and this made him feel at peace with himself and confident in a future that held only complete happiness. But then his world was destroyed: having become the laughing stock of all, even the most contemptible, Job's body and mind are besieged and tortured. He speaks to God with vehemence, "I cry out to you and you do not answer, I stand before you and you do not heed." Believing his words will now mean certain death, Job wonders in what way he could have possibly failed in his duties as God's servant, why he has been made to endure such suffering today.

Job then enumerates a number of specific sins only to declare, one by one, that he has never been guilty of any of them. He insists that he has been blameless and upright, honest and faithful, respectful to his slaves and generous with widows and orphans, magnanimous and disinterested, hospitable and open. He then pronounces himself ready to be duly punished if he has ever strayed in any way from the right path. He adds that his irreproachable conduct has never been motivated by the hope of receiving any reward from God, but out of his fear of God the Almighty. "Will anyone be brought to me who will listen?" cries Job after exhausting all his arguments.

At this point in the Book of Job a new figure appears, a certain Elihu, who says that neither Job nor his three friends are right. This speech, which fills chapters 32 to 37, was not part of the original version of the Book of Job and was added some centuries later. While attributing what Elihu considers Job's fallacious judgement to his present condition, Elihu also feels, contrary to Job's friends, that individual behavior cannot depend on divine retribution, for God transcends humanity. For Elihu, God is someone who educates men and opens their eyes. Instead of seeing suffering as punishment, it should therefore be considered a sign, an appeal for repentance, the price to be paid for deliverance. It is therefore up to Job to accept this re-evaluation of himself without anger, peacefully. Elihu concludes by praising the sublime nature of God and and again entreats Job to bend to this majesty and wisdom.

At this point in the Book of Job, the event so long-awaited comes to pass: Yahweh appears to Job and answers him. This dialogue will serve to re-establish a certain balance and allow for Job's "submission." Yahweh speaks to Job and to demonstrate the foolishness of his theories and the great distance that separates Man from God, he questions Job on the creation of the world and its workings. "Have you ever stood at the source of the sea, or walked along the bottom of its abyss? Have the gates of Death or of Darkness ever been shown to you?" Ironically, he fires a series of questions at Job about rain, rivers, the stars, clouds, lightening, snow, animals of all kinds such as deer, wild asses, onagers, buffalo, horses, birds of prey, as well as their habits.

Job, overwhelmed by such an obvious show of superior knowledge, is silent in a sign of his recognition of God's supremacy. God asks him, if he is capable, to destroy the evil forces surrounding him; but of course such a feat is not within the power of any man and therefore God must be left to act according to the plans of Providence. Divine action is neither an immediate reward for moral integrity nor automatic punishment of the impious. God rules over a world where evil is an element that must be reckoned with. God's actions are not

William Blake, ***When the Morning Stars Sing in Unison***

Texts in Egyptian and Mesopotamian literature exist in which a man wonders about his destiny marked by injustice or a reversal of fortune. Certain similarities with the Book of Job are notable.

aimed at eliminating evil, but rather at using it to manifest himself to men. For, the Lord calls upon all the means at his disposal, including suffering, to make his omnipotence known. To demonstrate this, Yahweh refers to the two monsters associated with the chaotic primeval forces of the world: Behemoth and Leviathan, both of them described in rich detail, and evokes these famous representatives of the forces of evil which God does not eliminate, but controls according to his overall plan for the universe.

At the end of God's illuminating intervention, Job totally recognizes the Lord's wisdom in all things. "I know you can do all and there is no task too great for you." Job therefore agrees that God's actions are right, even when they may be incomprehensible to men. No longer trying to obtain justifications, but eager to draw from God's teachings on human nature and divine plans and, above all, seeking direct contact upon which to base his faith, Job asks God for a new relationship to be born between them, a new "agreement." This new covenant will bind a God who listens to Man, and a faithful follower who feels his Lord is near him and present in his life, even in his suffering. Finally, Job retracts his accusations and expresses his regrets.

The text closes with a passage in prose, an epilogue in which Yahweh expresses his disapproval of Job's three friends who had spoken out of ignorance. He nevertheless forgives them out of respect for Job, his servant, whom Yahweh intends from now on to succor. He returns to Job twice of everything which he had lost, as well as the esteem and affection of those close to him. Once again a wealthy and fulfilled man, Job is later blessed with seven more sons and three daughters. He lives one hundred and forty years, that is, twice seventy years which represents the chronological cycle of perfection. Thus granted the exceptional longevity worthy of any of the great Patriarchs of Israel, he dies happy, old, and "full of days."

After all is said and done, Job's adventures consist of few events: a reversal of fortune, as sudden as it is radical and inexplicable, causes a long debate, the stages of which we have briefly outlined. Job's story, therefore, is a pretext for discussing theories circulating at the time concerning God's mysterious actions and his relationship with Man. For, though touching upon problems as fundamental and dramatic as the meaning of life and death and the origin of sin and suffering, the Book of Job does not, in fact, propose any doctrinal solutions. Job does not ask God to provide absolute answers to these questions, but rather to help him, in his difficult situation, to understand and accept his plight. This is what God will do, in fact, not through a universal message, but rather by appearing to Job and renewing contact with him and Job's trust, in other words, through reactivating Job's personal faith based upon knowing God and not through the "utiliarian" concept of divine retribution. In Job's case the reward for his conduct is the appearance of God and the new relationship born out of this meeting.

The Book of Job belongs to a genre known as Wisdom literature of which other examples exist in the Old Testament, notably in the Book of Proverbs or Ecclesiastes, though Job's Wisdom presents special features that would be too lengthy to develop in the scope of our work. We would rather like to turn our attention here to the way the figure of Job, and that of the righteous sufferer who questions his lot and questions God, fit into Near Eastern tradition where other important expressions have been preserved. In so doing we naturally do not intend to diminish in any way the literary or intellectual merits of the author of the Book of Job, whose exceptional talents and great originality are universally recognized.

If in Egyptian literature possible parallels from a formal and thematic point of view are offered, that is, texts where a man wonders about his destiny generally marked by an injustice or reversal of fortune, it is in Mesopotamian literature that we find the most striking similarities. A first text that bears the conventional title, *Man and His God* which has come down to us in Sumerian and in an extremely fragmentary state, describes the lot of a sick and unfortunate man who confides in his divine protector, expressing his despair and asking for the divinity's help to overcome the situation, though at the same time admitting that his misfortunes are due to his own impious conduct. This tale has a "happy end" in that the hero rediscovers his taste for life and the strength and joy to again worship his guardian divinity.

A second text, this time in Accadian, entitled *I Want to Praise the Lord of Wisdom*, expresses observations on the world and life in a poem of some five hundred verses containing the lamentations of a man whose fate is marked, as was Job's case, by illness, isolation, and his gods' abandonment. As Job, he asks himself for what reasons a pious man such as himself is so unjustly punished. Finally, through a special ritual he manages to drive away the "sins" that soiled him and regain the favor of his God, Marduk. In reading this text, re-baptized by scholars of Assyrian literature as *The Righteous Sufferer*, one cannot help being struck by its similarities with the Book of Job, in which certain statements about suffering and its effects, or on the feelings of solitude and injustice, find indisputable precedents.

Finally, the text which more than any other prefigures the Book of Job and confirms its traditional sapiential heritage, is a work entitled *Babylonian Theodicy* and consists of twenty-seven stanzas of eleven verses, written at the end of the second millenium B. C. It describes a sick man who speaks with a friend about his suffering, about the ups and downs of life, and the indifference of the gods. As Job, he wonders what there is to gain by being pious and righteous and, indignant, he notes that it is the wicked who rule the earth. Just as Job's friends, his interlocutor defends the "orthodox" viewpoint of divine retribution, the evil are punished and the righteous glorified, assuring the sick man that he will soon recover. Of course, missing here is the divine intervention which, in Job's case, solves the problem. In this story, the gods are simply asked to rescue the unfortunate man from his deadlock.

It goes without saying that each one of these texts presents obvious differences when compared with the Book of Job, but the similarities are such, as much in their form as in their content, that a common matrix is undeniable. Indeed the theme of the "righteous sufferer" throughout history has enjoyed great fame and exceptional popularity. Hercules, in classical mythology, is a significant example of this when he is made to perform twelve difficult labors though nothing in his conduct has justified such punishment, if not Hera's awful jealousy of a son born of adultery to her husband Zeus. Finally, Christ himself, through his life and death, perfectly illustrates this theme of which Job's life represents, we readily concede, one of the most remarkable stages.

DANIEL

The Prophet of the Apocalypse

... and Daniel scorned food and acquired knowledge.

Dante Alighieri

With the figure of Daniel, whose name means "God has rendered justice" or "God is my judge," an Israelite said to have been deported at the end of the seventh century B. C. to the court of king Nebuchadnezzar in Babylon where he demonstrates heroic attachment to Yahweh, we enter a new genre of biblical literature: apocalyptic writing. This presents, when compared with prophetic literature, some basic differences that will be discussed in the conclusion of our study. We will also consider the personages involved in these events from a historical point of view, beginning with Daniel himself, as well as the facts which are narrated or announced, since Daniel delivers prophetic visions which cover several centuries of Israel's history. As in many of the Books of the Old Testament, the Book of Daniel represents a text that is, in reality, the fruit of diverse writings. The best evidence of this is the fact that to the Hebrew text (referred to as "proto-canonical"), the Greek as well as the Latin Vulgate versions also add a passage in chapter 3 as well as two tales: "Susanna" and "Bel and the Dragon," additions known as deutero-canonical. One final feature of the Book of Daniel worth noting: its opening is written in Hebrew, followed by chapters in Aramaic and, finally, in its closing sections, it goes back to Hebrew again. The reason for this strange alternation of languages is unknown. In any case, we are obviously dealing with a composite work that combined several different sources through a complex literary process.

But now without further delay let us turn to the tale of Daniel's life as it has come down to us in the Old Testament. This will permit us to then look at this tale from a historical, literary, and theological perspective. The story begins in the third year of the reign of Jehoiachim, king of Judah, with the capture of Jerusalem by Nebuchadnezzar, the future king of Babylon, who orders that a few young Israelites of princely and noble rank be deported to the Babylonian court. This includes not only Daniel, but also three other young Israelites named Hananiah, Mishael, and Azariah. The chronological background given for this event, which of course marks a dramatic turning point in Daniel's life, does present certain problems. The famous massive deportation of the Jewish people by Nebuchadnezzar dates back to 597 B. C., after the taking of the city by the Babylonian troops. It was at that time that the prophet Ezekiel was deported, just as the king Jehoiachim himself. The operation was repeated a few years later in 586, then again in 582, but a taking of Jerusalem and a deportation in 605 B. C., since this is the date indicated for Daniel's transfer to Babylon, is a new element and not easily reconciled with other events of that year. In 605 B. C., in fact, Nebuchadnezzar, on behalf of his father Nabopolassar, then king of Babylon, won an important victory at Carchemish over the pharoah of Egypt, Neco. He pursued the Egyptian sovereign even up to the northern borders of Egypt then, having received the news of his father's death, Nebuchadnezzar

Michelangelo, *Daniel*
The artist suggests the youth and vigor of this very special prophet and shows him with a book, most likely to evoke Daniel's revelations concerning the future.

returned urgently to Babylon to succeed him on the throne. This critical period of transition obliged him to renounce undertaking any foreign campaigns for several years. It is therefore difficult to date the fall of Jerusalem referred to here. Perhaps while pursuing the pharoah across Palestine, Nebuchadnezzar stopped in Jerusalem just long enough to capture it and deport part of its population, but nothing is more uncertain. This may instead represent the first example of historical approximation of which there will be other instances in the Book of Daniel.

The young deported Israelites receive an excellent education at the palace of Babylon. They study the local writing and language, that is, the complex cuneiform system and the Babylonian tongue. After three years of "training," they become servants of the king and to sanction the change in their status, they are given new names. Daniel is re-baptized Belteshazzar, apparently a Babylonian name meaning "protect the life of the king!" and Hananiah becomes Shadrach, Mishael is renamed Meshach, Azariah is Abednego. However, this does not in any way convince Daniel to adopt Babylonian beliefs or customs. He swears he will continue to respect the Law of Yahweh and keep himself free from an "unclean" life. First of all, he refuses the food and wine provided for the servants, only eating vegetables and drinking water. Despite this austere diet Daniel and his unfortunate companions are in radiant health, a sign of Yahweh's favor and the protection of their God, to whom Daniel, trusting and deeply pious, has totally surrendered himself. Yahweh, in turn, as a reward, grants intelligence and wisdom to the young people and in addition, upon Daniel only, bestows the faculty to receive prophetic visions and dreams. For this reason the king Nebuchadnezzar consults Daniel and his friends regularly, so much greater is their wisdom than that of the local magicians and seers.

In the second year of his reign, Nebuchadnezzar has a dream which none of the experts are capable of interpreting, even under the king's threat to either annihilate those who are unable to help him, or bestow great honors on anyone who can satisfy his curiosity. Just as the king's officers are getting ready to execute all the wise men in Babylonia, Daniel and his acolytes, out of fear of being put to death as well, decide to give an explanation to the king's dream. During the night Daniel has a vision that reveals the key to Nebuchadnezzar's dream to him. Daniel naturally attributes this revelation to God's goodness and wisdom, and praises his God in a lyrical tone, in a manner that reminds us somewhat of Joseph who was also, with the help of divine intervention, an interpreter of dreams. Then he tells the amazed Nebuchadnezzar the solution to the dream and explains that this apocalyptic vision, that is, a revelation that deals with the end of the world, has been sent to him by God who has entrusted Daniel with the task of interpreting it.

Nebuchadnezzar had in fact dreamed of an immense and terrifying statue that rose up before him. Its head was of gold, its torso and arms of silver, the belly and thighs of brass, its legs of iron and finally, its feet half iron and half clay. Suddenly, a stone fell from a rock face and struck the statue on the feet, the entire statue collapsing and shattering into pieces that were scattered by the wind, leaving not the slightest trace. The stone that had destroyed the statue then began to grow, to the point of becoming a mountain that covered the entire earth. According to the interpretation Daniel gives to the king, the head made of gold symbolizes Nebuchadnezzar's kingdom destined to be taken over by another power, and then another after that, in a degeneration of earthly rule which the materials in the dream, of diminishing value, symbolize. The kingdom of iron will of course be quite resistent, but a mixed, hybrid empire will succeed it, in part strong and in part weak. It will be at that moment that God will send to earth, like a meteor appearing from out of the sky, a new kingdom which will sweep aside all the other preceding ones, and will establish an eternal indestructible power.

The strange statue in Nebuchadnezzar's dream, while evoking Hesiod's myth of the succession of the races where the race of gold is replaced by inferior races of silver, bronze, and iron, of progressively baser quality, has greatly interested commentators of the Book of Daniel who have asked themselves what empires, in historical terms, are thus evoked. The last empire may be that of the Seleucids, unless it is the Roman Empire; the third, that of Alexander the Great; the second the Median and Persian Empire; the first being the Babylonian kingdom. Some exegetes have defended another explanation: 1. Babylonian Empire 2. Median Empire 3. Persian Empire 4. Macedonian Empire, though this proposal has received less support.

Struck by the astuteness of Daniel's interpretation, Nebuchadnezzar bows down before the young man whom he showers with gifts and honors, appointing him commander of the Babylonian province and head of all the local wise men; the king also adopts the worship of Yahweh, whom he is now convinced is the wisest and most powerful of all the divinities, "the God of gods." The episode of Nebuchadnezzar's dream characterizes the theological aim of the entire Book of Daniel: to show that the course of history is not in the hands of men, but entirely in those of God. Vascillating paganism, like a colossus standing on feet of clay, is destined to disappear and when the "time of the end" comes, it will give way to the kingdom of God awaited by all his faithful.

The next episode in the Book of Daniel again has as its main "character" a gigantic golden statue (about 90 feet high) that Nebuchadnezzar has built near Babylon and which all the dignitaries of the country are urged to come and worship. The Hebrew version of the text does not give any chronological reference point for this inaugural ceremony but the Greek versions, by setting it in the eighteenth year of Nebuchadnezzar's reign, that is, in 587 or 586 B. C., relate it to the capture of Jerusalem. In any case, the king's decree that all must bow down before the effigy without exception is clear: whoever disobeys and refuses, will be thrown into a fiery furnace, in accordance with a practice well attested, moreover, in Babylonian law. However, Daniel's three companions Shadrach, Meshach, and Abednego, whom Daniel has engaged to assist him in his functions as commander of the Babylonian province, refuse to venerate the idol. They inform Nebuchadnezzar of their belief in their own God, whom they are certain will rescue them from the threat of the furnace and the king's despotism, swearing heroically that whatever the outcome, they will never be forced to worship the golden statue. Furious, Nebuchadnezzar has the three young people bound, a fire of exceptional intensity lit, and has them thrown into the furnace. However, while the men responsible for throwing them into the fire perish in the violent flames, Shadrach, Meshach, and Abednego go unscathed, continuing to praise God and his justice in the midst of the fire. Azariah (re-baptized Abednego), in particular, addresses a prayer of touching lyricism to God in which he regrets Israel's sins and the effects it has had, notably the Exile, then appeals to divine mercy. In the meantime, Nebuchadnezzar's slaves continue stoking the fire which grows greater and greater with more wood, pitch, coal, and other materials. But an angel of God comes down from the sky to protect our friends in the furnace who imperturbably continue glorifying Yahweh. We note that this passage is missing in the Hebrew version and that it is only included in the Greek texts and in the Vulgate. Nevertheless, its style, language, and content strongly suggest the existence of an original source in Semitic tongue, most likely one that initially existed independently from the tale of Daniel's life, and that was later inserted at this point in the story.

Nebuchadnezzar cannot believe his eyes: the three bound men, thrown into the furnace to meet their death, now appear to be four and are calmly walking about in the inferno, praying to God. The king then asks them to come out of the furnace and all the Babylonian officials certify that the fire has not left the slightest trace on their bodies or their clothes. The power of the Israelites' God has been revealed to all, and Nebuchadnezzar, once again, is obliged to recognize Yahweh's superiority. The king then decrees that whoever speaks against the God of Israel will be put to death and he then promotes the young people to even higher ranks in the Babylonian administration.

God then appears a second time to Nebuchadnezzar in a dream. Again, the Babylonian sages are incapable of interpreting the dream and the king calls upon Daniel's services. Nebuchadnezzar, in his dream, has seen a tree in the center of the earth that is so great and so tall that it touches the sky. The tree, covered with leaves and abundant fruit, feeds men and beasts and gives shade to all. We note in passing that in one of Nebuchadnezzar's historical inscriptions, the inscription of Wadi Brissa, the king is compared to a great tree whose shade protects all the people of the earth. We understand, therefore, that the tree's symbolism, imposing and fertile, must refer to Nebuchadnezzar's kingdom and that the animals, to his subjects. But then a messenger from the heavens commands the tree to be cut down, its branches, leaves and fruit to be chopped off, thus provoking the flight of the animals. The roots, nevertheless, will remain in the earth though the tree will be the victim of harsh punishment: chained up, given the heart of a beast, it will be abandoned for "seven periods," that is, for a very long time. In this way all will know that God alone rules over men, and therefore over the course of history, and that he places whomever he pleases on the earthly throne, even the most abject of men, if this is part of his unfathomable plans.

Daniel has absolutely no difficulty in giving Nebuchadnezzar the key to his dream. God is getting ready to destroy him, to punish him until he recognizes Yahweh's absolute supremacy, after which his kingdom will be restored to him. No matter how powerful he may be, Nebuchadnezzar cannot escape divine will which alone rules the world. And, in fact, a short while later the prophecy revealed by Daniel comes true and Nebuchadnezzar's arrogance earns him the foretold punishment. The king, however, immediately recognizes the omnipotence of Yahweh, whom he praises and glorifies. The king's power is therefore soon restored to him, stronger and more stable than ever. In reality, the history of Nebuchadnezzar's reign, as Babylonian sources have recounted it, makes no mention of a comparable fall and return of the king, notwithstanding a passage written by a late Jewish historian, Flavius Joseph who citing a more ancient source speaks of a prophecy pronounced by Nebuchadnezzar to Cyrus from the roof of his palace before his sudden disappearance. Nevertheless, beyond this historical aspect, the real objective is theological and, more precisely, apocalyptic. It is meant to nourish the hope of the coming of the kingdom of God, and to show that the Lord is far superior to any of the powerful of the earth, for he has the power to make or break them at will.

Medieval miniature, ***Daniel in the Lions' Den***

The iconography showing Daniel in the lions' den was a very popular theme in Christian imagery, notably in catacombs and on sarcophagi. It evoked the promise of humanity's rebirth and the establishment of the Kingdom of God.

The episode that follows no longer shows Nebuchadnezzar as its protagonist, but rather his alleged son who has become king under the name of Belshazzar. In reality, Babylonian sources give Evil-Merodach as Nebuchadnezzar's successor in 562 B. C., who was not at all, as the Book of Daniel claims in reference to Belshazzar, the last Babylonian sovereign before the establishment of the Median Empire of Darius. It was Nabonides who, in 539 B. C., witnessed the capture of Babylon and the fall of its empire, and this was only after three kings had preceded him on Nebuchadnezzar's throne. The Book of Daniel therefore shows great liberty in its use of historical facts, which reinforces our impression that an accurate historical reconstruction is not at all the author's objective for whom history is simply the instrument and vehicle of divine power. This being said, the figure of Belshazzar is not pure invention. Documents of the period tell us of the existence of a personage by this name, Nabonides' son, the "last emperor" who probably took an active role in his father's rule since his father spent much of his time outside Babylonia.

This Belshazzar, then, at the dawn of the fall of the Babylonian Empire, gathers a thousand dignitaries together for a grand banquet. In a drunken state, he asks to be brought the gold and silver cups which Nebuchadnezzar at the time of Daniel's deportation had taken from the Temple at Jerusalem. All the guests then drink wine from the cups and perform libations to their local gods. At that moment a miracle occurs: a hand appears and writes upon the wall of the royal hall, then disappears. The seers, summoned by the panicked king, are unable to read the message in spite of the promise of a fabulous reward. The queen, remembering Daniel's divining powers, who had intervened in this capacity under Nebuchadnezzar, has him called to the court. Without a second thought, Daniel refuses the gifts the king promises if he is successful, and then easily reads the terrible message. For, in fact, Belshazzar has ignored his predecessor's experience, when God humiliated and then rehabilitated him again. Showing even more arrogance than his predecessor, Belshazzar has disdained this God, even going so far as to desecrate the objects of his cult — referring here to the cups — and in so doing, will receive exemplary punishment. God has therefore decided to put his reign and his empire to an end and offer his power to the Medes and the Persians. Daniel, for his great clairvoyance, receives royal gifts and the position of third highest official in the empire. But Belshazzar cannot escape the destiny God has planned for him. He dies the same night, and at the age of 62 years, Darius the Mede succeeds him.

Here again, the historical facts we might reconstruct based on sources of the period are very different from the background presented in the Book of Daniel. Firstly, we know for a fact that Nabonidus, the last Babylonian sovereign, was not killed by new arrivals if only because he was not in

Babylon at the time. Once captured, he was exiled in Carmana while his capital fell easy prey to the invaders. Then, as another example, there is no trace in historical accounts of Darius, the son of a certain Xerxes, who is supposed to have ruled in Babylon after the fall of Nabonidus. According to Babylonian sources the conqueror of Babylon was Cyrus the Persian, whom the Book of Daniel gives as Darius's successor. It is therefore quite obvious that this personage is a literary invention and, as in other Old Testament writings, for example, the Books of Judith or Esther, history is used to provide the loose fabric, not always scrupulously respected, upon which the biblical editors "embroider," adding their own events which best illustrate divine action.

Because of his qualities, Daniel again assumes, as he had under Darius's imaginary predecessor, important responsibilities within the State, now organized into twenty-five satrapies, or provinces. The king's obvious esteem for Daniel incites the jealousy of the local officials who plot against him. They set a trap for Daniel by getting Darius to decree that any man, for the next thirty days, who worships another god but the king Darius himself will be thrown into the lions' den. In the ancient Near East, worshipping the king as a god was not at all rare and Alexander the Great, after his conquest of Asia, adopted this practice. As for the terrible fate that awaits those who disobey, this is surely no fruit of the imagination. Herodotus' account of Persian customs indicates that times were not kind to rebels.

Daniel, caught in the act of praying to Yahweh — which he does three times a day — is thrown into the lions' den, despite Darius's efforts to have him spared. The next day, however, to his enemies' great amazement, Daniel is discovered unhurt in the lions' den, protected by his all-powerful God who has recognized his innocence. In Daniel's place his detractors are thrown into the den with their wives and children, who are immediately torn to bits by the ferocious beasts. Then, as happened under the reigns of Nebuchadnezzar and Belshazzar, Darius recognizes the superiority of Yahweh.

With this event, which would like to appear as historical fact, the first part of the narrative of the Book of Daniel closes. It aims to demonstrate, through specific events, the great power of Yahweh who guides the course of history and whose kingdom, in an unspecified future, will come to rule. The chapters that follow then describe four visions which Daniel receives, again related to a historical period since they are set during the years of the reigns of the sovereigns mentioned previously: the first and third years of Belshazzar's reign, the first year of Darius's reign, and the third year of the reign of Cyrus, his successor. Daniel here is no longer a figure who interprets the dreams of others, but rather a prophet through whom God speaks to announce to men what the future holds.

The first vision, in the form of a dream, shows the sea agitated by the "four winds of the sky." Four great beasts, like monsters, rise from the waters. All have a hybrid, terrifying appearance: a lion with the wings of an eagle, a bear with three ribs in its jaws, a panther with four wings and four heads, a monster with ten horns and teeth made of iron. Then, a majestic old man surrounded by a great court climbs upon a throne and prepares to render justice to the beasts. The fourth monster is immediately eliminated and the others are deprived of their power until their time comes. Then, a being appears out of the sky who resembles a man — the original text calls him the "son of man" — and goes before the old judge who bestows power and majesty on him forever. This is very clearly a messianic vision, a foretelling of the coming of the one whom the Gospels often call the "Son of Man." He will, as ruler of the earth, replace all the other political powers symbolized by the four beasts. As previously represented in the four parts of the statue in Nebuchadnezzar's dream, we here have represented in the four beasts: the Babylonian Empire, the Median-Persian Empire, then that of Alexander the Great and his successors, and finally, the Seleucid Empire. Certain features of the monsters' physionomies can be explained, moreover, by the history or structure of these empires. For example, the four wings of the panther, which symbolize Alexander the Great, may refer to the four Diadochi, heirs to the Macedonian's empire. Very logically, the most terrible beast is the fourth, the one which belongs to the present, not so much in terms of Daniel's time, but of the period in which the author of the Book of Daniel was writing. For, and we will return to this point in our conclusion, it is very possible this author was a contemporary of the Seleucid king, Antiochus IV Epiphanes, who ruled between 175 and 163 B. C. and who was infamous for his persistent persecution of the Jews and his advocacy of the Hellenization of Israel. In fact, speaking of the fourth monster, our text highlights a king who rails against God and tries to exterminate his faithful, but God will annihilate him and establish his own kingdom for eternity. Antiochus, the enemy of the Jews, is therefore not only a historical figure here but rather the embodiment of the Antichrist, a prelude to the "end of time."

Two years later, Daniel has another vision, in Susa this time, the theater of Esther's adventures. The vision consists of a struggle between a ram and a goat, of which the latter emerges victor. From one of its horns four horns are born, and from one of these, a small horn then appears which wages war, like a man, against the celestial militia and desecrates the Temple, putting an end to sacrifices there. From a discussion between two angels, Daniel learns that this situation is destined to last eleven hundred and fifty days, that is, more than three years. After this time the angel Gabriel himself, Yahweh's messenger par excellence, will appear to Daniel to explain to him the meaning of his vision. The ram symbolizes the king of Persia; the goat, the king of Greece; and the horn, Alexander, upon whose death the empire is divided into four parts. These sovereigns will then be succeeded by a lawless faithless king who will lead the world to its downfall. As in the preceding vision, even as early as Saint Jerome, Antiochus IV Epiphanes is identified with a reign that was, in fact, marked from the beginning to its end by intrigue, ruthless ambition, and violence. In 168 B. C., after an unsuccessful campaign against Egypt,

Willem Drost, *The Vision of Daniel*

Unlike the other prophets, Daniel is not in direct contact with God. He receives symbolic or esoteric visions which God's messengers help him to decipher and understand.

Antiochus pillaged the Temple of Jerusalem and the next year, he desecrated it by erecting an altar to the Olympian god Zeus. Significantly, the purification of the Temple and the death of Antiochus came about some three years later. As in the first vision, the prophetic significance of Daniel's dream is God's victory over the pagan States which wage war against him and whose people, despite their desperate efforts to uproot the Israelites' faith and establish a stable universal empire, will fall victim to Yawheh, the supreme master of History.

The third vision, as we already know, comes to Daniel during the first year of the reign of Darius, the son of Xerxes. This vision is born out of the difficulty Daniel has in the reading and understanding of a passage by the prophet Jeremiah who speaks about a seventy-year deportation of the Jews of Babylon. Daniel prays to God for an explanation of what this means, most likely because he has confirmed that the prophecy has not been realized. As a result of his prayer, the angel Gabriel once again appears to Daniel. The angel tells him that the time necessary for the expiation of Israel's sins is very well seventy "weeks," but that this means seventy "seven year terms" or, in other words, 490 years. The angel Gabriel then reveals to Daniel the main stages in this countdown, at the end of which various events will take place, notably the advent of a personage who will wreak war and devastation, but who will finally be punished, thus permitting the establishment of a new kingdom. The aim is again, therefore, messianic and apocalyptic, in spite of the chronological "varnish" that gives a semblance of historical reality to these announcements for the future. We will avoid going into detail here on the innumerable interpretations that have been proposed of this passage which is, indeed, in many respects obscure; these types of esoterical calculations being, moreover, typical of all the literature of apocalyptic inspiration. Daniel's last vision, which takes place on the banks of the Tigris during the reign of Cyrus, is also explained by an angel who reveals to Daniel what is going to happen to him and his people when the "time of the end" comes. The prophecy again foresees the rule of three Persian kings, then a fourth one — this is Xerxes — who will send his armies against Greece (an allusion to the Median wars of the fifth century B. C.). Great power will then be concentrated in the hands of a bellicose king — referring to Alexander — but his empire will later be divided into four parts among his generals. The angel then paints a very detailed picture of the vicissitudes these latter will endure, the internal conflicts that will plague them. As usual, this historical progression is based on the "abject" Antiochus IV Epiphanes, violent usurper, brimming with wealth and arrogance, convinced that he is a god. The destructive political and religious action of this king is throroughly described as well as his dramatic end: "... he will meet his end, and no one will come to his rescue."

For, the liberator of the people will then rise up, Michael, the protector, the guardian angel of the Jewish people. Then, in the place of anguish will come deliverance and salvation. The dead will be resuscitated and receive universal judgement, the sages will be exalted as the stars in the firmament. The angel ends his discourse by urging Daniel to seal the book that holds these prophecies until the time of the end is upon them. Daniel would like to know when these prophecies will be realized and how he will recognize the first signs announcing such radical changes, but the angel remains vague indicating only that these events will take place, "for a time, two times, and half a time" that is, in three and a half years. Daniel, in any case, seems destined to die and be resting in peace before then, but when the messianic advent occurs, he will be resuscitated to take part in it.

The Book of Daniel in its Hebrew version ends here, but the Greek versions contain two more tales, one about Susanna, and the other about Bel and the Dragon. These stories most certainly go back to a Semitic original and both of them are included in the official canon in spite of their obscure origin. Susanna, whose name means "lily," is the wife of a certain Jehoiachim, a rich Hebrew who lives in Babylon. Susanna is a very beautiful woman and has been brought up according to the Law of Moses. Jehoiachim, one of the notables of the Hebrew community, lodges two elders in his residence who administer justice there. These two men, of a ripe old age, are attracted to Susanna and devise a plan to surprise her alone. One day, while they are hiding in the garden, Susanna goes to bathe after dismissing her servants and asking them to lock the garden gates as they leave. The two old men take advantage of the situation and demand that she surrender herself to them or threaten to accuse her of having brought a young lover into the garden. Susanna refuses to be blackmailed and begins to call for help. When the servants come running, the rejected admirers give their false version of the story.

The next day, all the people gather in Jehoiachim's house and the two judges accuse Susanna of adultery, intending to have her condemned to death. Accompanied by her parents, her children, and all of her relatives, she is forced to remove her veil and listen to the terrible accusations brought against her by the judges. Destined to be stoned, Susanna's only hope is Yahweh. He sends his holy Spirit to Daniel, then a very young man, and Daniel goes to protest against such hasty judgement. Accusing the two elders of false testimony, he questions them separately, demonstrating that their stories do not correspond. The two are thus put to death by the people who once again recognize Daniel's inspired wisdom.

The second tale takes place during the reign of Cyrus, king of Persia, to whom Daniel is counsel. In those days the Babylonians venerate, with offerings and sacrifices, an idol called Bel — this is most certainly the local god Marduk who has been given the title meaning, as Baal, "Lord." While the king venerates this god, Daniel, loyal to his traditions, worships Yahweh. Struck by his tenacity, Cyrus asks Daniel why he does not worship Bel, to which Daniel answers that Bel is nothing but an idol of bronze and clay whereas his God is creator of the world, the master of all forms of life. Furious, Cyrus then questions the priests of his God, seventy-two in all, asking them where the copious meals offered to Bel actually went: who eats them? Bel or the priests? If the first hypothesis is proven true, Daniel will be put to death for having blasphemed against Bel, if it is the second hypothesis, however, the priests can expect to be the victims of Cyrus's punishment. The priests ask the king to leave a meal in the temple and seal its doors so that the next morning he can see if the god has in fact consumed the offering. The priests, however, have built a secret access to the temple. Daniel is cleverer, however, and spreads ashes inside the temple before the king seals the doors. The next morning the seals are intact and the meal has disappeared. It is then that Daniel points out to Cyrus, who is already feeling triumphant, the footprints on the floor left by men, women, and children. The priests and their families have been inside the temple to eat the offerings meant for Bel. Cyrus puts the guilty to death and asks Daniel to destroy the idol of Bel and the temple.

But Bel is not the Babylonians' only god; they also have a dragon which Cyrus asks Daniel to worship, since this is a live god. Daniel, to show how weak this god really is, tells Cyrus that he can kill it without even using a sword or an arm. Daniel makes balls of pitch, fat, and fur, then feeds them to the dragon who dies instantly. But the people, angry at seeing this Jew destroy their idols and make their king a fool, threaten to kill the king unless he delivers Daniel to them. With no other alternative, Cyrus gives Daniel to the people who throw him in the lions' den where he remains for a full seven days. Although the animals in the pit are starved, they do not approach Daniel. A certain Habakkuk, namesake of a biblical prophet, is even sent to Babylon by an angel to take food to Daniel. When the king, after seven days, goes to the lions' den to mourn him, to his great surprise he finds Daniel perfectly safe and sound. As in the first episode that took place in the lions' den, Daniel's

Guido Reni, ***Susanna and the Elders***

Susanna is the wife of a rich Hebrew who lives in Babylon. Her beauty arouses the passionate feelings of two elders of the people who, though they are judges, do not hesitate to falsely accuse her of adultery.

accusors end up in the pit, easy prey for the hungry lions, and the king recognizes the supreme power of Daniel's god. The tale of Susanna, just as that of Bel and the dragon, are examples of the Jewish protest against pagan idolatry.

As we have seen, the Book of Daniel does not relate a linear biography of a historical personage, but rather holds a fundamental message which it expresses through events or visions set in a relatively inconsistent chronological framework. Nevertheless, it does refer to quite a vast period, spanning several centuries, from the presumed days of Daniel (seventh to sixth centuries B. C.) to that of Antiochus IV Epiphanes (second century B. C.), the probable period of the final editing of the work, and thus, quite logically, demonstrates familiarity with the history of distant centuries. The use of the first person in the text, therefore, is a literary device used to attribute authorship to the wise man, Daniel, of a work written at a much later date, as indicated notably by the use of certain terms of Persian and Greek origin.

The historical inaccuracies noted previously show that at every possible opportunity the Book of Daniel, modelling itself upon God's actions, transcends historical contingencies. This being said, the Book most certainly owed its writing to these same contingencies. We are led to believe, in fact, that the terrible persecution of the Jews for their beliefs by Antiochus gave rise to hopes for a new and better world where God would triumph over evil. These years were also, moreover, not far from the period that witnessed the insurrection of the Maccabeans against the oppressive power of the Seleucids. It has in fact been supposed that Daniel was associated with the "Hasidim" ("pious ones"), the "special forces" of the Maccabeans, a group which helped to inspire the famous movement of the Essenes of Qumran. Nevertheless, it would certainly be misleading to regard the Book of Daniel as solely a product of this period. It is undoubtedly, as are all the biblical Books, the vehicle of more ancient tales and traditions which at one time existed on their own but which are combined here, more or less successfully, with the intent of achieving a specific aim.

Probably the most notable feature of the figure of Daniel is his heroic attachment to his God, for whom he never hesitates to risk his life, completely trusting in Yahweh's unfailing protection. In addition, Daniel is also a sage, and a prophet capable of communicating indirectly with God through his acolytes who deliver him the keys to revelations of profound implications. Very significantly, in the Hebrew canon the Book of Daniel is not included in the same group as the other prophets, for Daniel is a very special kind of prophet, even if the Gospel according to Saint Matthew (24:15) refers to him as such. The prophetic Books, those of Isaiah or Jeremiah for example, consist of short prophecies that generally contain threats or promises of redemption expressed in a mixture of prose and poetry. Unlike these prophets, Daniel is not in direct contact with God but receives symbolic visions which God's messengers help him to decipher. For these reasons, and others that would be too lengthy to develop in the scope of this work, the Book of Daniel is considered the first example of apocalyptic writing, a literary type particularly in vogue in the world of Judaism between the third and second centuries B. C. It aims at giving, through revelations deciphered thanks to the intervention of knowing angels, an interpretation of the past and an idea of the future in terms of establishing justice in the world through the fulfillment of divine plans. In short, it represents a bona fide theology of history. From a formal point of view, these writings readily resort to symbolic, mysterious, and veiled expressions, to esoterical calculations and cosmic manifestations. At this level, moreover, the Book of Daniel reflects a traditional symbolic heritage of which we find echoes in ancient Canaanite literature. Thus, for example, do we note in the symbolism of the four winds that agitate the sea, an interesting parallel in the Mesopotamian myth of the creation of the world, while the figure of the Elder of Days reminds us of a title used for the god El in mythological Ugarit texts.

From this point of view, it is interesting to note that other characters who present similar qualities are known to bear the name Daniel. Ezekiel, on two occasions refers to a certain *Danel* known for his wisdom and justice, cited with Noah and Job, which seems to point to a distant past and ancient tradition. In Ugarit tradition the myth of *Aqhat* stages, in the role of the hero's father, a king named *Danil*, who is also a man of integrity and deeply pious. Finally, a Qumran document has shown such incredible similarities to chapter 4 of the Book of Daniel that specialists have put forth the hypothesis that a traditional cycle circulated with, as its hero, a certain Daniel/Danel renowned for his wisdom, of whom our Daniel would be but a reincarnation, "Israelized" to credibly bear an apocalyptic message.

Taking a distance from the philhellenizing atmosphere of the period (third to second centuries B. C.), the author of the Book of Daniel defends the prestige and superiority of the God of Israel who holds the government of the world in his hands. For the first time in the Old Testament, it is not so much history which is responsible for the expectancies of the righteous as is the hope for an otherworld. Salvation is no longer written in history but in a place beyond, and this presupposes that the world must come to a radical end. At the center of the religious thought in the Book of Daniel is therefore the announcement of the rebirth of humanity, desired by God and prepared by Daniel, with as its objective the establishment of the Kingdom of God. This Book contains, in fact, the only specific allusion to individual resurrection in the entire Hebrew Bible. Most probably this is the reason why the iconography showing Daniel in the lions' den enjoyed such success in Christian imagery, for example, in the obscurity of catacombs or on paleo-Christian sarcophagi. This theme was also often drawn upon in the context of hagiographic literature that recounted, in a very similar manner, the Passion of various Christian martyrs.

(*opposite page*)

Rembrandt, ***Susanna and the Two Elders***

Only Daniel's perspicacious intervention is able to save Susanna and unmask the two elders who are put to death.

GLOSSARY

Accadian: Language of Mesopotamia which was used for cuneiform inscriptions on clay tablets.

Apocrypha: Works that were not included in the Hebrew canon of the Bible.

Chtonian: This term refers to a divinity or cult related to the underworld, the world beyond.

Eponym: One who gives his name to a people, place, or institution.

Eschatology: Doctrine of "the last things" literally, and therefore of death, judgement, heaven, and hell.

Gnosticism: Doctrine that claims Man's salvation is to be acquired through knowledge, a belief severely opposed by the church fathers.

Hagiographa: Literature concerning the lives of the Saints.

Holocaust: A whole burnt offering in which no part of the sacrifical victim is kept for the officiating priests or for the faithful.

Messianism: Fervent hope in the reformation of mankind through an intervention by God and the belief in the advent of a Messiah.

Monotheism: Religious doctrine and worship based upon the belief that there is only one God.

Polytheism: Religious doctrine and worship based upon the belief that there are several gods that form a pantheon.

Pseudodepigrapha: A term that refers to a Book attributed to an author under an assumed name.

Sapiential (Books): Books of the Bible that concern the subject of wisdom notably Job, Proverbs, Ecclesiasticus (also called the "Wisdom of Jesus the Son of Sirach"), etc.

Syncretism: Process by which two divinities superimpose, merge with one another in virtue of attributions or functions they have in common.

Talmud: Body of Jewish law and legend subsequent to the Bible.

Theophany: A divine appearance.

CHRONOLOGY

NOTE: The dates above the line correspond to conventionally accepted periods, but this does not imply that the historical existence of the personages concerned is certain.

B. C.	
1750-1500	Abraham, Isaac, and Jacob
1300-1200	Israelites in Egypt (Joseph, Moses)
1200-1000	Exodus and Conquest of Canaan (Joshua); Epoch of the Judges (Samson, Samuel)

1020-1000	Saul and the establishment of the monarchy
1000-*c.* 965	David
965-*c.* 930	Solomon
930	Division of the Kingdom into Judah and Israel following the death of Solomon
873-852	Reign of Ahab and Jezebel; Elijah's ministry
842-814	Reign of Jehu, anointed by Elisha
8th Century	Hosea and Isaiah; Assyrians invade Judah
605	First deportation of Jews to Babylonia
597 and 587	Taking of Jerusalem by Nebuchadnezzar; destruction of Temple and Babylonian Exile
540	Return from Exile
559-529	Reign of Cyrus; Persian victory over the Babylonians
522-486	Reign of Darius I; First Median War
486-464	Reign of Xerxes I; Second Median War
440-*c.* 390	Ezra and Nehemiah
332	Alexander the Great defeats the Persians
323	Death of Alexander the Great; Palestine under the Ptolemies
198	Palestine falls under the Seleucids
167	Beginning of the Maccabean revolt against Antiochus IV (175-164)
63	Beginning of Roman domination; Pompey takes Jerusalem

ILLUSTRATIONS

Page numbers in **boldface**.

INDEX

Note: Indicated below in **boldface** are the names of personages mentioned in this volume but who are not treated specifically in any one chapter. Page numbers in *italics* refer to illustrations. Numbers in **boldface** refer to page numbers of the chapters themselves.